CHENG & TSUI

"Bringing Asia to the World"™

中文聽說讀寫

INTEGRATED

Traditional Characters

CHINESE

2

Textbook

4th Edition

Yuehua Liu and Tao-chung Yao
Nyan-Ping Bi, Liangyan Ge, Yaohua Shi

Original Edition by Tao-chung Yao and Yuehua Liu
Liangyan Ge, Yea-fen Chen, Nyan-Ping Bi, Xiaojun Wang, Yaohua Shi

CHENG & TSUI

"Bringing Asia to the World"™

Copyright © 2018, 2009, 2005, 1997 by
Cheng & Tsui Co., Inc.

Fourth Edition 2018
Third Edition 2009
Second Edition 2005
First Edition 1997

28 27 26 25 24   4 5 6 7 8   (Hardcover)
28 27 26 25 24   7 8 9 10 11 (Paperback)

ISBN 978-1-62291-138-7
[Fourth Edition, Traditional Characters,
Hardcover]

ISBN 978-1-62291-140-0
[Fourth Edition, Traditional Characters,
Paperback]

Library of Congress
Cataloging-in-Publication
Data [Third Edition]

Integrated Chinese = [Zhong wen ting shuo
du xie]. Traditional character edition. Level 1,
part 2 / Yuehua Liu . . . [et al.] – 3rd ed.
    p. cm.

Chinese and English.

Includes indexes.

Parallel title in Chinese characters.

ISBN 978-0-88727-673-6 (trad. hbk.)
– ISBN 978-0-88727-672-9 (trad. pbk.)
– ISBN 978-0-88727-671-2 (simp. hbk.)
– ISBN 978-0-88727-670-5 (simp. pbk.)
1. Chinese language–Textbooks for foreign
speakers–English. I. Liu, Yuehua. II. Title:
Zhong wen ting shuo du xie.

PL1129.E5I683 2008

495.1–dc22

Printed in the United States of America

The *Integrated Chinese* series encompasses
textbooks, workbooks, character workbooks,
teacher's resources, audio, video, a digital
edition on Cheng & Tsui FluencyLink™, and
more. Visit cheng-tsui.com for more
information on *Integrated Chinese*.

Publisher
JILL CHENG

Editorial Manager
BEN SHRAGGE

Editors
LEI WANG and MIKE YONG

Creative Director
CHRISTIAN SABOGAL

Designers
KATE PAPADAKI and LIZ YATES

Illustrator
KATE PAPADAKI

Photographs
© Adobe Stock
© Cheng & Tsui

Cheng & Tsui Co., Inc.
Phone (617) 988-2400
Fax (617) 426-3669
25 West Street
Boston, MA 02111-1213 USA
cheng-tsui.com

This Fourth Edition of *Integrated Chinese* is dedicated to the memory of our dearest colleague and friend Professor Tao-chung (Ted) Yao.

Publisher's Note

When Integrated Chinese was first published in 1997, it set a new standard with its focus on the development and integration of the four language skills (listening, speaking, reading, and writing). Today, to further enrich the learning experience of the many users of Integrated Chinese worldwide, Cheng & Tsui is pleased to offer this revised and updated Fourth Edition of Integrated Chinese. We would like to thank the many teachers and students who, by offering their valuable insights and suggestions, have helped Integrated Chinese evolve and keep pace with the many positive changes in the field of Chinese language instruction. Integrated Chinese continues to offer comprehensive language instruction, with many new features, including the Cheng & Tsui FluencyLink™, as detailed in the Preface.

The Cheng & Tsui Chinese Language Series is designed to publish and widely distribute quality language learning materials created by leading instructors from around the world. We welcome readers' comments and suggestions concerning the publications in this series at cheng-tsui.com.

Contents

Preface

The *Integrated Chinese* (IC) series is an internationally acclaimed Mandarin Chinese language course that delivers a cohesive system of print and digital resources for highly effective teaching and learning. First published in 1997, it is now the leading series of Chinese language learning resources in the United States and beyond. Through its holistic focus on the language skills of listening, speaking, reading, and writing, IC teaches novice and intermediate students the skills they need to function in Chinese.

What's New

It has been over eight years since the publication of the Third Edition of IC. We are deeply grateful for all the positive feedback, as well as constructive suggestions for improvement, from IC users. In the meantime, China and the world have seen significant transformations in electronic communications, commerce, and media. Additionally, the technology available to us is transforming the way teachers and students interact with content. The teaching of Chinese as a second language needs to keep pace with these exciting developments. Therefore, the time seems right to update IC across delivery formats.

In developing this latest edition of IC, we have consulted the American Council on the Teaching of Foreign Languages (ACTFL) *21st Century Skills Map for World Languages*. The national standards for foreign language learning in the 21st century focus on goals in five areas—communication, cultures, connections, comparisons, and communities. In addition to classifying the applicable **Language Practice** activities by communication mode (interpersonal, interpretive, and presentational), we have added a host of materials that address the 5 Cs. The delivery of IC via **Cheng & Tsui FluencyLink™** elevates the teaching and learning experience by presenting multimedia and interactive content in a truly blended and integrated way.

New, visually rich supplementary modules that recur in each lesson have been introduced. These can be taught in any sequence to serve as prompts for classroom discussion and student reflection:

- **Get Real with Chinese** draws on realia to situate language learning in real-life contexts. Students are required to analyze, predict, and synthesize before coming to conclusions about embedded linguistic and cultural meaning. Photos and questions connect the classroom to authentic Chinese experiences. To familiarize students with both character sets, students are exposed to realia in simplified characters and realia in traditional characters.

- **Chinese Chat** provides opportunities for language practice in the digital environment. Realistic texting, microblogging, and social media scenarios show students how the younger generation has adapted Chinese to new communication technologies.

- **Characterize It!** encourages students to approach Chinese characters analytically.

- While not a new segment, **How About You?** has been revamped for the Fourth Edition. This module encourages students to personalize their study of vocabulary and learn words and phrases that relate to their own interests and background. Questions now appear in both Chinese and English, while visual cues, which typically correspond to possible answers, promote vocabulary expansion and retention. Vocabulary items corresponding to the visual cues are listed in a separate index.

Moreover, to promote students' awareness of cultural diversity in a world of rapid globalization, we have included **Compare & Contrast** activities in the **Cultural Literacy** (formerly Culture Highlights) section. This section as a whole has been given a lavishly illustrated, magazine-style treatment to better engage students.

We have also updated the **Grammar** section to include exercises tailored to each grammar point, so students can immediately put into practice the language forms they have just learned. Additional practice exercises for each grammar point are accessible via FluencyLink.

Keeping It Casual (formerly That's How the Chinese Say It!) remains a review of functional expressions after Lessons 15 and 20 that encourages students to build their own personalized list of useful expressions.

Finally, the new **Lesson Wrap-Up** section includes context-based tasks that prepare students to communicate with native Chinese speakers. Also in this section are **Make It Flow!** exercises, which help students develop and apply strategies to organize information coherently and cohesively in written and spoken discourse. We created this activity to address the common phenomenon of novice and intermediate students speaking in choppy, isolated sentences.

The ultimate purpose of acquiring a language is communication, and a hallmark of effective communication is the ability to produce continuous discourse. The **Lesson Wrap-Up** activities are intended as assessment instruments for the **Can-Do Checklist**, which encourages students to measure their progress at the end of the lesson.

As previous users of IC will note, we have renamed the four-volume series. The new sequencing of Volumes 1 to 4 better reflects the flexibility of the materials and the diversity of our user groups and their instructional environments. However, we also recognize that Volumes 1 and 2 are often used together in the first year of language instruction, and Volumes 3 and 4 in the second. Thus, for ease of reference, we have retained the sequencing of the lessons from 1 to 20 in each half of the series.

As with the Third Edition, the Fourth Edition of IC features both traditional and simplified character versions of the Volume 1 and 2 textbooks and workbooks, and a combination of traditional and simplified characters in the Volume 3 and 4 textbooks and workbooks. However, in response to user feedback, we have updated the traditional characters to ensure they match the standard set used in Taiwan. For reference, we have consulted the Taiwan Ministry of Education's online *Revised Chinese Dictionary*.

The most significant change in the Fourth Edition is the incorporation of innovative educational technology. Users of the print edition have access to audio at cheng-tsui.com, while subscribers to FluencyLink have access to streaming audio plus additional, interactive content.

Users who choose to subscribe to FluencyLink will have access to:

- The Workbook (with auto-grading)
- The fully-downloadable Character Workbook
- Audio (Textbook and Workbook)
- Audio recording for teacher feedback
- Video of the lesson texts
- Additional cultural content

In addition to student subscriptions, teacher subscriptions are also available for FluencyLink. The teacher subscription to FluencyLink conveniently makes connections between the Textbook and the additional resources provided in the Teacher's Resources, such as video activity sheets, quizzes, and answer keys.

A key feature of FluencyLink is coherence. The innovative instructional design provides an integrated user experience, with multiple options for integration and Single Sign-on (SSO). Learners can move seamlessly between the transmission, practice, application, and evaluation stages, navigating the content to suit their particular learning needs and styles. For more information and a free trial, please visit cheng-tsui.com.

Both in its print and digital versions, the new IC features a contemporary layout that adds clarity and rigor to its instructional design. Rich new visuals complement the text's revised, user-friendly language and up-to-date cultural content. We hope that students and teachers find the many changes and new features timely and meaningful.

Organizational Principles

In the higher education setting, the IC series often covers two years of instruction, with smooth transitions from one level to the next. The lessons first cover topics from everyday life, then gradually move to more abstract subject matter. The materials do not follow one pedagogical methodology, but instead blend several effective teaching approaches. Used in conjunction with FluencyLink, incorporating differentiated instruction, blended learning, and the flipped classroom is even easier. Here are some of the features of IC that distinguish it from other Chinese language resources:

Integrating Pedagogy and Authenticity

We believe that students should be taught authentic materials even in their first year of language instruction. Therefore, authentic materials (produced by native Chinese speakers for native Chinese speakers) are included in every lesson.

Integrating Traditional and Simplified Characters

We believe that students should learn both traditional and simplified Chinese characters. However, we also realize that teaching students both forms from day one could be overwhelming. In the higher education setting, the IC series often covers two years of instruction, with the first two volumes usually used in the first year of study, and the final two volumes in the second. Therefore, the first two volumes of IC are available in separate traditional and simplified versions, with the alternative character forms of the texts included in the Appendix.

By their second year of study, we believe that all students should be exposed to both forms of written Chinese. Accordingly, the final two volumes of IC include both traditional and simplified characters. Students in second-year

Chinese language classes come from different backgrounds, and should be allowed to write in their preferred form. However, it is important that the learner write in one form only, and not a mix of both.

Integrating Teaching Approaches

Because no single teaching method can adequately train a student in all language skills, we employ a variety of approaches in IC. In addition to the communicative approach, we also use traditional methods such as grammar-translation and the direct method.

FluencyLink users can employ additional teaching approaches, such as differentiated learning and blended learning. Students can self-pace their learning, which is a very powerful instructional intervention. The product also facilitates breaking down direct instruction into more engaging "bites" of learning, which improves student engagement. Moreover, FluencyLink allows students to interact with the content at home and practice and apply their learning in the classroom with corrective teacher feedback, which has the potential to improve student outcomes. Additionally, teachers and learners do not need to follow the instructional flow of the underlying book. They can navigate using multiple pathways in flexible and customized ways and at varying paces for true individualized learning.

Acknowledgments

We would like to thank users around the world for believing in IC. We owe much of the continued success of IC to their invaluable feedback. Likewise, we would be remiss if we did not acknowledge the University of Notre Dame for sponsoring and inviting us to a one-day workshop on IC on April 9, 2016. Leading Chinese-language specialists from across the country shared their experiences with the IC authors. We are especially indebted to Professor Yongping Zhu, Chair of the Department of East Asian Languages and Cultures at Notre Dame, and his colleagues and staff for organizing the workshop.

Professors Fangpei Cai and Meng Li of the University of Chicago took time out from their busy teaching schedules to compile a detailed list of comments and suggestions. We are profoundly touched by their generosity. In completing this Fourth Edition, we have taken into consideration their and other users' recommendations for revision. Indeed, many of the changes are in response to user feedback. The authors are naturally responsible for any remaining shortcomings and oversights.

For two summers in a row, Professor Liangyan Ge's wife, Ms. Yongqing Pan, warmly invited the IC team to their home to complete the bulk of the work of revising the IC series. Words are inadequate to express our thanks to Ms. Pan for her gracious hospitality and her superb cooking day in and day out.

We are deeply grateful to our publisher Cheng & Tsui Company and to Jill Cheng in particular for her unswerving support for IC over the years. We would also like to express our heartfelt appreciation to our editor Ben Shragge and his colleagues for their meticulous attention to every aspect of this new edition.

As we look back on the evolution of IC, one person is never far from our thoughts. Without Professor Tao-chung Yao's commitment from its inception, IC would not have been possible. Sadly, Professor Yao passed away in September 2015. Throughout the summer, Professor Yao remained in close contact with the rest of the team, going over each draft of IC 1 with an eagle eye, providing us with the benefit of his wisdom by phone and email. This Fourth Edition of IC is a living tribute to his vision and guidance.

Note: Prefaces to the previous editions of IC are available at cheng-tsui.com.

Series Structure

The IC series has been carefully conceptualized and developed to facilitate flexible delivery options that meet the needs of different instructional environments.

Component per Volume	Description	Print/Other Formats	FluencyLink™
Textbook	· Ten engaging lessons per volume, each with readings, grammar explanations, communicative exercises, and culture notes	· Paperback or Hardcover · Simplified or Traditional Characters (Volumes 1 and 2) · Simplified and Traditional Characters (Volumes 3 and 4)	· *Student and Teacher subscriptions*
Workbook	· Wide range of integrated activities covering the three modes of communication (interpersonal, interpretive, and presentational)	· Paperback · Simplified or Traditional Characters (Volumes 1 and 2) · Simplified and Traditional Characters (Volumes 3 and 4)	· *Student and Teacher subscriptions*
Character Workbook	· Radical- and character-writing and stroke order practice	· Paperback · Simplified with Traditional Characters	· *Student and Teacher subscriptions*
Audio	· Audio for Textbook vocabulary and lesson texts, and in Volume 1, pronunciation exercises · Audio for Workbook listening exercises, and in Volume 1, pronunciation exercises · Normal and paused versions	· Audio available to print users at cheng-tsui.com	· *Student and Teacher subscriptions*
Video	· Volumes 1 and 2: acted dialogues and narratives presented in the Textbooks; also includes theme-related Culture Minutes sections in authentic settings · Volumes 3 and 4: documentary-style episodes correlating to the lesson themes in authentic settings	· One DVD per volume	· *Student and Teacher subscriptions*
Teacher's Resources	· Comprehensive implementation support, teaching tips, syllabi, tests and quizzes, answer keys, and supplementary resources	· Downloadable resources that include core lesson guides along with ancillary materials previously on the companion website	· *Teacher subscription*

Volume 2 Lesson Structure

All components of IC (Textbooks, Workbooks, and Teacher's Resources) are considered core and are designed to be used together to enhance teaching and learning. Recurrent lesson subsections are highlighted in the Textbook Elements column. Note that Supplementary Modules do not compose a separate section, but are rather discrete entities that appear throughout each lesson.

Section	Textbook Elements	Interactive Content	Workbooks	Teacher's Resources
Lesson Opener	· Learning Objectives state what students will be able to do by the end of the lesson · Relate & Get Ready helps students reflect on similarities and differences between Chinese culture and their own		· Opportunity for students to revisit learning objectives and self-assess	· Overview of language functions, vocabulary, grammar, pronunciation, and characters taught in the lesson · Sequencing recommendations and teaching aids
Text	· Two Chinese lesson texts demonstrate practical vocabulary and grammar usage · *Pinyin* versions of the texts provide pronunciation support · Language Notes elaborate on important structures and phrases in the lesson texts	· Audio builds receptive skills · Video provides insight into non-verbal cues and communication plus context through authentic settings	· Listening comprehension and speaking exercises based on the dialogues · Reading comprehension	· Strategies for teaching the lesson texts, plus question prompts · Dialogues as narratives · Pre- and post-video viewing activity worksheets and scripts
Vocabulary	· Vocabulary lists define and categorize new words from the lesson texts (proper nouns are listed last)	· Audio models proper pronunciation · Flashcards assist with vocabulary acquisition	· Handwriting and stroke order practice is provided in the Character Workbook · All exercises use lesson vocabulary to support acquisition	· Explanations, pronunciation tips, usage notes, and phrasal combinations · Vocabulary slideshows
Grammar	· Grammar points, which correspond to numbered references in the readings, explain and model language forms · Exercises allow students to practice the grammar points immediately	· Additional exercises deepen knowledge of the language	· Writing and grammar exercises based on grammar introduced in the lesson	· Explanations, pattern practice, and additional grammar notes · Grammar slideshows

Section	Textbook Elements	Interactive Content	Workbooks	Teacher's Resources
Language Practice	· Role-plays, pair activities, contextualized drills, and colorful cues prompt students to produce language		· Exercises and activities spanning the three modes of communication (interpersonal, interpretive, and presentational), plus *pinyin* and tone practice, to build communication and performance skills	· Student presentations, integrative practice, and additional practice activities · Additional activities categorized by macro-skill
Cultural Literacy	· Culture notes provide snapshots of contemporary and traditional Chinese-speaking cultures · Compare & Contrast draws connections between cultures	· Additional content further develops cultural literacy of the lesson theme	· Authentic materials to develop predictive skills	· Background notes expand on the section
Lesson Wrap-Up	· Make It Flow! develops students' ability to produce smooth discourse · Projects encourage review and recycling of lesson materials through different text types · Can-Do Checklist allows students to assess their fulfillment of the learning objectives			· Teaching tips for implementing self-diagnostic activities, answer keys for Make it Flow!, additional Make It Flow! exercises, and additional sample quizzes and tests · Slideshows that summarize content introduced in the lesson
Supplementary Modules	· How About You? encourages students to personalize their vocabulary · Get Real with Chinese teaches students to predict meaning from context · Characterize It! explores the structure of Chinese characters · Chinese Chat demonstrates how language is used in text messaging and social media	· Additional Characterize It! exercises increase understanding of characters		· Teaching tips and strategies for fully exploiting and implementing these new elements

Scope and Sequence

Lesson	Learning Objectives	Grammar	Cultural Literacy
11 Weather	· Talk about the weather in basic terms · Compare weather in two places · Talk about what you can do in nice or bad weather · Present a simple weather forecast	1. Comparative sentences using 比 (*bǐ*) (I) 2. The particle 了 (*le*) (III): 了 as a sentence-final particle 3. The modal verb 會 (*huì*) (will) (II) 4. Adjective + （一）點兒 (*[yì] diǎnr*) (a bit) 5. The adverb 又 (*yòu*) (again) 6. Adjective/verb + 是 (*shì*) + adjective/verb + 可是／但是… (*kěshì/dànshì…*)	· Place name transliteration · Weather · Units of measurement · Weather records
12 Dining	· Ask if there are seats available at a restaurant · Order some Chinese dishes · Describe your dietary preferences and restrictions · Ask for recommendations · Rush your order · Pay for your meal and get change	1. 一…也／都…不／沒… (*yī … yě/dōu … bù/méi …*) 2. 多／少 (*duō/shǎo*) + verb 3. Comparing 剛 (*gāng*) (just) and 剛才 (*gāngcái*) (just now) 4. Resultative complements (I) 5. 好 (*hǎo*) as a resultative complement 6. Adjective reduplication (I) 7. The verb 來 (*lái*)	· Four major schools of cooking · Utensils · Localization · Vegetarianism
13 Asking Directions	· Ask for and give directions · Identify locations by using landmarks as references · Describe whether two places are close to or far away from each other · State where you are heading and the reason for going there	1. Direction and location words 2. Comparative sentences using 沒（有） (*méi[yǒu]*) 3. Indicating degree using 那麼 (*nàme*) 4. 到 (*dào*) + place + 去 (*qù*) + action 5. The dynamic particle 過 (*guo*) 6. Verb reduplication (I) 7. Resultative complements (II) 8. 一…就… (*yī…jiù…*) (as soon as … then …)	· Feng shui · Chinatown · Casual greetings · Urban planning
14 Birthday Party	· Ask a friend to go to a party with you · Suggest things to bring to a get-together · Thank people for gifts · Describe a duration of time · Talk about the year of your birth and your Chinese zodiac sign	1. Indicating an action in progress using 呢 (*ne*) 2. Verbal phrases and subject-predicate phrases used as attributives 3. Time duration (I) 4. Sentences with 是…的 (*shì…de*) (I) 5. 還 (*hái*) (still) 6. 又…又… (*yòu…yòu…*) (both… and…)	· Chinese zodiac · Karaoke · Gift giving · Party etiquette

Abbreviations of Grammatical Terms

adj	adjective	pr	pronoun
adv	adverb	prefix	prefix
conj	conjunction	prep	preposition
interj	interjection	qp	question particle
m	measure word	qpr	question pronoun
mv	modal verb	t	time word
n	noun	v	verb
nu	numeral	**vc**	verb plus complement
p	particle	vo	verb plus object
pn	proper noun		

Legend of Digital Icons

The icons listed below refer to interactive content. Audio is available at chengtsui.co/resources to readers who have purchased the print edition. All other digital content is available exclusively to FluencyLink™ subscribers.

Audio — **Lesson Text, Vocabulary**

Video — **Lesson Text**

Flashcards — **Vocabulary**

More characters — **Characterize It!**

More exercises — **Grammar**

Continue to explore — **Cultural Literacy**

Cast of Characters

Wang Peng
王朋

A Chinese freshman from Beijing. He has quickly adapted to American college life and likes to play and watch sports.

Li You
李友

Amy Lee, an American student from New York State. She and Wang Peng meet each other on the first day of classes and soon become good friends.

Gao Wenzhong
高文中

Winston Gore, an English student. His parents work in the United States. Winston enjoys singing, dancing, and Chinese cooking. He has a secret crush on Bai Ying'ai.

Bai Ying'ai
白英愛

Baek Yeung Ae, an outgoing Korean student from Seoul. She finds Wang Peng very "cool" and very "cute."

Gao Xiaoyin
高小音

Jenny Gore, Winston's older sister. She has already graduated from college, and is now a school librarian.

Chang Laoshi
常老師

Chang Xiaoliang, originally from China and in her forties. She has been teaching Chinese in the United States for ten years.

Wang Hong
王紅

Wang Peng's younger sister. She is preparing to attend college in America.

Wang Peng's parents
王朋的父母

From Beijing, in their late forties.

Hailun
海倫

Helen, Gao Wenzhong's cousin. She has a one-year-old son, Tom.

Fei Xiansheng
費先生

Owen Fields, Gao Xiaoyin's high school classmate.

天氣

Tiānqì

WEATHER

Learning Objectives

In this lesson, you will learn to:

- Talk about the weather in basic terms
- Compare weather in two places
- Talk about what you can do in nice or bad weather
- Present a simple weather forecast

Relate & Get Ready

In your own culture/community:

- What is the typical weather in spring, summer, autumn, and winter?
- Where do people get weather information?
- What weather-dependent outdoor sports are popular, if any?
- How do people feel about rain or snow?

Tomorrow's Weather Will Be Even Better!

Dialogue 1

Audio

Video

（高小音跟弟弟高文中聊到天氣……）

今天天氣比[1]*昨天好，不下雪了[2]。

我約了朋友明天去公園滑冰，不知道天氣會[3]怎麼樣，冷不冷？

我剛才看了網上的天氣預報，明天天氣比今天更好。不但不會下雪，而且[a]會暖和一點兒[4]。

是嗎？太好了！

你約了誰去滑冰？

白英愛。

你約了白英愛？可是她今天早上坐飛機去紐約了。

真的啊？那我明天怎麼辦？

你還是在家看電視吧！

Integrated Chinese 2 | Textbook

* Here and throughout the book, the blue lesson text and numbers correspond to explanations in the **Grammar section**.

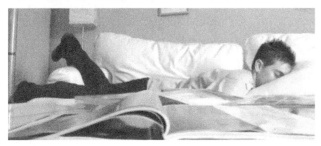

(Gāo Xiǎoyīn gēn dìdi Gāo Wénzhōng liáo dào tiānqì . . .)

 Jīntiān tiānqì bǐ[1] *zuótiān hǎo, bú xià xuě le*[2].

 Wǒ yuē le péngyou míngtiān qù gōngyuán huá bīng, bù zhīdào tiānqì huì[3] *zěnmeyàng, lěng bu lěng?*

 Wǒ gāngcái kàn le wǎng shang de tiānqì yùbào, míngtiān tiānqì bǐ jīntiān gèng hǎo. Búdàn bú huì xià xuě, érqiě[a] *huì nuǎnhuo yì diǎnr*[4].

 Shì ma? Tài hǎo le!

 Nǐ yuē le shéi qù huá bīng?

 Bái Yīng'ài.

 Nǐ yuē le Bái Yīng'ài? Kěshì tā jīntiān zǎoshang zuò fēijī qù Niǔyuē le.

 Zhēn de a? Nà wǒ míngtiān zěnme bàn?

Nǐ háishi zài jiā kàn diànshì ba!

Language Note

a 不但 (búdàn) · · · ，而且 (érqiě) · · ·

In a sentence with the 不但 (búdàn) · · ·，而且 (érqiě) · · · (not only . . . , but also . . .) structure, the conjunction 而且 (érqiě) in the second clause is generally required, while the conjunction 不但 (búdàn) in the first clause is optional.

Vocabulary

Audio

Flashcards

No.	Word	Pinyin	Part of Speech	Definition
1	天氣	tiānqì	n	weather
2	比	bǐ	prep/v	compared with (comparison marker); to compare [See Grammar 1.]
3	下雪	xià xuě	vo	to snow
4	約	yuē	v	to make an appointment
5	公園	gōngyuán	n	park
6	滑冰	huá bīng	vo	to ice skate
7	會	huì	mv	will [See Grammar 3.]
8	冷	lěng	adj	cold
9	剛才	gāngcái	t	just now, a moment ago
10	網上	wǎng shang		on the Internet
11	預報	yùbào	v/n	to forecast; forecast
12	更	gèng	adv	even more
13	不但⋯，而且⋯	búdàn⋯, érqiě⋯	conj	not only⋯, but also⋯
14	暖和	nuǎnhuo	adj	warm
15	辦	bàn	v	to handle, to do

You're in line to board your flight to Harbin, and you open up the weather app on your tablet. What are the chances that snow will fall during your trip? Can you identify any other details from the forecast?

GET Real WITH CHINESE

哈尔滨市

−20° 阴

今天有雪,天寒地冻,千万裹严实点!

湿度 79%   风力 2级

53 良

-15 | -24℃

明天 优
多云

今天 优
阵雪转多云

天气

15天预报

优

优

阵雪

多云

优

优

晴

轻

晴

你們那兒天氣
怎麼樣 ?

Nǐmen nàr tiānqì zěnmeyàng?
How's the weather over there?

我們這兒 _____ 。
Wǒmen zhèr _____ .

See index for corresponding vocabulary or research another term.

How About You?

Grammar

Comparative sentences using 比 (bǐ) (I)

You can use the pattern below to compare two entities.

X + 比 (bǐ) + Y + adjective

A 李友比她大姐高。

Lǐ Yǒu bǐ tā dàjiě gāo.

Li You is taller than her oldest sister.

B 今天比昨天冷。

Jīntiān bǐ zuótiān lěng.

Today is colder than yesterday.

C 第十課的語法比第九課的語法容易。

Dì shí kè de yǔfǎ bǐ dì jiǔ kè de yǔfǎ róngyì.

The grammar in Lesson Ten is easier than the grammar in Lesson Nine.

There are two ways in which the basic comparative construction can be further modified: the first is by adding a qualifying expression after the adjective, as shown in the following pattern. Note that the modifying expression must be placed *after* the adjective, not before it.

X + 比 (bǐ) + Y + adjective + 一點兒 (yì diǎnr)/得多 (de duō)/多了 (duō le)

D 今天比昨天冷一點兒。

Jīntiān bǐ zuótiān lěng yì diǎnr.

Today is a little colder than yesterday.

[✖ 今天比昨天一點兒冷。]

E 明天會比今天冷得多。

Míngtiān huì bǐ jīntiān lěng de duō.

Tomorrow will be much colder than today.

F 紐約比這兒冷多了/冷得多。

Niǔyuē bǐ zhèr lěng duō le/lěng de duō.

New York is much colder than here.

[✖ 紐約比這兒很冷。]

Note that "much colder" is 冷多了 (*lěng duō le*) or 冷得多 (*lěng de duō*), not 很冷 (*hěn lěng*) (very cold).

The second way to modify the basic comparative construction is by adding the adverb 更 (*gèng*) or the adverb 還 (*hái*) *before* the adjective, as shown in the following pattern.

X + 比 (*bǐ*) + Y + 更 (*gèng*)/還 (*hái*) + adjective

G 昨天冷，今天比昨天更冷/今天比昨天還冷。

Zuótiān lěng, jīntiān bǐ zuótiān gèng lěng/jīntiān bǐ zuótiān hái lěng.

Yesterday was cold. Today is even colder than yesterday.

跟 (*gēn*) and 和 (*hé*) can also be used to form a comparative sentence, as shown in the pattern below.

X + 跟 (*gēn*)/和 (*hé*) + Y + (不)一樣 (*[bù] yíyàng*) + adjective

However, unlike a comparative sentence using 比 (*bǐ*), a comparative sentence using 跟 (*gēn*) or 和 (*hé*) only indicates whether two entities do or don't exhibit an attribute to the same degree. Compare (H) with (I) and (J) with (K).

H 這個教室和那個教室一樣大。

Zhè ge jiàoshì hé nà ge jiàoshì yíyàng dà.

This classroom and that classroom are the same size.

I 這個教室跟那個教室不一樣大。

Zhè ge jiàoshì gēn nà ge jiàoshì bù yíyàng dà.

This classroom and that classroom are not the same size.

J 這個教室比那個教室大。

Zhè ge jiàoshì bǐ nà ge jiàoshì dà.

This classroom is larger than that classroom.

K	這個教室比那個教室大得多。

Zhè ge jiàoshì bǐ nà ge jiàoshì dà de duō.

This classroom is much larger than that classroom.

More exercises

EXERCISES

Turn the following sentences into comparative statements, inserting 比 where appropriate. Use exercise 1 as an example.

1 今天的天氣好，昨天的天氣不好。

→ 今天的天氣比昨天的好。

2 我的衣服貴，你的衣服不貴。

3 一月冷，十二月不冷。

---

2 | The particle 了 (le) (III): 了 as a sentence-final particle

When 了 *(le)* occurs at the end of a sentence, it usually indicates a change of status or the realization of a new situation. [See also Grammar 5, Lesson 5, and Grammar 5, Lesson 8, Volume 1.]

A	下雪了。		B	妹妹累了。

Xià xuě le.

It's snowing (now).

Mèimei lèi le.

My sister is tired (now).

C	我昨天沒有空兒，今天有空兒了。

Wǒ zuótiān méiyǒu kòngr, jīntiān yǒu kòngr le.

I didn't have time yesterday, but I do today.

D	你看，公共汽車來了。

Nǐ kàn, gōnggòng qìchē lái le.

Look, the bus is here.

When used in this sense, 了 *(le)* can still be used at the end of a negative sentence.

E 我沒有錢了，不買了。

Wǒ méiyǒu qián le, bù mǎi le.

I don't have any money left. I won't buy it anymore.

To negate 有 *(yǒu)* (to have), use 沒 *(méi)*, rather than 不 *(bù)*.

EXERCISES

More exercises

Answer the questions using 了 to suggest a change in state. Use exercise 1 as an example.

1　四月了，你們那兒冷嗎？（不冷）

　　→　我們這兒不冷了。

2　已經十二點半了，你餓不餓？（餓）

3　這種樣子的褲子你們上個星期沒有中號的，
　　這個星期呢？（有）

---

3 | **The modal verb 會 *(huì)* (will) (II)**

會 *(huì)* (will) indicates an anticipated event or action. [See also Grammar 9, Lesson 8.]

A 白老師現在不在辦公室，可是他明天會在。

Bái lǎoshī xiànzài bú zài bàngōngshì, kěshì tā míngtiān huì zài.

Teacher Bai is not in the office now, but he will be tomorrow.

B Q: 你明年做什麼？　　A: 我明年會去英國學英文。

Nǐ míngnián zuò shénme?　　　　*Wǒ míngnián huì qù Yīngguó xué Yīngwén.*

What are you going to do next year?　　I'm going to Britain to study English next year.

C 他說他晚上會給你發短信。

Tā shuō tā wǎnshang huì gěi nǐ fā duǎnxìn.

He said he'll send you a text message in the evening.

The negative form of 會 *(huì)* is 不會 *(bú huì)*.

D 小王覺得不舒服，今天不會來滑冰了。

Xiǎo Wáng juéde bù shūfu, jīntiān bú huì lái huá bīng le.

Little Wang is not feeling well. He won't come ice skating today after all.

E 她這幾天特別忙，晚上不會去聽音樂會。

Tā zhè jǐ tiān tèbié máng, wǎnshang bú huì qù tīng yīnyuèhuì.

She's very busy these days. She won't be going to the concert tonight.

F 天氣預報說這個週末不會下雪。

Tiānqì yùbào shuō zhè ge zhōumò bú huì xià xuě.

The weather forecast says that it won't snow this weekend.

EXERCISES

More exercises

Answer the questions using 會 or 不會 where appropriate. Use exercise 1 as an example.

1. 你明天會去看電影嗎？（我明天很忙⋯⋯）

   → 我明天很忙，不會去看電影。

2. 明天會下雪嗎？（明天天氣很好⋯⋯）

3. 你今年夏天會去中國學習中文嗎？（我今年夏天不在美國學校上課⋯⋯）

---

4 | **Adjective +（一）點兒** *([yì] diǎnr)* **(a bit)**

The expression （一）點兒 *([yì] diǎnr)* (a bit) can be placed after an adjective to indicate slight qualification. 一 *(yī)* is often omitted in casual speech.

A 前幾天我很不高興，可是昨天考試考得很好，我高興點兒了。

Qián jǐ tiān wǒ hěn bù gāoxìng, kěshì zuótiān kǎo shì kǎo de hěn hǎo, wǒ gāoxìng diǎnr le.

I was very unhappy a few days ago, but I did very well on the exam yesterday. I am a little bit happier now.

B 我妹妹比我姐姐高一點兒。

Wǒ mèimei bǐ wǒ jiějie gāo yì diǎnr.

My younger sister is a little taller than my older sister.

C 你得快點兒，看電影要晚了。

Nǐ děi kuài diǎnr, kàn diànyǐng yào wǎn le.

You'd better hurry up or you'll be late for the movie.

D 今天比昨天冷點兒。

Jīntiān bǐ zuótiān lěng diǎnr.

Today is a bit colder than yesterday.

E 老師，請您說話說得慢一點兒。

Lǎoshī, qǐng nín shuō huà shuō de màn yì diǎnr.

Teacher, please speak a little more slowly.

（一）點兒 (*[yì] diǎnr*) does not precede the adjective. The following sentences are incorrect:

[⊗ 我妹妹比我姐姐一點兒高。]
[⊗ 今天比昨天一點兒冷。]
[⊗ 老師，請您說話說得一點兒慢。]

EXERCISES

Paraphrase the sentences using 得多/多了 or 一點兒 where appropriate. Use exercise 1 as an example.

More exercises

1 今天有點兒冷，昨天不冷。

→ 今天比昨天冷一點兒。

2 坐地鐵很快，坐公共汽車很慢。

3 這家商店的東西很便宜，那家商店的東西很貴。

Language Practice

Let's compare

INTERPERSONAL

In pairs, role-play two friends shopping. Compare the colors, styles, and prices of these two pairs of shoes and help each other decide which pair to buy.

Afterwards, you wear your new shoes on a blind date. Use the prompts to tell each other your preferences and opinions, e.g.:

好吃 (hǎochī) (good to eat, delicious)

我喜歡吃美國菜。我覺得美國菜比中國菜好吃。你呢？

Wǒ xǐhuan chī Měiguó cài. Wǒ juéde Měiguó cài bǐ Zhōngguó cài hǎochī. Nǐ ne?

1   好喝 *hǎohē* (delicious to drink)

2   容易 *róngyì*

3   快 *kuài*

A new you

PRESENTATIONAL

Little Zhang has decided to change his old habits in order to lead a healthier lifestyle. Based on the images, describe how he does things differently these days using 了 (le), e.g.:

   (past) ✓ (present)

他以前不吃早飯，現在吃早飯了。

Tā yǐqián bù chī zǎofàn, xiànzài chī zǎofàn le.

1	✅ (past)	❌ (present)
2	✅ (past)	❌ (present)
3	❌ (past)	✅ (present)

What about you? Share a list of lifestyle changes that you would like to make.

C | **Super-fan** | INTERPERSONAL

In pairs, show how much of a fan you are of the IC characters. Answer the questions affirmatively by using 不但⋯而且⋯ (búdàn . . . érqiě . . .) and add that they possess other qualities or capacities.

Q: 王朋帥嗎？ 　　　　　　　　　　高
Wáng Péng shuài ma? 　　　　　　*gāo*

A: 王朋不但很帥，而且很高。
Wáng Péng búdàn hěn shuài, érqiě hěn gāo.

Q: 王朋喜歡看球嗎？ 　　　　　　打球
Wáng Péng xǐhuan kàn qiú ma? 　*dǎ qiú*

A: 王朋不但喜歡看球，而且喜歡打球。
Wáng Péng búdàn xǐhuan kàn qiú, érqiě xǐhuan dǎ qiú.

1 Q: 高文中高嗎？ 　　　　　　　　帥
Gāo Wénzhōng gāo ma? 　　　　*shuài*

A: _____

Q: 高文中喜歡唱歌嗎？ 　　　　　跳舞
Gāo Wénzhōng xǐhuan chàng gē ma? 　*tiào wǔ*

A: _____

2 Q: 白英愛寫字寫得快嗎？

Bái Yīng'ài xiě zì xiě de kuài ma?

漂亮

piàoliang

A: _____

Q: 白英愛會說英文嗎？

Bái Yīng'ài huì shuō Yīngwén ma?

中文

Zhōngwén

A: _____

3 Q: 李友的衣服好看嗎？

Lǐ Yǒu de yīfu hǎokàn ma?

便宜

piányi

A: _____

Q: 李友常常復習生詞語法嗎？

Lǐ Yǒu chángcháng fùxí shēngcí yǔfǎ ma?

預習

yùxí

A: _____

D | **Weather forecast** | PRESENTATIONAL

Use the images below to give a weather report to the class, e.g.:

北京

Běijīng

天氣預報說北京明天會下雪。

Tiānqì yùbào shuō Běijīng míngtiān huì xià xuě.

1 北京

Běijīng

2 紐約

Niǔyuē

3 紐約 ✕

Niǔyuē

Dating dilemma

INTERPERSONAL

You can't make up your mind: "Who should I go out with, Student A or Student B?" Student A has many good qualities. Your friend argues that Student B at least equals Student A, perhaps even surpasses him/her. Or your friend reminds you that Student B is better than Student A in some other way. Use ···跟···一樣··· (...gēn...yíyàng...) or 比 (bǐ) to compare the two based on their attributes, e.g.:

You

我覺得Student A很帥／漂亮。

Wǒ juéde Student A hěn shuài/piàoliang.

Friend

可是 Student B 跟 Student A一樣帥／漂亮。

Kěshì Student B gēn Student A yíyàng shuài/piàoliang.

不，不，不，Student B比 Student A帥／
漂亮多了。

Bù, bù, bù, Student B bǐ Student A shuài/piàoliang duō le.

1 高
   gāo

2 酷
   kù

3 學習　好
   xuéxí　*hǎo*

4 打球打得好
   dǎ qiú dǎ de hǎo

5 跳舞跳得好
   tiào wǔ tiào de hǎo

Then give a conclusion about whom you should go out with, using ···比 (bǐ)···好 (hǎo).

❶ 冷   ❷ 冰

What do the characters mean?

What is the common radical?

What does the radical mean?

How does the radical relate to the overall meaning of the characters?

Chinese Chat

The IC cast is discussing plans to go ice skating on WeChat. Which of the characters are planning to go?

9:41 PM   85%

‹ WeChat   **朋友們**

7:20 PM

明天我想去滑冰。誰想一起去？

我！

我也想去，可是我現在在紐約……

明天天氣很好，那我也去吧！

The Weather Here Is Awful!

Dialogue 2

（高文中在網上找白英愛聊天兒。）

英愛，紐約那麼好玩兒，你怎麼在網上，沒出去？

這兒的天氣非常糟糕。

怎麼了？[a]

昨天下大雨，今天又[5]下雨了。

這個週末這兒天氣很好，你快一點兒回來吧。

這個週末紐約也會暖和一點兒。我下個星期有一個面試，還不能回去。

我在加州找了一個工作，你也去吧。加州冬天不冷，夏天不熱，春天和秋天更舒服。

加州好是好[6]，可是我更喜歡紐約。

Language Note

[a] 怎麼了？(Zěnme le?)
This question may be asked upon encountering an unusual situation.

Pinyin Dialogue

(Gāo Wénzhōng zài wǎng shang zhǎo Bái Yīng'ài liáo tiānr.)

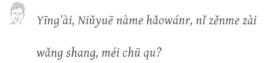 Yīng'ài, Niǔyuē nàme hǎowánr, nǐ zěnme zài

wǎng shang, méi chū qu?

Zhèr de tiānqì fēicháng zāogāo.

Zěnme le?[a]

Zuótiān xià dà yǔ, jīntiān yòu[5] xià yǔ le.

Zhè ge zhōumò zhèr tiānqì hěn hǎo, nǐ kuài yì

diǎnr huí lai ba.

Zhè ge zhōumò Niǔyuē yě huì nuǎnhuo yì diǎnr.

Wǒ xià ge xīngqī yǒu yí ge miànshì, hái bù néng

huí qu.

Wǒ zài Jiāzhōu zhǎo le yí ge gōngzuò, nǐ yě qù

ba. Jiāzhōu dōngtiān bù lěng, xiàtiān bú rè,

chūntiān hé qiūtiān gèng shūfu.

Jiāzhōu hǎo shi hǎo[6], kěshì wǒ gèng xǐhuan

Niǔyuē.

Vocabulary

No.	Word	Pinyin	Part of Speech	Definition
1	那麼	*nàme*	pr	(indicating degree) so, such
2	好玩兒	*hǎowánr*	adj	fun, amusing, interesting
3	非常	*fēicháng*	adv	very, extremely, exceedingly
4	糟糕	*zāogāo*	adj	in a terrible mess, how terrible
5	下雨	*xià yǔ*	vo	to rain
6	又	*yòu*	adv	again [See Grammar 5.]
7	面試	*miànshì*	v/n	to interview; interview (for a job or school admission)
8	回去	*huí qu*	vc	to go back, to return
9	冬天	*dōngtiān*	n	winter
10	夏天	*xiàtiān*	n	summer
11	熱	*rè*	adj	hot
12	春天	*chūntiān*	n	spring
13	秋天	*qiūtiān*	n	autumn, fall
14	舒服	*shūfu*	adj	comfortable
15	加州	*Jiāzhōu*	pn	California

Audio

Flashcards

You see these decorations alongside a neighbor's door in Chinatown. What season is being celebrated?

Calligraphy courtesy of Zhongli Zhang

大地回春

冬去山明水秀

春來鳥語花香

GET Real WITH CHINESE

如果天氣不好，
你想在家做什麼？

Rúguǒ tiānqì bù hǎo, nǐ xiǎng zài jiā zuò shénme?

If the weather is bad, what would you like to do at home?

How About You?

我想在家 ＿＿＿＿＿＿ 。

Wǒ xiǎng zài jiā ＿＿＿＿＿＿.

See index for corresponding vocabulary or research another term.

Grammar

5 | **The adverb 又 *(yòu)* (again)**

又 *(yòu)* (again) indicates the recurrence of an action.

A 昨天早上下雪，今天早上又下雪了。

Zuótiān zǎoshang xià xuě, jīntiān zǎoshang yòu xià xuě le.

It snowed yesterday morning, and snowed again this morning.

B 媽媽上個星期給我打電話，這個星期又給我打電話了。

Māma shàng ge xīngqī gěi wǒ dǎ diànhuà, zhè ge xīngqī yòu gěi wǒ dǎ diànhuà le.

My mom called me last week, and she called me again this week.

C 他昨天復習了第八課的語法，今天又復習了。

Tā zuótiān fùxí le dì bā kè de yǔfǎ, jīntiān yòu fùxí le.

He reviewed the grammar in Lesson Eight yesterday, and reviewed it again today.

If the verb is 是 *(shì)* or a modal verb, 又 *(yòu)* is required regardless of the timing of the action.

D 明天又是星期一了。

Míngtiān yòu shì xīngqīyī le.

Tomorrow is Monday again.

E 妹妹上個星期買了很多衣服，明天又要去買衣服。

Mèimei shàng ge xīngqī mǎi le hěn duō yīfu, míngtiān yòu yào qù mǎi yīfu.

My younger sister bought a lot of clothes last week. She'll go clothes shopping again tomorrow.

Like 又 *(yòu)*, 再 *(zài)* also signifies the recurrence of an action, but refers to the future.

F 同學們剛才練習打球練習得不錯，不過老師說明天得再練習。

Tóngxué men gāngcái liànxí dǎ qiú liànxí de búcuò, búguò lǎoshī shuō míngtiān děi zài liànxí.

The students did well practicing playing ball just now, but the teacher said that they need to keep practicing tomorrow.

G 我昨天去跳舞了，我想明天晚上再去跳舞。

Wǒ zuótiān qù tiào wǔ le, wǒ xiǎng míngtiān wǎnshang zài qù tiào wǔ.

I went dancing yesterday. I'd like to go dancing again tomorrow night.

More exercises

EXERCISES

Using 又, combine the sentences to create a new one to indicate that something happened again. Use exercise 1 as an example.

1　昨天我媽媽給我打電話了。

　　今天我媽媽給我打電話了。

　　→　今天我媽媽又給我打電話了。

2　我們上個星期考試了。我們這個星期考試了。

3　這裡昨天下雪了。這裡今天下雪了。

---

6 | **Adjective/verb + 是** (shì) **+ adjective/verb +**
可是/但是··· (kěshì/dànshì...)

Sentences in this pattern usually imply that the speaker accepts the validity of a certain point of view but wishes to offer an alternative perspective or emphasize a different aspect of the matter.

A Q: 滑冰難不難？

Huá bīng nán bu nán?

Is ice skating difficult?

A: 滑冰難是難，可是很有意思。

Huá bīng nán shì nán, kěshì hěn yǒu yìsi.

It is difficult, but it is very interesting.

B Q: 在高速公路上開車，你緊張嗎？

Zài gāosù gōnglù shang kāi chē, nǐ jǐnzhāng ma?

Do you get nervous driving on the highway?

A: 緊張是緊張，可是也很好玩兒。

Jǐnzhāng shì jǐnzhāng, kěshì yě hěn hǎowánr.

I do get nervous, but I find it a lot of fun, too.

C Q: 明天學校開會，你去不去？

Míngtiān xuéxiào kāi huì, nǐ qù bu qù?

There's a meeting at school tomorrow. Are you going?

A: 我去是去，可是會晚一點兒。

Wǒ qù shì qù, kěshì huì wǎn yì diǎnr.

I am going, but I'll be a little bit late.

D Q: 你喜歡這張照片嗎？

Nǐ xǐhuan zhè zhāng zhàopiàn ma?

Do you like this photo?

A: 喜歡是喜歡，可是這張照片太小了。

Xǐhuan shì xǐhuan, kěshì zhè zhāng zhàopiàn tài xiǎo le.

I do, but this picture is too small.

This pattern can be used only when the adjective or verb in it has already been mentioned, e.g., 難 (nán) in (A), 緊張 (jǐnzhāng) in (B), 去 (qù) in (C), and 喜歡 (xǐhuan) in (D). In this regard, it is different from the pattern 雖然···可是/但是··· (suīrán . . . kěshì/dànshì . . .).

EXERCISES

In pairs, take turns completing the exchanges using 是⋯可是/但是⋯ where appropriate. Use exercise 1 as an example.

1 **Student A** 坐公共汽車很麻煩。（很便宜）

   Student B 坐公共汽車麻煩是麻煩，可是很便宜。

2 **Student A** 打車去機場很方便。（很貴）

   Student B ＿＿＿＿＿＿＿＿＿＿＿＿。

3 **Student A** 這件襯衫大小很合適。（樣子不好）

   Student B ＿＿＿＿＿＿＿＿＿＿＿＿。

Chinese Chat

Your friend is chatting with you on Google Hangouts to arrange an outing. How would you reply?

Language Practice

| | Depends on the weather | INTERPERSONAL |

When you plan something and the weather does not cooperate, what do you do? In pairs, take turns suggesting alternatives using 還是···吧··· (*háishi . . . ba . . .*) and see if you can settle on plans.

Student A   我想出去玩兒，可是下雨了。

Wǒ xiǎng chū qu wánr, kěshì xià yǔ le.

Student B   別出去了！還是在家看電視吧。

Bié chū qu le! Háishi zài jiā kàn diànshì ba.

1   Student A   我想去買點兒東西，可是雪下得很大。

Wǒ xiǎng qù mǎi diǎnr dōngxi, kěshì xuě xià de hěn dà.

Student B   _____

2   Student A   我想出去看朋友，可是天氣很糟糕。

Wǒ xiǎng chū qu kàn péngyou, kěshì tiānqì hěn zāogāo.

Student B   _____

3   Student A   我想去公園打球，但是太熱。

Wǒ xiǎng qù gōngyuán dǎ qiú, dànshì tài rè.

Student B   _____

Same old, same old

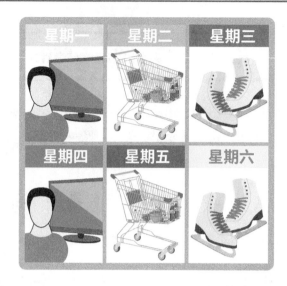

Based on the above calendar, recap what Little Zhang did last week by using 又 (yòu), e.g.:

小張星期一看電視，星期四又看電視了。

Xiǎo Zhāng xīngqīyī kàn diànshì, xīngqīsì yòu kàn diànshì le.

1

2

H

Two sides to every coin

In pairs, take turns reminding each that there is another side to consider by using

⋯是⋯，可是⋯ (…shì…, kěshì…), e.g.:

加州　　漂亮

Jiāzhōu　　*piàoliang*

Student A　加州很漂亮。

Jiāzhōu hěn piàoliang.

Student B　加州漂亮是漂亮，可是東西太貴了。

Jiāzhōu piàoliang shì piàoliang, kěshì dōngxi tài guì le.

1 紐約
Niǔyuē

有意思
yǒu yìsi

2 坐地鐵
zuò dìtiě

便宜
piányi

3 坐公共汽車
zuò gōnggòng qìchē

慢
màn

4 北京的冬天
Běijīng de dōngtiān

下雪
xià xuě

Weather report

PRESENTATIONAL

It's winter, and you're the newly hired weatherperson at the student TV station. Report on the weather in Beijing for the next three days. Describe which days will be colder/warmer and how the weather will change. After finishing up your report, compare the weather in Beijing with the weather in your town.

next Monday
28°F

next Tuesday
37°F

next Wednesday
40°F

What do the characters mean?

What is the common radical?

What does the radical mean?

How does the radical relate to the overall meaning of the characters?

Characterize it!

❶ 春

❷ 暖

More characters

文化

Continue
to explore

A section of the Great Wall near Beijing

Peach blossoms in Wuyuan, Jiangxi Province

波士頓
Bōshìdùn
BOSTON

倫敦
Lúndūn
LONDON

柏林
Bólín
BERLIN

PLACE NAME TRANSLITERATION

Some Chinese names for places in the West were invented
by early Chinese immigrants, for example, San Francisco was
dubbed 舊金山 *(Jiùjīnshān)* (lit. Old Gold Mountain) after
gold was discovered in Victoria, Australia. For a period of time,
Melbourne was called 新金山 *(Xīnjīnshān)* (lit. New Gold
Mountain). However, the vast majority of Chinese names for
places in the West are transliterations. California, for instance,
is transliterated as 加利福尼亞州 *(Jiālìfúníyàzhōu)*,
which is often shortened to 加州 *(Jiāzhōu)*. The character
州 *(zhōu)* means "state." Today, Melbourne is known by its
transliteration 墨爾本 *(Mò'ěrběn)* as well.

Weather

Across China, climatic conditions differ dramatically. In general terms, the north is cold and snowy in winter; the south, hot and wet in summer. 重慶 (*Chóngqìng*), 武漢 (*Wǔhàn*), and 南京 (*Nánjīng*), are nicknamed the "Three Furnaces on the Yangtze River" for their scorching hot summer temperatures. Some cities are known for being temperate year-round— 昆明 (*Kūnmíng*), for instance, is famous for being like spring all year, 四季如春 (*sìjì rú chūn*). In the lower Yangtze (長江) (*Chángjiāng*) valley, the rainy season called 梅雨 (*méi yǔ*) starts in mid-June and lasts until early July, bringing copious rain and high humidity. 梅 (*méi*) (plum) is a homophone of 霉 (*méi*) meaning "mold." In southern China, the rainy season generally starts in July and ends in August, swelling nearly all rivers to flood levels. In winter, the warmth and resorts of the island of 海南 (*Hǎinán*) provide a respite to tourists from the north, while many southerners brave the cold in the northern city of 哈爾濱 (*Hā'ěrbīn*) for its annual ice sculpture festival.

A snow-covered house in Xuexiang Village, Heilongjiang Province

UNITS OF MEASUREMENT

China uses the metric system: thus, temperatures are given in Celsius, distances in kilometers, and weights in kilograms in China. However, on occasion, people do still use traditional Chinese units of measurement such as the 里 (*lǐ*), equal to half a kilometer or 0.311 miles, and the 斤 (*jīn*), equal to half a kilogram or 1.102 pounds. The 里 (*lǐ*) is referred to in a famous Chinese proverb from the Tao Te Ching, 道德經 (*Dàodéjīng*), attributed to Laozi: 千里之行，始於足下 (*qiān lǐ zhī xíng, shǐ yú zú xià*) (A journey of a thousand li begins with a single step).

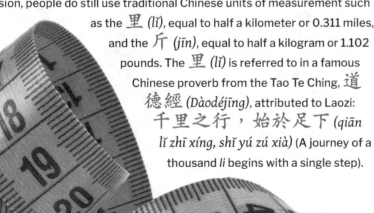

COMPARE & CONTRAST

The traditional Chinese calendar, which is strictly speaking a lunisolar calendar, is divided into twenty-four solar terms called 節氣 (*jiéqi*). One term, 冬至 (*dōngzhì*) (winter solstice), marks the longest night of the year in the Northern Hemisphere. Traditionally, people eat dumplings (餃子) (*jiǎozi*), in the north, and wonton (餛飩) (*húntun*) and glutinous rice balls (湯圓) (*tāngyuán*) in the south. It is also the day to make ritual offerings to one's ancestors and visit the graves of deceased relatives. Is the December solstice observed in any special way in your culture? Are there any foods or traditions associated with it?

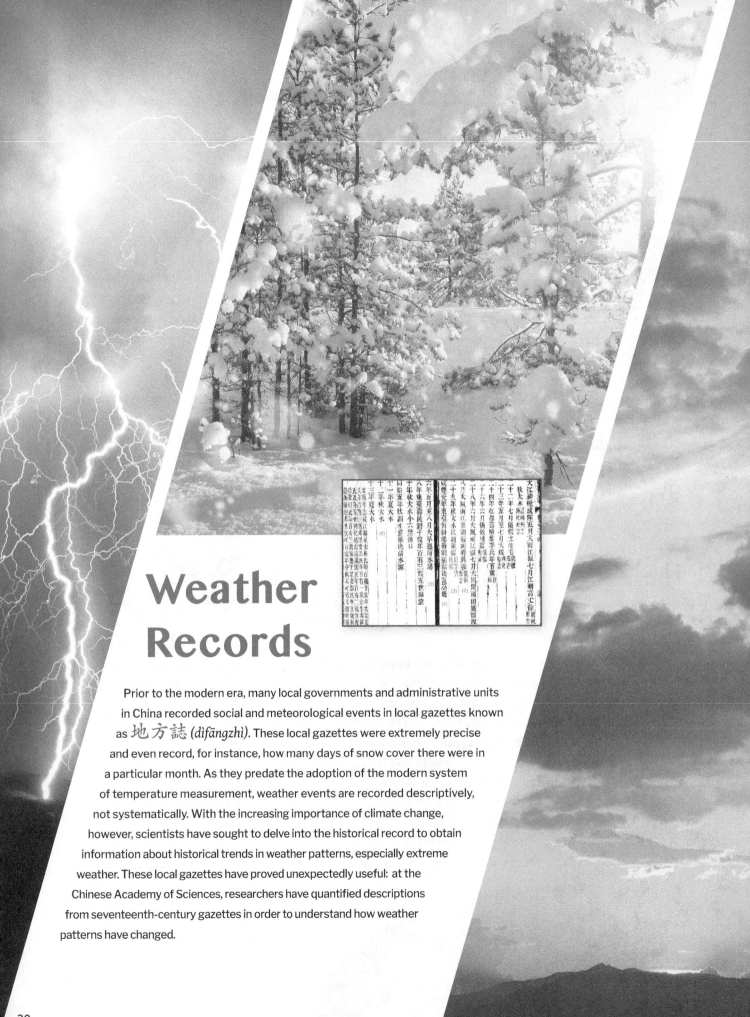

Weather Records

Prior to the modern era, many local governments and administrative units in China recorded social and meteorological events in local gazettes known as 地方誌 (*difāngzhì*). These local gazettes were extremely precise and even record, for instance, how many days of snow cover there were in a particular month. As they predate the adoption of the modern system of temperature measurement, weather events are recorded descriptively, not systematically. With the increasing importance of climate change, however, scientists have sought to delve into the historical record to obtain information about historical trends in weather patterns, especially extreme weather. These local gazettes have proved unexpectedly useful: at the Chinese Academy of Sciences, researchers have quantified descriptions from seventeenth-century gazettes in order to understand how weather patterns have changed.

Lesson Wrap-Up

Rearrange the sentences below into a logical sequence. Then combine the sentences into a coherent narrative. Replace nouns with pronouns and change periods to commas where appropriate. Delete identical subject pronouns. Add the connective devices 而且 (érqiě) and 所以 (suǒyǐ), the location word 這兒 (zhèr), and the time word 晚上 (wǎnshang) where desirable.

_____晚上高文中在網上跟白英愛聊天。

_____高文中告訴白英愛學校那邊的天氣很好。

__1__白英愛昨天來紐約找工作。

_____高文中讓白英愛快點回去。

_____紐約今天又下雨了。

_____白英愛說紐約的天氣非常糟糕。

_____紐約昨天下大雨了。

_____白英愛說紐約的天氣週末也會好一點。

_____白英愛說下星期一她有一個面試。

_____白英愛說她不能回去。

Pretend that you are a Chinese cable TV weatherperson and give a national two-day weather forecast to the class or make a video and share it with your classmates. Look up the two-day weather forecasts for five cities in five different regions of your country—e.g., New England, Florida, the Midwest, the Pacific Northwest, and California—for any two-day period. Is there any rain or snow in the forecasts? How do the temperatures compare across the two-day period?

Interview a friend about what the seasons are like in his/her hometown.

你家那兒的冬天怎麼樣？冷不冷？常常下雪嗎？

冬天可以做什麼？

你家那兒的春天呢？長不長？舒服不舒服？

夏天熱不熱？常常下雨嗎？

夏天可以做什麼？

秋天天藍不藍？

你喜歡你家那兒的春天、夏天、秋天還是冬天？為什麼？

Can-Do Check List

I can

Before proceeding to Lesson 12, make sure you can complete the following tasks in Chinese:

- ☐ Provide a simple description of the weather
- ☐ Describe the climate where I live
- ☐ Describe basic weather changes
- ☐ Compare the weather in two places

吃飯
Chī fàn

DINING

Learning Objectives

In this lesson, you will learn to:

- Ask if there are seats available at a restaurant
- Order some Chinese dishes
- Describe your dietary preferences and restrictions
- Ask for recommendations
- Rush your order
- Pay for your meal and get change

Relate & Get Ready

In your own culture/community:

- Do people order and eat their own dishes, or do they share their dishes with others?
- Do people prefer hot or cold beverages with their meals?
- How do most people pay for their meals: in cash or with a credit card?

Dining Out

Dialogue 1

Audio

Video

（在飯館兒……）

請進，請進。

人怎麼這麼[a]多？好像一個位子[b]都沒[1]有了。

服務員，請問，還有沒有位子？

有，有，有。那張桌子沒有人。

……

兩位想吃點兒什麼？

王朋，你點菜吧。

好。先給我們兩盤餃子，要素的。

除了餃子以外，還要什麼？

李友，你說呢？

還要一盤家常豆腐，不要放肉，我吃素。

我們的家常豆腐沒有肉。

還要兩碗[c]酸辣湯，請別放味精，少[2]放點兒鹽。有小白菜嗎？

對不起，小白菜剛[3]賣完[4]。

那就不要青菜了。

那喝點兒什麼呢？

我要一杯冰茶。李友，你喝什麼？

我很渴，請給我一杯可樂，多放點兒冰。

好，兩盤餃子，一盤家常豆腐，兩碗酸辣湯，一杯冰茶，一杯可樂，多放冰。還要別的嗎？

不要別的了，這些夠^d了。服務員，我們都餓了，請上菜快一點兒^e。

沒問題，菜很快就能做好⁵。

(Zài fànguǎnr . . .)

🗣 *Qǐng jìn, qǐng jìn.*

🗣 *Rén zěnme zhème^a duō? Hǎoxiàng yí ge wèizi^b*

dōu méi¹ yǒu le.

🗣 *Fúwùyuán, qǐng wèn, hái yǒu méiyǒu wèizi?*

🗣 *Yǒu, yǒu, yǒu. Nà zhāng zhuōzi méiyǒu rén.*

. . .

🗣 *Liǎng wèi xiǎng chī diǎnr shénme?*

🗣 *Wáng Péng, nǐ diǎn cài ba.*

🗣 *Hǎo. Xiān gěi wǒmen liǎng pán jiǎozi, yào sù de.*

🗣 *Chúle jiǎozi yǐwài, hái yào shénme?*

🗣 *Lǐ Yǒu, nǐ shuō ne?*

🗣 *Hái yào yì pán jiācháng dòufu, bú yào fàng ròu,*

wǒ chī sù.

🗣 *Wǒmen de jiācháng dòufu méiyǒu ròu.*

🗣 *Hái yào liǎng wǎn^c suānlàtāng, qǐng bié fàng*

wèijīng, shǎo² fàng diǎnr yán. Yǒu xiǎo báicài ma?

🗣 *Duìbuqǐ, xiǎo báicài gāng³ mài wán⁴.*

🗣 *Nà jiù bú yào qīngcài le.*

🗣 *Nà hē diǎnr shénme ne?*

🗣 *Wǒ yào yì bēi bīngchá. Lǐ Yǒu, nǐ hē shénme?*

🗣 *Wǒ hěn kě, qǐng gěi wǒ yì bēi kělè, duō fàng*

diǎnr bīng.

🗣 *Hǎo, liǎng pán jiǎozi, yì pán jiācháng dòufu, liǎng*

wǎn suānlàtāng, yì bēi bīngchá, yì bēi kělè, duō

fàng bīng. Hái yào bié de ma?

🗣 *Bú yào bié de le, zhè xiē gòu^d le. Fúwùyuán,*

wǒmen dōu è le, qǐng shàng cài kuài yì diǎnr^e.

🗣 *Méi wèntí, cài hěn kuài jiù néng zuò hǎo⁵.*

a 這麼 *(zhème/zème)*

In Beijing, 這麼 *(zhème)* is commonly pronounced as *zème.*

b 位子 *(wèizi)* **and** 椅子 *(yǐzi)*

Seat is 位子 *(wèizi)*; chair is 椅子 *(yǐzi)*.

c 碗 *(wǎn)*

Nouns for objects that contain things can function as measure words, as in 一碗飯 *(yì wǎn fàn)* (a bowl of rice), 一杯水 *(yì bēi shuǐ)* (a glass of water), and 一盤餃子 *(yì pán jiǎozi)* (a plate of dumplings). When these words are used as nouns rather than as measure words, some have to take a suffix such as 子 *(zi)*, as in 杯子 *(bēizi)* (cup), 盤子 *(pánzi)* (plate), and 瓶子 *(píngzi)* (bottle). Note that these words are defined in the vocabulary list according to the part of speech in which they appear in the text.

d 夠 *(gòu)*

When used as an adjective, 夠 *(gòu)* can only be a predicate; it cannot come before the noun being modified. Thus you can say 我的錢不夠 *(Wǒ de qián bú gòu)* (I don't have enough money), but never ✕ 我沒有夠錢. In an affirmative statement, 夠 *(gòu)* usually cannot be modified by 很 *(hěn)*. Additionally, 夠 *(gòu)* can be used after a verb as a complement, e.g.: 玩（兒）夠了 *(wán[r] gòu le)* (to have played enough) and 買夠了 *(mǎi gòu le)* (to have bought enough).

e **Topic-comment sentences**

請上菜快一點兒 *(qǐng shàng cài kuài yì diǎnr)* is a topic-comment sentence. [See also Grammar 1, Lesson 10, Volume 1.] 上菜 *(shàng cài)* is known information and the topic of the sentence. 快一點兒 *(kuài yì diǎnr)* is new information, hence the word order.

Vocabulary

No.	Word	Pinyin	Part of Speech	Definition
1	飯館（兒）	fànguǎn(r)	n	restaurant
2	好像	hǎoxiàng	adv	to seem, to be like
3	位子	wèizi	n	seat
4	服務員	fúwùyuán	n	waiter, attendant
	服務	fúwù	v	to serve, to provide service
5	桌子	zhuōzi	n	table
6	點菜	diǎn cài	vo	to order food
7	盤	pán	n	plate, dish
8	餃子	jiǎozi	n	dumplings (with vegetable and/or meat filling)
9	素	sù	adj	vegetarian (lit. plain)
10	家常	jiācháng	n	home-style
11	豆腐	dòufu	n	tofu, bean curd
12	放	fàng	v	to put, to place
13	肉	ròu	n	meat
14	碗	wǎn	n	bowl
15	酸辣湯	suānlàtāng	n	hot-and-sour soup
	酸	suān	adj	sour
	辣	là	adj	spicy, hot
	湯	tāng	n	soup
16	味精	wèijīng	n	monosodium glutamate (MSG)
17	鹽	yán	n	salt
18	小白菜	xiǎo báicài	n	baby bok choy
19	剛	gāng	adv	just [See Grammar 3.]

Audio

Flashcards

GET Real WITH CHINESE

素菜

酸辣白菜............	¥20
蒜蓉青菜............	¥18
拍黄瓜............	¥18
麻婆豆腐............	¥22
凉拌豆腐............	¥20

荤菜

酸辣肥牛.........	¥48
水煮肉片.........	¥68
红烧肉............	¥38
椒盐牛仔骨.........	¥48
糖醋鱼............	¥45

汤类

¥18

面类

No.	Word	Pinyin	Part of Speech	Definition
20	賣完	mài wán	vc	to be sold out [See Grammar 4.]
	完	wán	c	finished
21	青菜	qīngcài	n	green, leafy vegetable
22	冰茶	bīngchá	n	iced tea
	冰	bīng	n	ice
23	渴	kě	adj	thirsty
24	些	xiē	m	(measure word for an indefinite amount), some
25	夠	gòu	adj	enough
26	餓	è	adj	hungry
27	上菜	shàng cài	vo	to serve food

去中餐館吃飯，你想點什麼菜？

Qù Zhōngcānguǎn chī fàn, nǐ xiǎng diǎn shénme cài?

What dishes would you like to order at a Chinese restaurant?

我想點 ＿＿＿＿＿＿＿＿ 。

Wǒ xiǎng diǎn ＿＿＿＿＿＿＿＿ .

How About You?

See index for corresponding vocabulary or research another dish.

Grammar

<u>1</u> | 一…也／都…不／沒… (yī…yě/dōu…bù/méi…)

These structures are used for emphatic negation; they express the meaning "not at all" or "not even one."

Subject + 一 + measure word + object + 也／都 + 不／沒（有）(+ verb)
(yī)　　　　　　　　　　　　　(yě/dōu)　(bù/méi[yǒu])

A | 小李一個朋友也沒有。

Xiǎo Lǐ yí ge péngyou yě méiyǒu.

Little Li doesn't have a single friend.

B | 爸爸今天一杯茶都沒喝。

Bàba jīntiān yì bēi chá dōu méi hē.

My father didn't have a single cup of tea today.

Topic (object) + subject + 一 + measure word + 也／都 + 不／沒 + verb
(yī)　　　　　　　　　　　(yě/dōu)　(bù/méi)

C | 這些襯衫我一件也不喜歡。

Zhè xiē chènshān wǒ yí jiàn yě bù xǐhuan.

I don't like any of these shirts.

D | 哥哥的鞋，弟弟一雙都不能穿。

Gēge de xié, dìdi yì shuāng dōu bù néng chuān.

The younger brother cannot wear a single pair of his older brother's shoes.

Subject + 一點兒 + object + 也／都 + 不／沒 + verb
(yì diǎnr)　　　　　(yě/dōu)　(bù/méi)

E | 他去了商店，可是一點兒東西也沒買。

Tā qù le shāngdiàn, kěshì yì diǎnr dōngxi yě méi mǎi.

He went to the store, but didn't buy anything at all.

媽媽做菜一點兒味精都不放。

Māma zuò cài yì diǎnr wèijīng dōu bú fang.

Mom doesn't use any MSG in her cooking.

If the noun after 一 *(yī)* is countable, a proper measure word should be used between 一 *(yī)* and the noun, as in (A), (B), (C), and (D). If the noun is uncountable, the phrase 一點兒 *(yì diǎnr)* is usually used instead, as in (E) and (F).

The following sentences are incorrect:

[✖ 小李沒有一個朋友。]

[✖ 這些襯衫我不喜歡一件。]

[✖ 他東西沒買一點兒。]

The construction 一點兒 *(yìdiǎnr)* + 也 / 都 *(yě/dōu)* + 不 / 沒 *(bù/méi)* can also be used before an adjective to express emphatic negation, as in (G), (H), and (I).

G

這兒的冬天一點兒也不冷。

Zhèr de dōngtiān yì diǎnr yě bù lěng.

Winter here isn't cold at all.

H

那個學校一點兒也不漂亮。

Nà ge xuéxiào yì diǎnr yě bú piàoliang.

That school is not pretty at all.

I

這杯冰茶一點都不好喝。

Zhè bēi bīngchá yì diǎnr dōu bù hǎohē.

This glass of iced tea doesn't taste good at all.

EXERCISES

More exercises

Make the sentences more emphatic by using the 一···也/都···不/沒··· structure and appropriate measure words. Use exercise 1 as an example.

1   她不喜歡這個飯館兒的菜。

→ 這個飯館兒的菜她一個都不喜歡。

2   我今年沒有買衣服。

3   小王昨天沒有預習中文生詞。

多 / 少 (duō/shǎo) + verb

The way the two adjectives 多 (duō) and 少 (shǎo) are used is non-typical of adjectives in general. To express doing something "more" or "less," place 多 (duō) or 少 (shǎo) before the verb.

A　爸爸告訴媽媽做菜的時候少放鹽，
多放點兒糖。

Bàba gàosu māma zuò cài de shíhou shǎo fàng yán, duō fàng diǎnr táng.

Dad asked Mom to add less salt and more sugar when cooking.

B　上中文課得多説中文，少説英文。

Shàng Zhōngwén kè děi duō shuō Zhōngwén, shǎo shuō Yīngwén.

In Chinese class, one should speak more Chinese and less English.

The "多 / 少 (duō/shǎo) + verb" construction is sometimes used to denote a deviation from the correct amount or number.

C　你多找了我一塊錢。

Nǐ duō zhǎo le wǒ yí kuài qián.

You gave me one dollar too many.

D　老師説要寫五十個字，我寫了四十五個，
少寫了五個。

Lǎoshī shuō yào xiě wǔshí ge zì, wǒ xiě le sìshíwǔ ge, shǎo xiě le wǔ ge.

The teacher told us to write fifty characters. I wrote forty-five. I was five short.

EXERCISES

Fill in the blanks with 多 or 少. Use exercise 1 as an example.

1　醫生説我們得少喝可樂，多喝水。

2　爸爸希望我 ＿＿＿ 吃青菜 ＿＿＿ 吃肉。

3　這雙鞋一百七十五塊，我給了售貨員兩百塊，
她找了我三十五塊，＿＿＿ 找了十塊。

More
exercises

Comparing 剛 (gāng) (just) and 剛才 (gāngcái) (just now)

As an adverb, 剛 (gāng) (just) denotes that an action or change in situation took place in the very recent past.

A 我哥哥剛從中國來，在這兒一個朋友都沒有。

Wǒ gēge gāng cóng Zhōngguó lái, zài zhèr yí ge péngyou dōu méiyǒu.

My older brother just came from China. He doesn't have a single friend here.

B 我剛洗完澡，舒服極了。

Wǒ gāng xǐ wán zǎo, shūfu jí le.

I just showered, and feel great.

剛才 (gāngcái) (just now) is a time word that refers to the period just moments before.

C Q: 你知道王朋在哪兒嗎？

Nǐ zhīdào Wáng Péng zài nǎr ma?

Do you know where Wang Peng is?

A: 他剛才在這兒，我不知道他去哪兒了。

Tā gāngcái zài zhèr, wǒ bù zhīdao tā qù nǎr le.

He was here a moment ago. I don't know where he went.

D 弟弟剛才吃了十五個餃子，喝了兩碗酸辣湯。

Dìdi gāngcái chī le shíwǔ ge jiǎozi, hē le liǎng wǎn suānlàtāng.

My younger brother ate fifteen dumplings and two bowls of hot-and-sour soup a moment ago.

Although 剛 (gāng) and 剛才 (gāngcái) are similar in meaning, they are classified as different parts of speech and are therefore used differently. First, unlike 剛才 (gāngcái), 剛 (gāng) cannot be followed by 不 (bù) or 沒 (méi).

E Q: 你剛才為什麼沒說？

Nǐ gāngcái wèishénme méi shuō?

Why didn't you say anything a moment ago?

A: 我剛才不想說。

Wǒ gāngcái bù xiǎng shuō.

I didn't want to say anything a moment ago.

[✖ 你剛為什麼沒說？]
[✖ 我剛不想說。]

Second, sentences that include 剛才 (*gāngcái*) often end with 了 (*le*). By contrast, sentences that include 剛 (*gāng*) cannot end with 了 (*le*).

F Q: 你剛才去哪兒了？老師要你去辦公室找他。

Nǐ gāngcái qù nǎr le? Lǎoshī yào nǐ qù bàngōngshì zhǎo tā.

Where were you a moment ago? The teacher wanted you to go to his office.

A: 我剛才去圖書館了。

Wǒ gāngcái qù túshūguǎn le.

I went to the library just now.

G Q: 明天的考試你開始準備了嗎？

Míngtiān de kǎoshì nǐ kāishǐ zhǔnbèi le ma?

Have you started preparing for tomorrow's test?

A: 剛開始準備。

Gāng kāishǐ zhǔnbèi.

I just started.

[✖ 剛開始準備了。]

EXERCISES

Fill in the blanks with 剛 or 剛才. Use exercise 1 as an example.

More exercises

1　高文中 ＿＿＿＿ 從英國來。

　　→ 高文中剛從英國來。

2　她 ＿＿＿＿ 給我發了一個短信。

3　你 ＿＿＿＿ 吃完飯，現在別去洗澡。

Resultative complements (I)

Following a verb, an adjective or another verb can be used to denote the result of the action, hence the term resultative complement.

A　小白菜賣完了。

Xiǎo báicài mài wán le.

The baby bok choy is sold out.

B　你找錯錢了。

Nǐ zhǎo cuò qián le.

You gave me the wrong change.

C　那個人是誰你看清楚了嗎?

Nà ge rén shì shéi nǐ kàn qīngchu le ma?

Did you see clearly who that person was?

(清楚 [qīngchu] [clear] [See Dialogue 2.])

D　太好了，這個字你寫對了。

Tài hǎo le, zhè ge zì nǐ xiě duì le.

Great! You wrote this character correctly.

Generally, the negative form of a resultative complement is formed by placing 沒 (*méi*) (no, not) or 沒有 (*méiyǒu*) (have not) before the verb.

E　小白菜沒賣完。

Xiǎo báicài méi mài wán.

The baby bok choy isn't sold out.

F　那個人我沒看清楚。

Nà ge rén wǒ méi kàn qīngchu.

I didn't see clearly who that person was.

G　糟糕，這個字你沒有寫對。

Zāogāo, zhè ge zì nǐ méiyǒu xiě duì.

Yikes! You didn't write this character correctly.

The use of an adjective as a resultative complement is not random. It is advisable to take the combination of the verb and the complement as a whole unit.

EXERCISES

Fill in the blanks with the appropriate resultative complement: 完, 到, 錯, 對, or 懂.
Use exercise 1 as an example.

1 　你說錯了，她的名字不是王小英。

2 　你說 _____ 了，白英愛是韓國人。

3 　老師的話你聽 _____ 了嗎？

---

5 | 好 *(hǎo)* **as a resultative complement**

好 *(hǎo)* can serve as a complement following a verb to signify the completion of an action
and readiness to start another.

A 飯做好了，快來吃吧。

Fàn zuò hǎo le, kuài lái chī ba.

The food is ready. Come and eat.

B 功課做好了，我要睡覺了。

Gōngkè zuò hǎo le, wǒ yào shuì jiào le.

My homework is done, and I'm going to bed.

C 衣服我已經幫你買好了，明天晚會
你就可以穿了。

Yīfu wǒ yǐjīng bāng nǐ mǎi hǎo le, míngtiān wǎnhuì nǐ jiù kěyǐ chuān le.

I've already bought clothes for you. You can wear them to the party tomorrow night.

EXERCISES

Fill in the blanks with the appropriate verbs: 看, 做, 買, or 準備, and add 好 to indicate
that one is ready for the next action. Use exercise 1 as an example.

More
exercises

1 　飯做好了，可以吃飯了。

2 　電影票 _____ 了，我們進去吧。

3 　_____ 了嗎？可以開始考試了嗎？

Language Practice

I'll pass

PRESENTATIONAL

Your friend is hard to please and doesn't like any of the items he/she sees while out shopping with you. In pairs, discuss his/her shopping haul using 一⋯也/都⋯不/沒⋯ (yì . . . yě/dōu . . . bù/méi), e.g.:

那兒的襯衫他/她都不喜歡，一件都沒買。

Nàr de chènshān tā dōu bù xǐhuan, yí jiàn dōu méi mǎi.

 1　　 2　　 3　　 4　　 5

One of those days

PRESENTATIONAL

Everything went wrong for Wang Peng today. Li You, on the other hand, had a great day today. Recap what happened to them to the class using 了 (le), e.g.:

Wang Peng rode the wrong bus.

王朋今天坐錯車了。

Wáng Péng jīntiān zuò cuò chē le.

1　Wang Peng wore the wrong clothes.

2　Wang Peng did the wrong homework.

3　Li You understood what the teacher said.

4　Li You finished her homework.

5　Li You saw her good friend Bai Ying'ai.

Getting it done

In pairs, take turns asking each other whether you have finished one task and are ready for the next one, using 好 (hǎo), e.g.:

練習　　　漢字

liànxí　　　*Hànzì*

Q: 你漢字練習好了嗎？

Nǐ Hànzì liànxí hǎo le ma?

A: 漢字我練習好了。(affirmative)

Hànzì wǒ liànxí hǎo le.

A: 我練習漢字沒練習好。/
漢字我沒練習好。(negative)

Wǒ liànxí Hànzì méi liànxí hǎo./Hànzì wǒ méi liànxí hǎo.

1　做　　　中文功課

zuò　　　*Zhōngwén gōngkè*

2　復習　　生詞語法

fùxí　　　*shēngcí yǔfǎ*

3　準備　　考試

zhǔnbèi　　*kǎoshì*

Characterize it!

What do the characters mean?

What is the common radical?

What does the radical mean?

How does the radical relate to the overall meaning of the characters?

❶ 飯　❷ 館　❸ 餃　❹ 餓

More characters

What do Chinese-language teachers hope for from their students? Form complete sentences using 多 *(duō)* or 少 *(shǎo)*, e.g.:

老師希望學生：
多來上課
老師希望学生多來上課。

Lǎoshī xīwàng xuésheng:

duō lái shàng kè

Lǎoshī xīwàng xuésheng duō lái shàng kè.

1 多預習課文
   duō yùxí kèwén

2 多聽錄音
   duō tīng lùyīn

3 多復習生詞語法
   duō fùxí shēngcí yǔfǎ

4 多練習寫漢字
   duō liànxí xiě Hànzì

5 上課少說英文
   shàng kè shǎo shuō Yīngwén

6 少玩兒
   shǎo wánr

Then, in pairs, come up with your own list of what you or would like your teacher to do more or less, using 學生希望老師……… *(xuésheng xīwàng lǎoshī …)*.

Chinese Chat

Li You just posted a restaurant review on Dianping (大眾點評) *(Dàzhòng diǎnpíng)*, a popular Chinese review app. What dishes do you think she would recommend?

 李友
★★★★☆ 口味：4   環境：5   服務：4   人均：¥35

酸辣湯太好喝了！家常豆腐也很好吃，一點兒味精都沒放。不過素餃子不太好吃……

10-22 心美小館   讚(9)   回應(2)   收藏   舉報

At the Dining Hall

Dialogue 2

Audio

Video

（今天是星期四，學生餐廳有中國菜，
師傅是上海人。）

師傅[a]，請問今天晚飯有什麼好吃的？

我們今天有糖醋魚，甜甜的[6]、酸酸的，
好吃極了[b]，你買一個吧。

好。今天有沒有紅燒牛肉？

沒有。你已經要魚了，別吃肉了。來[7]個
涼拌黃瓜吧？

好。再來一碗米飯。一共多少錢？

糖醋魚，四塊五，涼拌黃瓜，一塊七；
一碗米飯，五毛錢。一共六塊七。

師傅，糟糕，我忘了帶飯卡了。這是十塊錢。

找你三塊三。

師傅，錢你找錯了，多找了我一塊錢。

對不起，我沒有看清楚。

沒關係[c]。

下個星期四再來。

好，再見。

Pinyin Dialogue

(Jīntiān shì xīngqīsì, xuéshēng cāntīng yǒu
Zhōngguó cài, shīfu shì Shànghǎi rén.)

 Shīfu[a], qǐng wèn jīntiān wǎnfàn yǒu shénme hàochī de?

 Wǒmen jīntiān yǒu tángcùyú, tián tián de[6], suān
suān de, hǎochī jí le[b], nǐ mǎi yí ge ba.

 Hǎo. Jīntiān yǒu méiyǒu hóngshāo niúròu?

 Méiyǒu. Nǐ yǐjīng yào yú le, bié chī ròu le. Lái[7] ge
liángbàn huánggua ba?

 Hǎo. Zài lái yì wǎn mǐfàn. Yígòng duōshao qián?

 Tángcùyú, sì kuài wǔ, liángbàn huánggua, yí kuài
qī; Yì wǎn mǐfàn, wǔ máo qián. Yígòng liù kuài qī.

 Shīfu, zāogāo, wǒ wàng le dài fànkǎ le. Zhè shì shí
kuài qián.

 Zhǎo nǐ sān kuài sān.

 Shīfu, qián nǐ zhǎo cuò le, duō zhǎo le wǒ yí kuài qián.

 Duìbuqǐ, wǒ méiyǒu kàn qīngchu.

 Méi guānxi[c].

Xià ge xīngqīsì zài lái.

Hǎo, zàijiàn.

Language Notes

a 師傅 (shīfu)

The term 師傅 (shīfu) (master worker) is commonly
used in Mainland China for addressing strangers,
particularly taxi drivers, chefs, and other skilled service
workers. [See also Cultural Literacy, Lesson 9, Volume 1.]

b 極了 (jí le)

When used after an adjective or verb, 極了 (jí le)
usually indicates a superlative degree, as in
今天熱極了 (Jīntiān rè jí le) (It is extremely hot today)
and 他高興極了 (Tā gāoxìng jí le) (He is overjoyed).

c 沒關係 (méi guānxi)

To respond to 對不起 (duìbuqǐ), it is common
to say 沒關係 (méi guānxi) (it doesn't matter).

Vocabulary

Audio

Flashcards

No.	Word	Pinyin	Part of Speech	Definition
1	師傅	shīfu	n	master worker
2	好吃	hǎochī	adj	delicious
3	糖醋魚	tángcùyú	n	sweet-and-sour fish
	糖	táng	n	sugar
	醋	cù	n	vinegar
4	甜	tián	adj	sweet
5	酸	suān	adj	sour
6	極	jí	adv	extremely
7	紅燒	hóngshāo	v	to braise in soy sauce (to red-cook)
8	牛肉	niúròu	n	beef
	牛	niú	n	cow, ox
9	魚	yú	n	fish
10	涼拌	liángbàn	v	(of food) cold "blended," cold tossed
11	黃瓜	huánggua	n	cucumber
12	米飯	mǐfàn	n	cooked rice
13	忘	wàng	v	to forget
14	帶	dài	v	to bring, to take, to carry, to come with
15	飯卡	fànkǎ	n	meal card
16	錯	cuò	adj	wrong

1	冰珍珠奶茶 半糖	65
3	熱拿鐵咖啡	225
1	冰拿鐵咖啡	75
1	熱卡布奇諾	75
合計:		440

GET Real WITH CHINESE

No.	Word	Pinyin	Part of Speech	Definition
17	清楚	*qīngchu*	adj	clear
18	沒關係	*méi guānxi*		it doesn't matter
19	上海	*Shànghǎi*	pn	Shanghai

你希望能在學校餐廳吃到什麼菜？

Nǐ xīwàng néng zài xuéxiào cāntīng chī dào shénme cài?

What dishes would you like to be able to eat at the school cafeteria?

我希望 _____ 。

Wǒ xīwàng _____ .

How About You?

See index for corresponding vocabulary or research another term.

Grammar

Adjective reduplication (I)

Some Chinese adjectives can be reduplicated. When monosyllabic adjectives are reduplicated, the accent usually falls on the second occurrence. Reduplication of adjectives often suggests an approving and appreciative attitude on the speaker's part when they are attributives and predicates.

A 王朋高高的，很帥。

Wáng Péng gāo gāo de, hěn shuài.

Wang Peng is tall and handsome.

B 可樂涼涼的，很好喝。

Kělè liáng liáng de, hěn hǎo hē.

The cola is nicely cold and tasty.

C 酸辣湯酸酸的、辣辣的，非常好喝。

Suānlàtāng suān suān de, là là de, fēicháng hǎo hē.

The hot-and-sour soup is a bit sour and a bit hot; it tastes great.

Reduplication of adjectives usually does not appear in negative form.

EXERCISES

Paraphrase the sentences by repeating the adjectives to show your approval or appreciation. Use exercise 1 as an example.

More
exercises

1 這碗湯　　辣　　很好喝

→ 這碗湯辣辣的，很好喝。

2 冰咖啡　　涼　　很好喝

3 紅燒牛肉　甜　　很好吃

The verb 來 (lái)

In colloquial Chinese, the verb 來 (lái) can serve as a substitute for certain verbs, mostly in imperative sentences.

A Q: 先生，你們想吃點兒什麼？

Xiānsheng, nǐmen xiǎng chī diǎnr shénme?

Sir, what would you like?

A: 來一盤糖醋魚，一碗酸辣湯，和一碗米飯。

Lái yì pán tángcùyú, yì wǎn suānlàtāng, hé yì wǎn mǐfàn.

Give us a plate of sweet-and-sour fish, a bowl of hot-and-sour soup, and a bowl of rice, please.

At a concert, when the singer has sung the last song:

B 再來一個！

Zài lái yí ge!

Encore!

The use of 來 (lái) in this sense is rather limited. It is usually used at restaurants, stores, and parties, especially when buying small things or coaxing someone to sing another song and so on.

Language Practice

	Try the special	PRESENTATIONAL

Role-play as a waiter in a restaurant. Use the images below to make recommendations to the class, e.g.:

我們的青菜好吃極了。

Wǒmen de qīngcài hǎochī jí le.

1

2

3

4

Now, role-play as a customer and complain about the food, e.g., it's too expensive, sour, sweet, spicy . . . Note: the opposites of 好吃 *(hǎochī)* and 好喝 *(hǎohē)* are 難吃 *(nánchī)* and 難喝 *(nánhē)*.

How do you pronounce the characters?

What is the common component?

How do you pronounce the common component?

How does the component relate to the pronunciation of the characters?

Characterize it!

❶ 請 ❷ 精 ❸ 清

More characters

May I take your order?

Pretend you and your classmates are in a restaurant in China, and the waiter is taking your order. The easiest way to place an order in a Chinese restaurant is to use 來 (lái), e.g.:

Q: 您想喝點兒什麼？

Nín xiǎng hē diǎnr shénme?

x2　A: 服務員，來兩杯冰茶。

Fúwùyuán, lái liǎng bēi bīngchá.

1 x3

2 x1

3 x1

4 x2

5 x2

It doesn't agree with me

Tell the waiter that you have a special diet and would like the chef not to use certain ingredients or seasonings, e.g.:

我不吃鹽，請師傅一點兒鹽都不要／別放。

Wǒ bù chī yán, qǐng shīfu yìdiǎnr yán dōu bú yào/bié fàng.

1　MSG

2　meat

3　vinegar

4　sugar

INTERPERSONAL	**At your service**	PRESENTATIONAL

You're helping your friend to prepare for an interview for a part-time job at a restaurant. In groups, brainstorm and create a protocol cheat sheet on how to greet and seat customers, recommend dishes, address customers' dietary restrictions, ensure customer satisfaction, etc. Compare each group's suggestions and vote for the best.

Q: 如果客人問："服務員，還有沒有位子？"服務員說什麼？

Rúguǒ kèrén wèn: "Fúwùyuán, hái yǒu méiyǒu wèizi?" Fúwùyuán shuō shénme?

A: 服務員說："有，有，有，那兒有位子。"

Fúwùyuán shuō: "Yǒu, yǒu, yǒu, nàr yǒu wèizi."

Chinese Chat

A customer is texting your restaurant to place a takeout order. How would you respond?

心美小館

我想點餐。 *15 minutes ago*

... *13 minutes ago*

姓張。一個家常豆腐，一碗酸辣湯，一碗米飯。 *12 minutes ago*

... *10 minutes ago*

豆腐賣完了？那有什麼好吃的素菜？ *8 minutes ago*

... *7 minutes ago*

好，一共多少錢？能刷卡嗎？ *6 minutes ago*

... *5 minutes ago*

什麼時候能做好？ *3 minutes ago*

... *1 minute ago*

Send

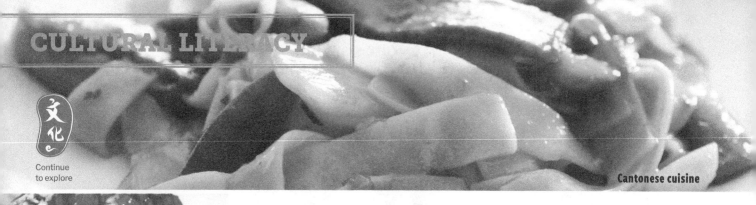

文化

Continue
to explore

Cantonese cuisine

FOUR
MAJOR SCHOOLS OF
Cooking

Shandong cuisine

The term 中國菜 (Zhōngguó cài) encompasses the great variety of Chinese cuisine. There are said to be four major schools of cooking: 魯菜 (Lǔcài), from northern Shandong Province; 川菜 (Chuāncài), from Sichuan Province; 粵菜 (Yuècài), from Guangdong Province; and 淮揚菜 (Huáiyángcài), from the lower Yangtze Valley. Chinese restaurants typically specialize in one particular style, but some are more eclectic.

Traditionally, the Chinese meal is built around a staple (主食) (zhǔshí)—in the south, this is typically rice, whereas in the north, it can be noodles (麵條) (miàntiáo), dumplings (餃子) (jiǎozi), or Chinese steamed bread (饅頭) (mántou).

Huaiyang cusine

Sichuanese cuisine

Utensils

In Chinese food culture, knives (刀) (*dāo*) belong in the kitchen, not at the dining table. The cook preempts the diner's need for a knife by cutting up food, especially meat, into small pieces before cooking. Most Chinese people prefer to eat with chopsticks (筷子) (*kuàizi*).

COMPARE&CONTRAST

1 In China as in many other countries, there are regional differences in cuisine. Can you think of any similar regional differences in your own country?

2 In what ways are Chinese restaurants in China different from those in your country? How do diners in China feel about ice-cold beverages? For Chinese diners, is it not a meal without soup? How about desserts and fortune cookies?

Localization

Since the 1990s, American fast food restaurants such as KFC (肯德基) (*Kěndéjī*), McDonald's (麥當勞) (*Màidāngláo*), and Pizza Hut (必勝客) (*Bìshèngkè*) have flourished in Chinese cities. The dubious reputation of American fast food as "fattening" has not scared many Chinese customers away. The success of these American restaurants in China has been, at least in part, due to their efforts at adapting to local tastes. KFC, for instance, offers soy milk (豆漿) (*dòujiāng*) and deep-fried dough sticks (油條) (*yóutiáo*) for breakfast, while McDonald's has chicken rolls (雞肉捲) (*jīròujuǎn*) on the menu.

Vege tarian ism

Historically, vegetarianism (吃素) (chī sù) in China has been related to the practice of Buddhism. According to orthodox standards, 吃素 entails abstaining from not only meat but also pungent vegetables and herbs such as onions, garlic, and chives. Many vegetarian dishes, however, try to emulate the texture and flavor of meat. This is why Buddhist temple dishes regularly feature "mock chicken" and "mock duck." Nowadays, people in China become vegetarian for a wide variety of reasons, like health, that are unrelated to religious practices.

Lesson Wrap-Up

Rearrange the sentences below into a logical sequence. Then combine the sentences into a coherent narrative. Replace nouns with pronouns and change periods to commas where appropriate. Delete identical subject pronouns. Add the connective devices 後來 (hòulái), 就 (jiù), 除了⋯以外 (chúle ... yǐwài), 還⋯ (hái ...), 可是 (kěshì), and 就 (jiù) where necessary.

_____ 飯館裡好像一個位子都沒有了。

_____ 李友又要了兩碗酸辣湯。

_____ 小白菜已經賣完了。

_____ 王朋和李友看到有一張桌子沒有人。

_____ 王朋和李友點了兩盤素餃子。

_____ 王朋和李友還點了一盤家常豆腐。

__1__ 昨天王朋和李友去一家中國飯館吃飯。

_____ 飯館裡吃飯的人很多。

_____ 李友覺得點的菜夠了。

_____ 李友覺得不用點別的了。

_____ 王朋和李友坐了下來。

_____ 李友還想點小白菜。

_____ 李友讓服務員上菜快一點兒。

Role-Play

Student A You have a part-time job working as a server at a Chinese restaurant. Welcome customers to the restaurant. Find out what they would like to drink first. Take their orders. Suggest a dish that they can share. Assure them that the food will be prepared according to their dietary restrictions.

Student B Customer, vegetarian, does not like MSG, likes tofu, likes dumplings; would like a Coke while waiting for the food.

Student C Customer, loves meat, does not like salty food, likes dumplings; would like tea while waiting for the food.

Presentation

Make a slideshow presentation about your favorite Chinese dish. Include these points:

- Ingredients: 這個菜裡有哪些材料 (cáiliào) (ingredient) ？
- Seasonings: 這個菜裡有哪些調料 (tiáoliào) (seasoning) ？
- Flavors of the dish: 這個菜甜不甜，辣不辣⋯⋯ ？
- Reason for liking the dish: 我喜歡這個菜，因為⋯⋯

Can-Do Check List ✓ **I can**

Before proceeding to Lesson 13, make sure you can complete the following tasks in Chinese:

- ☐ Ask if there are seats available
- ☐ Name some Chinese dishes and place an order
- ☐ Tell the waiter my dietary preferences and restrictions
- ☐ Ask for recommendations
- ☐ Pay my bill
- ☐ Get correct change after payment

問路

Wèn lù

ASKING DIRECTIONS

Learning Objectives

In this lesson, you will learn to:

- Ask for and give directions
- Identify locations by using landmarks as references
- Describe whether two places are close to or far away from each other
- State where you are heading and the reason for going there

Relate & Get Ready

In your own culture/community:

- Besides "hello," "how are you," and "what's up," what are some common greetings?
- What phrases do people often use when giving directions?

Where Are You Off To?

Dialogue 1

Audio

Video

（白英愛剛下課……）

 小白，下課了？上哪兒去[a]？

您好，常老師。我想去學校的電腦中心，不知道怎麼走，聽說就在運動場旁邊[1]。

電腦中心沒有[2]運動場那麼[3]遠。你知道學校圖書館在哪裡[b]嗎？

知道，離王朋的宿舍不遠。

電腦中心離圖書館很近，就在圖書館和學生活動中心中間。

常老師，您去哪兒呢？

我想到學校書店去買書[4]。

書店在什麼地方[c]？

就在學生活動中心裡邊。我們一起走吧。

好。

(Bái Yīng'ài gāng xià kè . . .)

 Xiǎo Bái, xià kè le? Shàng nǎr qù [a]?

 Nín hǎo, Cháng lǎoshī. Wǒ xiǎng qù xuéxiào de

diànnǎo zhōngxīn, bù zhīdào zěnme zǒu, tīngshuō

jiù zài yùndòngchǎng pángbiān [1].

 Diànnǎo zhōngxīn méiyǒu [2] *yùndòngchǎng nàme* [3]

yuǎn. Nǐ zhīdào xuéxiào túshūguǎn zài nǎli [b] *ma?*

 Zhīdào, lí Wáng Péng de sùshè bù yuǎn.

 Diànnǎo zhōngxīn lí túshūguǎn hěn jìn,

jiù zài túshūguǎn hé xuéshēng huódòng

zhōngxīn zhōngjiān.

 Cháng lǎoshī, nín qù nǎr ne?

 Wǒ xiǎng dào xuéxiào shūdiàn qù mǎi shū [4].

 Shūdiàn zài shénme dìfang [c]?

 Jiù zài xuéshēng huódòng zhōngxīn lǐbian.

Wǒmen yìqǐ zǒu ba.

 Hǎo.

a 上哪兒去 (shàng nǎr qu)

This is a more casual way of asking 去哪兒 (qù nǎr).

b 哪裡 (nǎli)

This is a question word meaning "where." It is interchangeable with 哪兒 (nǎr). People in northern China, especially in Beijing, end many words with the 兒 (ér) sound. For example, some people say 明兒 (míngr) for "tomorrow" instead of 明天 (míngtiān), and 這兒 (zhèr) for "here" instead of 這裡 (zhèli).

c 什麼地方 (shénme dìfang)

This phrase literally means "what place." It is generally interchangeable with 哪兒 (nǎr) or 哪裡 (nǎli).

Vocabulary

Audio

Flashcards

No.	Word	Pinyin	Part of Speech	Definition
1	上	shàng	v	to go [colloq.]
2	中心	zhōngxīn	n	center
3	聽說	tīngshuō	v	to be told, to hear of
4	運動	yùndòng	n	sports
5	場	chǎng	n	field
6	旁邊	pángbiān	n	side [See Grammar 1.]
7	遠	yuǎn	adj	far
8	離	lí	prep	away from
9	近	jìn	adj	near
10	活動	huódòng	n	activity
11	中間	zhōngjiān	n	middle
12	書店	shūdiàn	n	bookstore
13	地方	dìfang	n	place
14	裡邊	lǐbian	n	inside [See Grammar 1.]

你下課以後想
上哪兒去？

Nǐ xià kè yǐhòu xiǎng shàng nǎr qu?

Where are you going after class?

我想 ＿＿＿＿＿＿＿＿。

Wǒ xiǎng ＿＿＿＿＿＿＿＿.

How About You?

See index for corresponding vocabulary or research another term.

Grammar

Direction and location words

The direction words 上／下／前／後／左／右／東／南／西／北／裡／外／旁 (shàng/xià/qián/hòu/zuǒ/yòu/dōng/nán/xī/běi/lǐ/wài/páng) are often combined with suffixes such as 邊 (biān), 面 (miàn), and 頭 (tóu). As shown below, such compounds become location words.

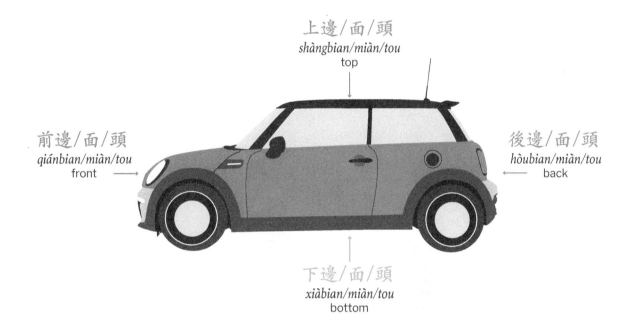

上邊／面／頭
shàngbian/miàn/tou
top

前邊／面／頭
qiánbian/miàn/tou
front

後邊／面／頭
hòubian/miàn/tou
back

下邊／面／頭
xiàbian/miàn/tou
bottom

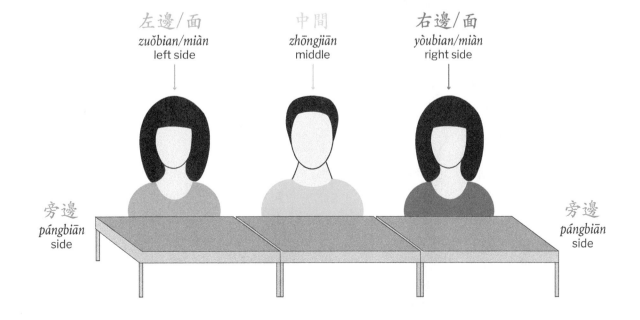

左邊／面
zuǒbian/miàn
left side

中間
zhōngjiān
middle

右邊／面
yòubian/miàn
right side

旁邊
pángbiān
side

旁邊
pángbiān
side

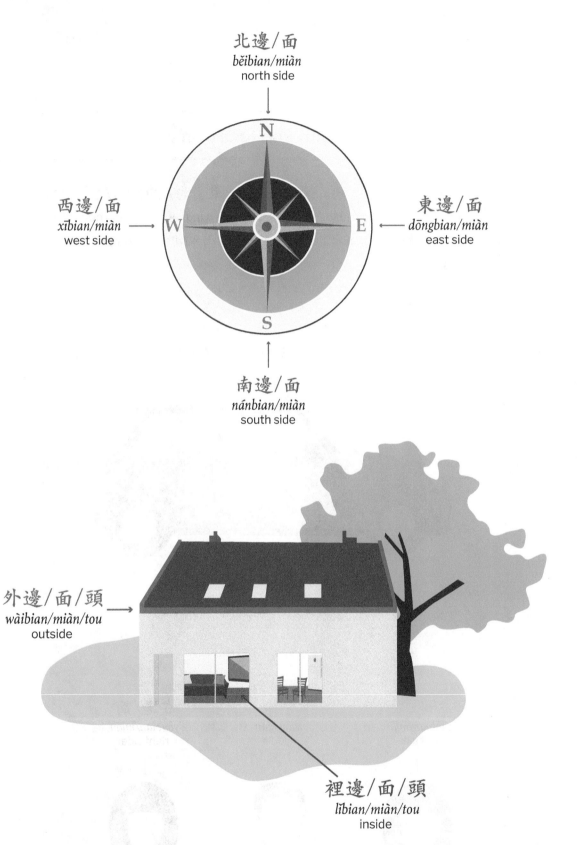

北邊/面
běibian/miàn
north side

西邊/面
xībian/miàn
west side

東邊/面
dōngbian/miàn
east side

南邊/面
nánbian/miàn
south side

外邊/面/頭
wàibian/miàn/tou
outside

裡邊/面/頭
lǐbian/miàn/tou
inside

The direction word 上 (*shàng*) (on) or 裡 (*lǐ*) (in) can be combined with a noun to form a location expression, as in (A). Other examples include 桌子上 (*zhuōzi shang*) (on the table), 衣服上 (*yīfu shang*) (on the clothes), 書上 (*shū shang*) (in/on the book), 學校裡 (*xuéxiào li*) (in the school), 辦公室裡 (*bàngōngshì li*) (in the office), 教室裡 (*jiàoshì li*) (in the classroom), and 電視裡 (*diànshì li*) (on TV). Note that 裡 (*lǐ*) cannot be used after some proper nouns, such as countries or cities, as shown in (B).

A 學校裡有很多學生。

Xuéxiào li yǒu hěn duō xuésheng.

There are many students at school.

B 北京有很多學生。

Běijīng yǒu hěn duō xuésheng.

There are many students in Beijing.

[⊗ 北京裡有很多學生。]

The combination of a direction word plus 邊 *(biān)*/面 *(miàn)*/頭 *(tóu)* can follow a noun to indicate a location, e.g., 圖書館（的）旁邊 *(túshūguǎn [de] pángbiān)* (near the library), 學校（的）裡面 *(xuéxiào [de] lǐmiàn)* (inside the school), 桌子（的）上頭 *(zhuōzi [de] shàngtou)* (on the table), 教室（的）外面 *(jiàoshì [de] wàimiàn)* (outside the classroom), and 城市（的）北邊 *(chéngshì [de] běibian)* (north of the city). In these expressions, the particle 的 *(de)* following the noun is optional.

GET Real WITH CHINESE

You see this sign while touring Sun Moon Lake. What is it pointing toward, and would you want to make this part of your itinerary?

EXERCISES

Complete the sentences with the appropriate location words: 上邊/頭, 前面/頭,
後面/頭, 裡面/頭, or 中間. Use exercise 1 as an example.

1 　教室 ＿＿＿＿ 有很多學生。

　　→ 教室裡面有很多學生。

2 　桌子 ＿＿＿＿ 有三本書。

3 　圖書館和電腦中心的 ＿＿＿＿ 是宿舍。

2	**Comparative sentences using 沒（有）** *(méi[yǒu])*

Besides using 比 *(bǐ)*, another way to make a comparison is to use 沒（有）*(méi[yǒu])*.
The two are opposites in meaning, as shown in the table below. In a comparative sentence
using 沒有 *(méiyǒu)*, the pronoun 那麼 *(nàme)* is sometimes added to the sentence, as
seen in (C) and (D).

X 比 *(bǐ)* Y 大 *(dà)* 　　　　　　　　X > Y
= Y 沒有 *(méiyǒu)* X 大 *(dà)* 　　　　　Y < X

A 我比弟弟高。 　　　　　　or 弟弟沒有我高。

Wǒ bǐ dìdi gāo. 　　　　　　　　*Dìdi méiyǒu wǒ gāo.*

I am taller than my younger brother. 　My younger brother is not as tall as I am.

B 上海比北京熱。 　　　　　or 北京沒有上海熱。

Shànghǎi bǐ Běijīng rè. 　　　　　*Běijīng méiyǒu Shànghǎi rè.*

Shanghai is hotter than Beijing. 　It is not as hot in Beijing as in Shanghai.

C 他哥哥比他姐姐喜歡買東西。

Tā gēge bǐ tā jiějie xǐhuan mǎi dōngxi.

His older brother likes shopping more than his older sister does.

or 他姐姐沒有他哥哥那麼喜歡買東西。

Tā jiějie méiyǒu tā gēge nàme xǐhuan mǎi dōngxi.

His older sister does not like shopping as much as his older brother does.
(His older sister might like shopping too, but not as much as his older brother.)

D 她比我喜歡刷卡買東西。

Tā bǐ wǒ xǐhuan shuā kǎ mǎi dōngxi.

She likes to use credit cards for shopping more than I do.

or 我沒有她那麼喜歡刷卡買東西。

Wǒ méiyǒu tā nàme xǐhuan shuā kǎ mǎi dōngxi.

I don't like to use credit cards for shopping as much as she does.
(I do use credit cards for shopping, but she likes to use them more than I do.)

EXERCISES

Paraphrase the sentences by inserting 沒有 where appropriate. Use exercise 1 as an example.

More
exercises

1 王老師說話不快，李老師說話快。

　→　王老師說話沒有李老師快。

2 那篇課文沒有意思，這篇課文有意思。

3 紅色的鞋不貴，黑色的鞋貴。

<u>3</u>　**Indicating degree using 那麼** *(nàme)*

那麼 *(nàme)* is often placed before adjectives or verbs such as 想 *(xiǎng)*, 喜歡 *(xǐhuan)*,
會 *(huì)*, 能 *(néng)*, and 希望 *(xīwàng)*, to denote a high degree, as in (A). 沒有⋯那
麼⋯ *(méiyǒu … nàme …)* means "not reaching the point of," as in (B), (C), (D), and (E).

A 你那麼不喜歡發短信，就別發了吧。

Nǐ nàme bù xǐhuan fā duǎnxìn, jiù bié fā le ba.

Since you dislike sending text messages so much, stop doing it then.

B 弟弟沒有哥哥那麼帥，那麼酷。

Dìdi méiyǒu gēge nàme shuài, nàme kù.

The younger brother is not as handsome and cool as the older brother.

C 坐地鐵沒有坐公共汽車那麼麻煩。

Zuò dìtiě méiyǒu zuò gōnggòng qìchē nàme máfan.

Taking the subway is not as much of a hassle as taking the bus.

D 這件衣服沒有那件衣服那麼舒服。

Zhè jiàn yīfu méiyǒu nà jiàn yīfu nàme shūfu.

This outfit is not as comfortable as that one.

E 這個電腦沒有那個電腦那麼新。

Zhè gè diànnǎo méiyǒu nà gè diànnǎo nàme xīn.

This computer is not as new as that one.

By using 那麼 (nàme), the speaker attributes a certain quality or characteristic to something or somebody. By stating that the younger brother does not reach the same level of handsomeness and coolness as the older brother, for instance, (B) confirms that the older brother is handsome and cool.

More exercises

EXERCISES

Paraphrase the sentences by inserting 沒有···那麼··· where appropriate. Use exercise 1 as an example.

1 那件衣服比這件衣服便宜。

→ 這件衣服沒有那件衣服那麼便宜。

2 我弟弟比我喜歡打球。

3 寫中文比說中文難。

到 (dào) + place + 去 (qù) + action

In this structure, the combination of "到 (dào) + place + 去 (qù) + action" denotes the purpose of going somewhere. It is the same as "去 (qù) + place + action."

A 我要到電腦中心去上網。
or 我要去電腦中心上網。

Wǒ yào dào diànnǎo zhōngxīn qù shàng wǎng. or *Wǒ yào qù diànnǎo zhōngxīn shàng wǎng.*

I want to go to the computer center to use the Internet.

B 他到朋友的宿舍去聊天兒了。
or 他去朋友的宿舍聊天兒了。

Tā dào péngyou de sùshè qù liáo tiānr le. or *Tā qù péngyou de sùshè liáo tiānr le.*

He went to his friend's dorm to chat.

C 我們到公園去滑冰吧。
or 我們去公園滑冰吧。

Wǒmen dào gōngyuán qù huábīng ba. or *Wǒmen qù gōngyuán huábīng ba.*

Let's go ice skating in the park.

EXERCISES

Rephrase the following sentences with 到…去…. Use exercise 1 as an example.

More exercises

1   我要去圖書館看書。
　　→ 我要到圖書館去看書。

2   王朋要去商店買東西。

3   我們週末要去朋友家吃飯。

Language Practice

Lost and found	INTERPERSONAL

Little Peng can't find anything in his room; his mom has to tell him where everything is. In pairs, role-play Little Peng, who cannot find anything and keeps asking "Where is my . . . ?" and his mother, who has to tell him where everything is. Use direction and location words, e.g.:

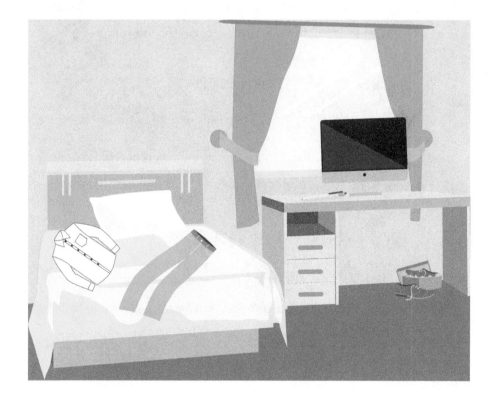

Q: 我的電腦呢？

Wǒ de diànnǎo ne?

A: 你的電腦在桌子上。

Nǐ de diànnǎo zài zhuōzi shang.

 1   2   3   4

This and that

PRESENTATIONAL

Based on the given clues, use 沒有⋯（那麼）⋯ *(méiyǒu…[nàme]…)* to make comparisons, e.g.:

 今天沒有昨天（那麼）暖和。

Jīntiān méiyǒu zuótiān (nàme) nuǎnhuo.

1 6′ 1″　5′ 11″

2  ￥45.00　￥60.00

3

4  size 32　size 30

5

Near and far

INTERPERSONAL

In pairs, locate each city on the map and form a question-and-answer about whether the city is close to or far away from where you live, e.g.:

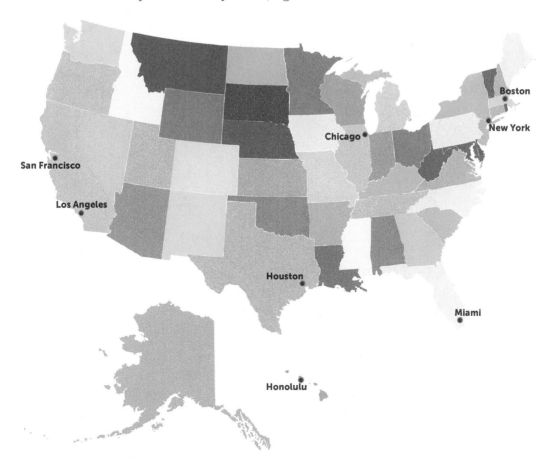

Q: 紐約離我們這兒遠嗎？

Niǔyuē lí wǒmen zhèr yuǎn ma?

A: 紐約離我們這兒很遠／不遠／很近。

Niǔyuē lí wǒmen zhèr hěn yuǎn/bù yuǎn/hěn jìn.

1	Boston	**3**	Houston	**5**	Miami	**7**	Honolulu
2	Chicago	**4**	Los Angeles	**6**	San Francisco		

D Hot spots and cool places   `INTERPERSONAL`

In pairs, role-play a friend coming to visit your school and make suggestions for showing him/her around. Pick a place and an activity depicted below, and use the "到 *(dào)* + place + 去 *(qù)* + action" or "去 *(qù)* + place + action" patterns to discuss possible itineraries, e.g.:

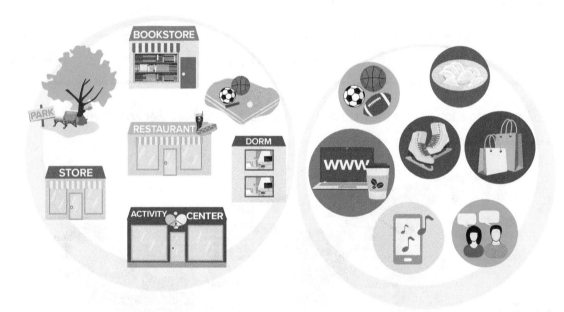

Student A 我們到公園去滑冰，好嗎？／
我們去公園滑冰，好嗎？

Wǒmen dào gōngyuán qù huá bīng, hǎo ma?/Wǒmen qù gōngyuán huá bīng, hǎo ma?

Student B 好，什麼時候去？ (affirmative)

Hǎo, shénme shíhou qù?

Student B 我們還是⋯⋯吧。 (negative)

Wǒmen háishi... ba.

You're interning at a local market research company and have been asked to survey students' consumer behaviors. Collect the results and make a presentation to your class.

1 你喜歡到哪兒去跳舞？

Nǐ xǐhuan dào nǎr qù tiào wǔ?

2 你週末晚上常常到哪兒去吃飯？

Nǐ zhōumò wǎnshang chángcháng dào nǎr qù chī fàn?

3 你喜歡到哪兒去看電影？

Nǐ xǐhuan dào nǎr qù kàn diànyǐng?

4 你常常到哪兒去買衣服？

Nǐ chángcháng dào nǎr qù mǎi yīfu?

Chinese Chat

The student union just published a new post on Weibo. Where do you think people on campus will be headed tonight?

9:48 PM 85%

PU學生會 ☆
01-22 16:20 來自華為榮耀8

同學們，現在已經不下雪了，也沒有那麼冷了。晚上一起來學校新的學生活動中心看電影吧！

轉發 431　　　評論 82　　　讚 602

白英愛 👍 32 💬
01-22 16:28

太好了！新的學生活動中心在哪兒啊？

PU學生會：就在圖書館和電腦中心中間。

↗ 轉發　│　評論　│　👍 讚

Going to Chinatown

Dialogue 2

Audio

Video

（高文中找王朋去中國城吃飯⋯⋯）

我們去中國城吃中國飯吧！

我沒去過[5]中國城，不知道中國城在哪兒。

沒問題[a]，你開車，我告訴你怎麼走。

你有谷歌地圖嗎？拿給我看看[6]。

手機在宿舍裡，我忘了帶了。

沒有地圖，走錯了怎麼辦？

沒有地圖沒關係，中國城我去過很多次，
不用地圖也能找到[7]。你從這兒一直往南
開，到第三個路口，往西一拐[b]就[8]到了。

哎，我不知道東南西北[c]。

那你一直往前開，到第三個紅綠燈，
往右一拐就到了。

（到了第三個路口……）

不對，不對。你看，這個路口只能往左拐，不能往右拐。

那就是下一個路口。往右拐，再往前開。到了，到了，你看見了嗎？前面有很多中國字。

那不是中文，那是日文，我們到了小東京了。

是嗎？那我們不吃中國飯了，吃日本飯吧！

(Gāo Wénzhōng zhǎo Wáng Péng qù Zhōngguóchéng chī fàn.)

 Wǒmen qù Zhōngguóchéng chī Zhōngguó fàn ba!

 Wǒ méi qù guo[5] Zhōngguóchéng, bù zhīdào Zhōngguóchéng zài nǎr.

 Méi wèntí[a], nǐ kāi chē, wǒ gàosù nǐ zěnme zǒu.

 Nǐ yǒu Gǔgē dìtú ma? Ná gěi wǒ kàn kan[6].

 Shǒujī zài sùshè li, wǒ wàng le dài le.

 Méiyǒu dìtú, zǒu cuò le zěnmebàn?

 Méiyǒu dìtú méi guānxi, Zhōngguóchéng wǒ qù guo hěn duō cì, bú yòng dìtú yě néng zhǎo dào[7].

Nǐ cóng zhèr yìzhí wǎng nán kāi, dào dì sān ge lùkǒu, wǎng xī yì guǎi[b] jiù[8] dào le.

 Āi, wǒ bù zhīdào dōng nán xī běi[c].

 Nà nǐ yìzhí wǎng qián kāi, dào dì sān ge hónglùdēng, wǎng yòu yì guǎi jiù dào le.

(Dào le dì sān ge lùkǒu . . .)

 Bú duì, bú duì. Nǐ kàn, zhè ge lùkǒu zhǐ néng wǎng zuǒ guǎi, bù néng wǎng yòu guǎi.

 Nà jiù shì xià yí ge lùkǒu. Wǎng yòu guǎi, zài wǎng qián kāi. Dào le, dào le, nǐ kàn jiàn le ma? Qiánmiàn yǒu hěn duō Zhōngguó zì.

 Nà bú shì Zhōngwén, nà shì Rìwén, wǒmen dào le Xiǎo Dōngjīng le.

 Shì ma? Nà wǒmen bù chī Zhōngguó fàn le, chī Rìběn fàn ba.

a 沒問題 *(méi wèntí)* **vs.** 沒關係 *(méi guānxi)*

You can use 沒問題 *(méi wèntí)* (no problem) to assure someone that their request will be met or a problem will be solved, e.g.: 開車送你去機場？沒問題! *(Kāi chē sòng nǐ qù jīchǎng? Méi wèntí!)* (Drive you to the airport? No problem!). 沒關係 *(méi guānxi)* (it doesn't matter), on the other hand, downplays the severity or impact of an issue, and is often used in response to someone's apology for a minor mistake.

b 拐 *(guǎi)*

拐 *(guǎi)*, in the sense of "to turn," is used mainly in northern China. In the south, 轉 *(zhuǎn)* is more common. It is also the more formal substitute for 拐 *(guǎi)* in the north.

c 東南西北 *(dōng nán xī běi)*

Chinese speakers customarily mention the four directions in a set sequence, 東南西北 *(dōng nán xī běi)* or 東西南北 *(dōng xī nán běi)*. Unlike in English, intermediate directions are given with east or west first. Hence, for southeast and northeast, one says 東南 *(dōng nán)* and 東北 *(dōng běi)*, never ✗ 南東 *(nán dōng)* or ✗ 北東 *(běi dōng)*. Similarly, for southwest and northwest, one says 西南 *(xī nán)* and 西北 *(xī běi)*, never ✗ 南西 *(nán xī)* or ✗ 北西 *(běi xī)*. The speaker means he can't tell which way is east, south, etc.

Vocabulary

Audio

Flashcards

No.	Word	Pinyin	Part of Speech	Definition
1	中國城	Zhōngguóchéng	n	Chinatown
	城	chéng	n	town, city
2	過	guo	p	(particle used after a verb to indicate a past experience) [See Grammar 5.]
3	地圖	dìtú	n	map
4	拿	ná	v	to take, to get
5	次	cì	m	(measure word for frequency)
6	從	cóng	prep	from
7	一直	yìzhí	adv	straight, continuously
8	往	wǎng	prep	towards
9	南	nán	n	south
10	路口	lùkǒu	n	intersection
11	西	xī	n	west
12	拐	guǎi	v	to turn
13	哎	āi	excl	(exclamatory particle to express surprise or dissatisfaction)
14	東	dōng	n	east
15	北	běi	n	north
16	前	qián	n	forward, ahead
17	紅綠燈	hónglǜdēng	n	traffic light
	燈	dēng	n	light
18	右	yòu	n	right
19	左	zuǒ	n	left

You're taking a bus from Beijing to Zhangjiakou to go skiing, and you see this sign as you look out the window. What message does the sign have for motorcyclists and for drivers of large buses and trucks?

GET Real WITH CHINESE

No.	Word	Pinyin	Part of Speech	Definition
20	前面	qiánmiàn	n	ahead, in front of
21	谷歌	Gǔgē	pn	Google
22	日文	Rìwén	pn	Japanese (language)
23	東京	Dōngjīng	pn	Tokyo
24	日本	Rìběn	pn	Japan

你的中文教室在
圖書館的哪邊？

Nǐ de Zhōngwén jiàoshì zài túshūguǎn de nǎ bian?

Where is your Chinese classroom located relative to the library?

How About You?

我的中文教室在 _____ 。

Wǒ de Zhōngwén jiàoshì zài _____ .

See index for corresponding vocabulary or refer to Language Note c to combine the cardinal directions.

Grammar

5 | **The dynamic particle 過 (guo)**

The dynamic particle 過 (guo) is used to denote a past experience or occurrence that has not continued to the present but, typically, has a bearing on the present.

A 我在中國城工作過一年，所以我知道怎麼走。

> *Wǒ zài Zhōngguóchéng gōngzuò guo yì nián, suǒyǐ wǒ zhīdào zěnme zǒu.*
>
> I worked in Chinatown for a year, so I know how to get there.
>
> [The fact that the speaker worked in Chinatown for a year is the reason why he/she knows how to get there.]

B 我見過李友，（所以知道）她很高。

> *Wǒ jiàn guo Lǐ Yǒu, (suǒyǐ zhīdào) tā hěn gāo.*
>
> I've met Li You before, (so I know) she is tall.

C Q: 運動場遠不遠，你知道嗎？

> *Yùndòngchǎng yuǎn bu yuǎn, nǐ zhīdào ma?*
>
> Do you know if the sports field is far from here?

A: 運動場我去過，（所以我知道）不遠，很近。

> *Yùndòngchǎng wǒ qù guo, (suǒyǐ wǒ zhīdào) bù yuǎn, hěn jìn.*
>
> I've been to the sports field, (so I know) it is not far away. It's very close.

In this kind of sentence, expressions of time are often either unspecific or completely absent. If there is no time expression, the implied time for the action or event is 以前 (yǐqián) (before, previously). Sometimes 以前 (yǐqián) can appear in the sentence as well.

D 我以前去過中國城，知道怎麼走。

> *Wǒ yǐqián qù guo Zhōngguóchéng, zhīdào zěnme zǒu.*
>
> I've been to Chinatown before. I know how to get there.

E 以前我們見過面，可是沒說過話。

Yǐqián wǒmen jiàn guo miàn, kěshì méi shuō guo huà.

We've met before, but we've never spoken to each other.

An expression indicating a specific time can also occasionally appear in a sentence with 過 (guo).

F Q: 你見過李小姐嗎？

Nǐ jiàn guo Lǐ xiǎojiě ma?

Have you ever met Miss Li?

A: 見過，上個月還見過她。

Jiàn guo, shàng ge yuè hái jiàn guo tā.

Yes. I saw her as recently as last month.

More exercises

EXERCISES

Use 過 to find out whether someone has or hasn't done something.
Use exercise 1 as an example.

1 你媽媽　　去　　英國
   → 你媽媽去過英國嗎？

2 你　　　　吃　　素餃子

3 你爸爸　　喝　　酸辣湯

---

6 | **Verb reduplication (I)**

Like adjectives [see Grammar 6, Lesson 12], verbs can also be reduplicated in imperative sentences. Verb reduplication softens the tone of a request or suggestion.

A 老師，您再說說什麼時候用"了"，好嗎？

Lǎoshī, nín zài shuō shuo shénme shíhou yòng "le," hǎo ma?

Teacher, would you say a bit more about when to use "le," please?

B　媽，您看看，我這樣寫對不對？

Mā, nín kàn kan, wǒ zhèyàng xiě duì bu duì?

Mom, take a look—did I write this correctly or not?

C　我用用你的電腦可以嗎？

Wǒ yòng yong nǐ de diànnǎo kěyǐ ma?

Could I use your computer for a minute?

D　你幫我找找我的筆，好嗎？

Nǐ bāng wǒ zhǎo zhao wǒ de bǐ, hǎo ma?

Could you help me look for my pen for a second?

E　你考完試，我們一起去公園走走，
聊聊天兒。

Nǐ kǎo wán shì, wǒmen yìqǐ qù gōngyuán zǒu zou, liáo liao tiānr.

After your exam, let's take a walk in the park and have a chat.

If a sentence includes both a modal verb and an action verb, only the action verb can
be reduplicated.

F　她想看看我的新手機。

Tā xiǎng kàn kan wǒ de xīn shǒujī.

She wants to take a look at my new cell phone.

EXERCISES

Repeat the verb to soften the tone of voice. Use exercise 1 as an example.

More
exercises

1　你看，這件衣服我穿合適不合適？（看）
　→ 你看看，這件衣服我穿合適不合適？

2　你說，他那麼做對不對？（說）

3　王朋，我用你的筆，行嗎？（用）

7

Resultative complements (II)

Let's review all the resultative complements that you have come across so far, and learn some new ones that can be formed from the verbs and complements you already know.

完 (wán):

A 看完

kàn wán

finish reading, finish watching

B 吃完

chī wán

finish eating

C 喝完

hē wán

finish drinking

D 考完

kǎo wán

finish taking a test

E 買完

mǎi wán

finish buying

F 賣完

mài wán

finish selling, sell out

到 (dào):

G 找到

zhǎo dào

find (something or someone) successfully

H 看到

kàn dào

see (something or someone)

I 聽到

tīng dào

hear (something or someone)

J 買到

mǎi dào

buy (something) successfully

見 (jiàn):

K 看見

kàn jiàn

see (something or someone)—
same as 看到 (*kàn dào*)

L 聽見

tīng jiàn

hear (something or someone)—
same as 聽到 (*tīng dào*)

好 (hǎo):

M 做好

zuò hǎo

complete doing something (and now be ready for the next action)

N 買好

mǎi hǎo

complete buying something (and now be ready for the next action)

O 準備好

zhǔnbèi hǎo

prepare something (and now be ready for the next action)

錯 (cuò):

P 買錯

mǎi cuò

buy the wrong thing

S 說錯

shuō cuò

say (something) incorrectly

Q 找錯

zhǎo cuò

give the wrong change, find
the wrong person or thing

T 走錯

zǒu cuò

go the wrong way

R 寫錯

xiě cuò

write (something) incorrectly

懂 (dǒng):

U 聽懂

tīng dǒng

comprehend what one hears

V 看懂

kàn dǒng

comprehend what one reads or sees

清楚 (qīngchu):

W 看清楚

kàn qīngchu

see (something) clearly

X 聽清楚

tīng qīngchu

hear (something) clearly

會 (huì):

Y 學會

xué huì

acquire a skill (to do something that one was previously unable to do)

Collocations such as these, made up of a verb and a resultative complement, are best learned as set phrases. Some resultative complements are semantically related to the verb. For instance, in the sentence 我昨天看見她了 (Wǒ zuótiān kàn jiàn tā le) (I saw her yesterday), the complement is semantically related to 看 (kàn), the verb of the sentence. Some resultative complements are semantically related to the object. In the sentence 我寫錯了兩個字 (Wǒ xiě cuò le liǎng ge zì) (I wrote two characters incorrectly), for instance, it is the object "characters" 字 (zì) that are "wrong" 錯 (cuò). Some resultative complements are related to the subject, e.g., in the sentence 我學會了 (Wǒ xué huì le) (I have learned it), the complement 會 (huì) is semantically related to 我 (wǒ), the subject of the sentence.

More exercises

EXERCISES

Fill in the blanks with the appropriate complements. Use exercise 1 as an example.

完　懂　錯　清楚　對　到

1　我沒有買到電影票。

2　你聽 ＿＿＿＿ 了，她不叫李文英。

3　這篇課文你看 ＿＿＿＿ 了嗎？

8

一⋯就⋯ (yī . . jiù . . .) (as soon as . . . then . . .)

This structure combines two habitual or two one-time actions. In a habitual situation, whenever the first action occurs, the second action immediately follows.

A 他一上課就想睡覺。

Tā yí shàng kè jiù xiǎng shuì jiào.

He feels sleepy every time class starts.

B 小張平常只吃青菜，一吃肉就不舒服。

Xiǎo Zhāng píngcháng zhǐ chī qīngcài, yì chī ròu jiù bù shūfu.

Little Zhang normally eats only vegetables. He feels sick whenever he eats meat.

C 李律師一累就喝咖啡。

Lǐ lùshī yí lèi jiù hē kāfēi.

Attorney Li drinks coffee whenever he feels tired.

In a one-time situation, the second action takes place as soon as the first is completed:

D 我們一進飯館兒，服務員就告訴我們
沒位子了。

Wǒmen yí jìn fànguǎnr, fúwùyuán jiù gàosù wǒmen méi wèizi le.

As soon as we entered the restaurant, the waiter told us there were
no seats available.

E 這課的語法很容易，我一看就懂。

Zhè kè de yǔfǎ hěn róngyì, wǒ yí kàn jiù dǒng.

The grammar in this lesson was very easy (to understand).
I understood it as soon as I read it.

F 活動中心離這兒不遠，到第二個路口，
往右一拐就到了。

Huódòng zhōngxīn lí zhèr bù yuǎn, dào dì èr ge lùkǒu, wǎng yòu yì guǎi jiù dào le.

The activity center is not far from here. Turn right at the second intersection, and you'll be there.

More exercises

EXERCISES

In pairs, ask and answer the following questions. Use exercise 1 as an example.

1 你一起床就做什麼？（洗澡）

→ 我一起床就洗澡。

2 你一吃完早飯就做什麼？（去學校上課）

3 你一做完功課就做什麼？（聽音樂）

Characterize it!

More characters

❶ ❷ ❸ ❹ ❺

運　邊　近　過　遠

What do the characters mean?

What is the common radical?

What does the radical mean?

How does the radical relate to the overall meaning of the characters?

Language Practice

Have you ever?

INTERPERSONAL

In pairs, form a question-and-answer about whether your partner has tried the following things. Ask a follow-up question if the answer is affirmative. Ask if he/she wishes to try them if the answer is negative. Use 過 (guo) to denote the past experience, e.g.:

Q: 你打過球嗎？

Nǐ dǎ guo qiú ma?

A: 我打過（球）。

Wǒ dǎ guo (qiú).

Q: 你覺得打球有意思嗎？

Nǐ juéde dǎ qiú yǒu yìsi ma?

A: 我覺得打球很有意思/沒有意思。

Wǒ juéde dǎ qiú hěn yǒu yìsi/méiyǒu yìsi.

1   **2** **3**

Then find out how adventurous an eater your partner is. Use 過 (guo) to ask whether they have tried a certain dish, e.g.:

Student A 你吃過家常豆腐嗎？

Nǐ chī guo jiācháng dòufu ma?

Student B 我沒吃過。家常豆腐好吃嗎？

Wǒ méi chī guo. Jiācháng dòufu hǎochī ma?

Student A 我覺得（家常豆腐）很好吃/不好吃。

Wǒ juéde (jiācháng dòufu) hěn hǎochī/bù hǎochī.

4   5   6

<u>G</u>

One thing after another   INTERPERSONAL

In pairs, take turns asking questions about each other's habits. Use 一···就···
(yī . . . jiù . . .) to denote the sequence.

1   Q: 你平常一吃完早飯就做什麼？

        Nǐ píngcháng yì chī wán zǎofàn jiù zuò shénme?

    A: _____

2   Q: 你平常一下中文課就做什麼？

        Nǐ píngcháng yí xià Zhōngwénkè jiù zuò shénme?

    A: _____

3   Q: 你平常一高興就做什麼？

        Nǐ píngcháng yì gāoxìng jiù zuò shénme?

    A: _____

4   Q: 你昨天早上一起床就做什麼了？

        Nǐ zuótiān zǎoshang yì qǐ chuáng jiù zuò shénme le?

    A: _____

5   Q: 你昨天一回家就做什麼了？

        Nǐ zuótiān yì huí jiā jiù zuò shénme le?

    A: _____

Location, location, location

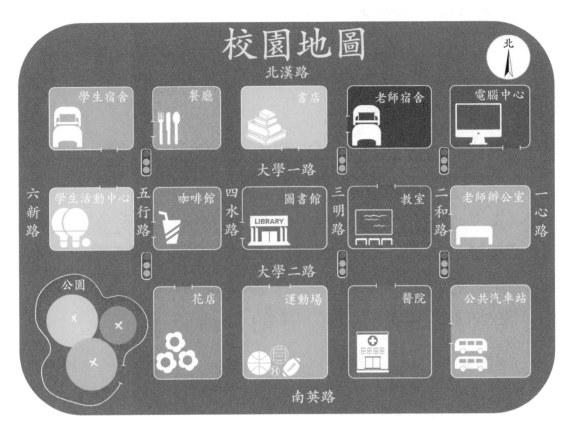

Locate the following places using landmarks and direction and location words, e.g.:

Q: 請問圖書館在哪兒？

Qǐng wèn túshūguǎn zài nǎr?

A: 圖書館在運動場（的）北邊。/
圖書館在教室和咖啡館（的）中間。

Túshūguǎn zài yùndòngchǎng (de) běibian./
Túshūguǎn zài jiàoshì hé kāfēiguǎn (de) zhōngjiān.

1 公園

gōngyuán

3 運動場

yùndòngchǎng

2 餐廳

cāntīng

4 公共汽車站

gōnggòng qìchē zhàn

Getting there from here

In pairs, use the map from the previous exercise to ask for and give directions with your partner, e.g.:

公園 → 老師辦公室

gōngyuán ⟶ lǎoshī bàngōngshì

Q: 從公園到老師辦公室怎麼走？

Cóng gōngyuán dào lǎoshī bàngōngshì zěnme zǒu?

A: 你從公園出來，上五行路，往北走，到第一個路口，往東拐，一直走，到第三個路口往左一拐，就到了。/
老師辦公室就在你（的）右邊兒。

Nǐ cóng gōngyuán chū lai, shàng Wǔxínglù, wǎng běi zǒu, dào dì yī ge lùkǒu, wǎng dōng guǎi, yìzhí zǒu, dào dì sān ge lùkǒu wǎng zuǒ yì guǎi, jiù dào le./
Lǎoshī bàngōngshì jiù zài nǐ (de) yòubianr.

1 電腦中心 → 運動場

diànnǎo zhōngxīn ⟶ yùndòngchǎng

2 學生宿舍 → 公共汽車站

xuéshēng sùshè ⟶ gōnggòng qìchē zhàn

3 書店 → 花店

shūdiàn ⟶ huādiàn (florist)

You're exchanging WeChat messages with a friend to confirm where you'll meet. What would you type?

9:41 PM   85%

8:23 PM

你在哪兒？

 我們不是約在運動中心見面嗎？你在哪兒？

…

 你聽錯了！是運動中心，不是運動場……

…

 不遠。往東一直走，到第三個紅綠燈往左一拐就到了。

哪兒是東？還是你來找我吧！☺

Characterize it!

What do the characters mean?

What is the common radical?

What does the radical mean?

How does the radical relate to the overall meaning of the characters?

❶ 城   ❷ 地   ❸ 場

More characters

文化

Continue
to explore

A courtyard in a traditional house
in Pingyao, Shanxi Province

FENG SHUI

Most Chinese people would prefer to have their houses face south, 坐北朝南 (zuò běi cháo nán) (situated in the north and facing south). Just look at the palaces of the Forbidden City in Beijing! In terms of 風水 (fēngshuǐ) (lit. wind and water), the ages-old Chinese practice of harmonizing human existence with nature, south is the most auspicious direction for one's home to face because it balances yin, 陰 (yīn), and yang, 陽 (yáng), and optimizes the flow of qi, 氣 (qì) (lit. air), a metaphysical life force. This is hardly surprising, considering that in the northern hemisphere facing south allows for maximum sun and light exposure.

COMPARE&CONTRAST

1 Chinese people prefer south-facing homes. Is home orientation a big deal in your culture? Which direction do you prefer your windows to face?

2 The so-called Four Symbols (四象) (Sìxiàng) are four Chinese mythological animals, each with its own cardinal direction. They are the Blue Dragon (青龍) (Qīnglóng) of the east, Vermilion Bird (朱雀) (Zhūquè) of the south, White Tiger (白虎) (Báihǔ) of the west, and Black Turtle (玄武) (Xuánwǔ) of the north. Culturally, they have been important in China, Korea, Japan, and Vietnam, and they appear in modern popular entertainment such as manga and anime. Are there similar ideas in your culture?

Chinatown

中國城 (*Zhōngguóchéng*) (Chinatown), also known as 唐人街 (*Tángrénjiē*) (lit. street for the people of Tang, Tang referring to the Tang dynasty in Chinese history), were originally ethnic enclaves for Chinese immigrants in large metropolitan areas in the United States and other countries. However, with the mingling of immigrants from across Asia, especially East Asia, many Chinatowns are becoming increasingly "pan-Asian" rather than specifically Chinese. However, Chinatowns remain a meaningful window on Chinese culture.

Casual greetings

In Chinese culture, people commonly greet each other by asking a casual question about the routine activity that the other person is engaged in at the moment. Thus, upon seeing a friend on her way to a grocery store, you could ask 買菜呀？(*Mǎi cài ya?*) (Going grocery shopping, eh?). Running into a fellow student who is leaving a classroom, you could ask 下課了？(*Xià kè le?*) (Just had your class?). As the situation is usually very obvious, the speaker does not expect, and is not interested in, an elaborate answer. Nor are these questions considered intrusive or personal.

A view of Beijing from north of the Forbidden City

URBAN

The Forbidden City

Beijing is essentially laid out around a symmetrical grid of large, straight thoroughfares, at the center of which is the Forbidden City. The urban planning principles that undergird the city of Beijing are based on Chinese cosmology. "The sky is round and the earth square" (天圓地方) (*tiān yuán dì fāng*), as the familiar saying goes. Situating the emperor, known as "the Son of Heaven" (天子) (*Tiānzǐ*) at the center of the square capital was therefore highly symbolic. The emperor performed his most important ceremonial duties enthroned in the Hall of Supreme Harmony facing the south. The influence of Beijing's Ming-era planning persists into the present: the names of many subway stations, such as 東直門 (*Dōngzhímén*) and 西直門 (*Xizhímén*), refer to old gates in the demolished Beijing city wall.

PLANNING

Lesson Wrap-Up

Rearrange the following sentences into a logical sequence. Then combine the sentences into a coherent narrative. Replace nouns with pronouns and change periods to commas where appropriate. Delete identical subject pronouns. Add the connective devices 這個時候 (zhè ge shíhou), 就 (jiù), and 所以 (suǒyǐ) where appropriate.

_____白英愛看見常老師來了。

_____白英愛問常老師。

__1__白英愛要去學校的電腦中心。

_____常老師告訴白英愛電腦中心就在圖書館和學生活動中心中間。

_____白英愛現在知道去電腦中心怎麼走了。

_____白英愛不知道去電腦中心怎麼走。

_____常老師告訴白英愛電腦中心離圖書館很近。

_____白英愛知道圖書館離王朋住的地方不遠。

Skit

As you come out of the student activity center, you see a Chinese visitor looking lost. Greet him/her in Chinese and find out where he/she would like to go. The Chinese visitor is very glad that you speak Chinese. He/she thinks your campus is nice-looking and tells you where he/she is from. He/she is trying to find the library. Explain how to get to the library from the student activity center. Offer to walk there with him/her. The Chinese visitor thanks you and asks you about your school. At the entrance to the library, he/she thanks you again, and you say goodbye to each other.

Asking Directions

You are home on break. A Chinese friend is coming to stay with you for a couple of days. He/she calls you from the road. He/she is lost, but thinks that he/she is only several blocks from your house. Decide where your friend is and tell him/her how to get to your house. Incorporate the useful expressions 一直往東/西/南/北開 (yìzhí wǎng dōng/xī/nán/běi kāi), 到第 X 個路口 (dào dì x ge lùkǒu), 往左/右拐 (wǎng zuǒ/yòu guǎi), 然後··· (ránhòu . . .), and ···就到了 (. . . jìu dào le). Optional: After you've recorded your directions, exchange your recording with a classmate. Listen to each other's recordings and draw a map indicating the driving route. Exchange maps and let each other know how the other person did.

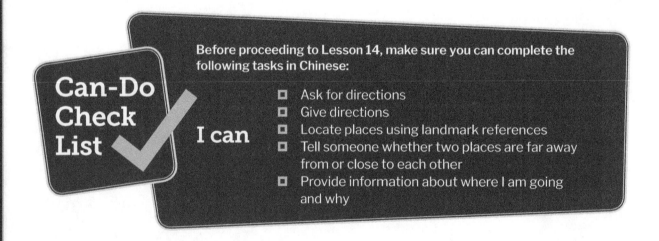

Can-Do Check List ✓

I can

Before proceeding to Lesson 14, make sure you can complete the following tasks in Chinese:

- ☐ Ask for directions
- ☐ Give directions
- ☐ Locate places using landmark references
- ☐ Tell someone whether two places are far away from or close to each other
- ☐ Provide information about where I am going and why

生日晚會

Shēngrì wǎnhuì

BIRTHDAY PARTY

Learning Objectives

In this lesson, you will learn to:

- Ask a friend to go to a party with you
- Suggest things to bring to a get-together
- Thank people for gifts
- Describe a duration of time
- Talk about the year of your birth and your Chinese zodiac sign

Relate & Get Ready

In your own culture/community:

- How are birthdays usually celebrated?
- What do people bring to a birthday party?
- Are there any gift-giving taboos?
- Are people supposed to open gifts in front of the gift giver?

Let's Go to a Party!

Dialogue 1

Audio

Video

（李友給王朋打電話。）

王朋，你做什麼呢[1]？

我看書呢。

今天高小音過生日[a]，晚上我們在她家開舞會，你能去嗎？

能去。幾點？

七點。我們先吃飯，吃完飯再唱歌跳舞。

有哪些人？

小音和她的男朋友、小音的表姐[b]、白英愛、你妹妹王紅，聽說還有小音的中學同學。

你要送給小音什麼生日禮物？

我買了一本書送給她。

那我帶什麼東西？

飲料或者水果都可以。

那我帶一些飲料，再買一把花兒。

小音愛吃水果，我再買一些蘋果、梨和西瓜吧。

你住的地方[2]離小音家很遠，水果很重，我開車去接你，我們一起去吧。

好，我六點半在樓下等你。

(Lǐ Yǒu gěi Wáng Péng dǎ diànhuà.)

 Wáng Péng, nǐ zuò shénme ne[1]?

 Wǒ kàn shū ne.

 Jīntiān Gāo Xiǎoyīn *guò shēngrì*[a], wǎnshang wǒmen zài tā jiā kāi wǔhuì, nǐ néng qù ma?

 Néng qù. Jǐ diǎn?

 Qī diǎn. Wǒmen xiān chī fàn, chī wán fàn zài chàng gē tiào wǔ.

 Yǒu nǎ xiē rén?

 Xiǎoyīn hé tā de nánpéngyou, Xiǎoyīn de *biǎojiě*[b], Bái Yīng'ài, nǐ mèimei Wáng Hóng, tīng-shuō hái yǒu Xiǎoyīn de zhōngxué tóngxué.

 Nǐ yào sòng gěi Xiǎoyīn shénme shēngrì lǐwù?

 Wǒ mǎi le yì běn shū sòng gěi tā.

 Nà wǒ dài shénme dōngxi?

 Yǐnliào huòzhě shuǐguǒ dōu kěyǐ.

 Nà wǒ dài yì xiē yǐnliào, zài mǎi yì bǎ huār.

 Xiǎoyīn ài chī shuǐguǒ, wǒ zài mǎi yì xiē píngguǒ, lí hé xīgua ba.

 Nǐ *zhù de dìfang*[2] lí Xiǎoyīn jiā hěn yuǎn, shuǐguǒ hěn zhòng, wǒ kāi chē qù jiē nǐ, wǒmen yìqǐ qù ba.

 Hǎo, wǒ liù diǎn bàn zài lóu xià děng nǐ.

Language Notes

a 過 *(guò)*

Apart from 過生日 *(guò shēngrì)* (to celebrate one's birthday), the verb 過 *(guò)* (to live [a life], to observe [a holiday], to celebrate [a festival]) appears in many other expressions, such as 過年 *(guò nián)* (to celebrate the New Year), 過節 *(guò jié)* (to celebrate a festival), and 過日子 *(guò rìzi)* (to live one's life, to live from day to day).

b 表姐 *(biǎojiě)* **and** 堂姐 *(tángjiě)*

The kinship term 表姐 *(biǎojiě)* is more narrowly defined than its translation "older female cousin" would suggest. Your "older female cousin" is a 表姐 *(biǎojiě)* if she is a daughter of your father's sister or your mother's sister or brother. But if she is your paternal uncle's daughter, she is a 堂姐 *(tángjiě)*, not a 表姐 *(biǎojiě)*. Therefore, your 堂姐 *(tángjiě)* typically shares your family name. For more Chinese kinship terms, see Grammar 5 in Lesson 20.

Vocabulary

Audio

Flashcards

No.	Word	Pinyin	Part of Speech	Definition
1	過	guò	v	to live (a life), to observe (a holiday), to celebrate (a festival), to pass
2	舞會	wǔhuì	n	dance party, ball
3	表姐	biǎojiě	n	older female cousin
4	中學	zhōngxué	n	middle school, secondary school
5	送	sòng	v	to give as a gift
6	禮物	lǐwù	n	gift, present
7	本	běn	m	(measure word for books)
8	飲料	yǐnliào	n	beverage
9	水果	shuǐguǒ	n	fruit
10	把	bǎ	m	(measure word for things with handles, for handfuls of things)
11	花	huā	n	flower
12	愛	ài	v	to love, to like, to be fond of
13	蘋果	píngguǒ	n	apple
14	梨	lí	n	pear
15	西瓜	xīgua	n	watermelon
16	住	zhù	v	to live (in a certain place)
17	重	zhòng	adj	heavy, serious
18	接	jiē	v	to catch, to meet, to welcome

On a pamphlet from your favorite cookie bakery in Tainan, you notice this box set being advertised. Is this meant to be given as a gift? What do you think 入 *(rù)* and the numbers indicate?

超值分享包 / 7種口味〔NT110元〕

18入綜合禮盒
煎・餅・禮・盒・系・列
Fried Cookies

小瓦煎燒9入 / 海苔煎餅4入 /
格子煎餅4入 / 檸檬捲心5入 /
草莓捲心5入

每盒 / 〔NT220元〕

No.	Word	Pinyin	Part of Speech	Definition
19	樓	*lóu*	n	multi-story building, floor (of a multi-level building)
20	王紅	*Wáng Hóng*	pn	a personal name

你愛吃什麼水果？

Nǐ ài chī shénme shuǐguǒ?
What fruits do you like to eat?

我愛吃 ＿＿＿＿＿＿＿。
Wǒ ài chī ＿＿＿＿＿＿.

See index for corresponding vocabulary or research another term.

Grammar

1 **Indicating an action in progress using 呢 (ne)**

呢 (ne) at the end of a sentence indicates that the action denoted by the verb is in progress. In this sense, it is similar to 在 (zài). However, 在 (zài) is not used at the end of a sentence, but before the verb.

A 你寫什麼呢？

Nǐ xiě shénme ne?

What are you writing?

B 你找什麼呢？

Nǐ zhǎo shénme ne?

What are you looking for?

呢 (ne) can also be used in conjunction with 在 (zài).

C 你在寫什麼呢？

Nǐ zài xiě shénme ne?

What are you writing?

D 你在找什麼呢？

Nǐ zài zhǎo shénme ne?

What are you looking for?

在 (zài) by itself can indicate that an action is in progress; therefore, the 呢 (ne) in (C) and (D) can be omitted.

在 (zài) can also be preceded by 正 (zhèng). The phrase 正在 (zhèngzài) further emphasizes that the action is ongoing.

E 我昨天給他打電話的時候，
他正在做功課呢。

Wǒ zuótiān gěi tā dǎ diànhuà de shíhou, tā zhèngzài zuò gōngkè ne.

When I called him yesterday, he was right in the middle of doing his homework.

F 別去找他，他正在睡覺呢。

Bié qù zhǎo tā, tā zhèngzài shuì jiào ne.

Don't go looking for him. He's sleeping at the moment.

More
exercises

EXERCISES

Complete the sentences with 正在⋯呢. Use exercise 1 as an example.

1　我回家的時候

　　媽媽（做飯）

　　→　我回家的時候，媽媽正在做飯呢。

2　姐姐給我打電話的時候

　　我（聽音樂）

3　老師進教室的時候

　　小高（復習生詞）

Verbal phrases and subject-predicate phrases used as attributives

In Chinese, attributives, often followed by the particle 的 (de), always appear before what they modify. Verbs, verbal phrases, and subject-predicate phrases can all serve as attributives.

A 吃的東西

chī de dōngxi

things to eat

B 穿的衣服

chuān de yīfu

clothes to wear, or clothes being worn

C 新買的飯卡

xīn mǎi de fànkǎ

newly bought meal card

D 昨天來的同學

zuótiān lái de tóngxué

classmate/classmates who came yesterday

E 以前認識的朋友

yǐqián rènshi de péngyou

friend/friends one previously got to know

F 我媽媽做的豆腐

wǒ māma zuò de dòufu

the tofu dish my mother makes/made

G 老師給我們的功課

lǎoshī gěi wǒmen de gōngkè

the homework the teacher assigned us

H 朋友送的蘋果

péngyou sòng de píngguǒ

apples given by a friend

I 請你跳舞的那個人

qǐng nǐ tiào wǔ de nà gè rén

that person who asked you to dance

J 我妹妹喜歡去的那個很酷的地方

wǒ mèimei xǐhuan qù de nà ge hěn kù de dìfang

that very cool place that my younger sister loves to go to

EXERCISES

Modify the nouns with a verb phrase or subject-predicate phrase. Use exercise 1 as an example.

1 筆（我剛買）→ 我剛買的筆
2 書（你送給我）
3 衣服（哥哥新買）
4 朋友（昨天認識）

More exercises

What do the characters mean?
What is the common radical?
What does the radical mean?
How does the radical relate to the overall meaning of the characters?

Characterize it!

❶ 禮 ❷ 視 ❸ 票 ❹ 祝

More characters

Language Practice

In the midst	INTERPERSONAL

In pairs, form a question-and-answer about what these people are doing. Use 呢 *(ne)* to indicate the action is in progress, e.g.:

Q: 她（在）做什麼呢？

Tā (zài) zuò shénme ne?

A: 她（在）喝湯呢。

Tā (zài) hē tāng ne.

 1   2   3   4   5

Then ask your partner what he/she was doing last night at 7:00 and 9:00.

B

Oh, that one!	PRESENTATIONAL

Combine the two short sentences into one, using the highlighted verb and phrase to form an attributive. Add 的 *(de)* where appropriate, e.g.:

他買了一件衣服。那件衣服很貴。

Tā mǎi le yí jiàn yīfu. Nà jiàn yīfu hěn guì.

他買的那件衣服很貴。

Tā mǎi de nà jiàn yīfu hěn guì.

1 他寫了一個字。那個字很漂亮。

   Tā xiě le yí ge zì. Nà ge zì hěn piàoliang.

2 她買了一件襯衫。那件襯衫是中號的。

   Tā mǎi le yí jiàn chènshān. Nà jiàn chènshān shì zhōng hào de.

3 我哥哥給了我一枝筆。那枝筆是黑色的。

Wǒ gēge gěi le wǒ yì zhī bǐ. Nà zhī bǐ shì hēisè de.

4 妹妹帶了一些水果。那些水果很貴。

Mèimei dài le yì xiē shuǐguǒ. Nà xiē shuǐguǒ hěn guì.

5 表姐賣了一些花。那些花很漂亮。

Biǎojiě mài le yì xiē huā. Nà xiē huā hěn piàoliang.

C | **Who's who?** | INTERPERSONAL

Help your new classmate match people in your class to their names, using a verb phrase or subject-predicate phrases as an attributive. Add 的 (de) where appropriate, e.g.:

Q: Jamal是誰？

Jamal *shì shéi?*

A: Jamal是那個穿藍色襯衫的學生。

Jamal *shì nà ge chuān lánsè chènshān de xuésheng.*

Q: Katy是誰？

Katy *shì shéi?*

A: Katy是那個正在看書的女孩。

Katy *shì nà ge zhèngzài kàn shū de nǚ hái.*

Then quiz the new classmate, e.g.:

Q: 那個穿藍色襯衫的學生是誰？

Nà ge chuān lánsè chènshān de xuésheng shì shéi?

A: 那個穿藍色襯衫的學生是Jamal。

Nà ge chuān lánsè chènshān de xuésheng shì Jamal.

Birthday Bash

Dialogue 2

Audio

Video

（在高小音家……）

王朋，李友，快進來。

小音，祝你生日快樂！這是送給你的生日
禮物。

謝謝！……太好了！我一直想買這本書。
帶這麼多東西，你們太客氣了。

哥哥，李友，你們來了[a]。

啊[b]。小紅，你怎麼樣？

我很好。每天都在學英文。

小紅，你每天練習英文練習多長時間[3]？

三個半鐘頭[c]。還看兩個鐘頭的英文電視。

哎，你們兩個是什麼時候到的[4]？

剛到。

白英愛沒跟你們一起來嗎？

她還[5]沒來？我以為[d]她已經來了。

王朋，李友，來，我給你們介紹一下，
這是我表姐海倫，這是她的兒子湯姆。

你好，海倫。

你好，王朋。文中和小音都說你又聰明[e]又用功[6]。

哪裡，哪裡。你的中文說得真好，是在哪兒學的？

在暑期班[f]學的。

哎，湯姆長[g]得真可愛！你們看，他笑了。他幾歲了？

剛一歲，是去年生的，屬狗。

你們看，他的臉圓圓的，眼睛大大的，鼻子高高的，嘴不大也不小，長得很像海倫。

媽媽這麼漂亮，兒子長大一定也很帥。

來，來，來，我們吃蛋糕吧。

等等白英愛吧。她最愛吃蛋糕。

(Zài Gāo Xiǎoyīn jiā . . .)

Wáng Péng, Lǐ Yǒu, kuài jìn lai.

Xiǎoyīn, zhù nǐ shēngrì kuàilè! Zhè shì sòng gěi nǐ de shēngrì lǐwù.

Xièxiè! . . . Tài hǎo le! Wǒ yìzhí xiǎng mǎi zhè běn shū. Dài zhème duō dōngxi, nǐmen tài kèqi le.

Gēge, Lǐ Yǒu, *nǐmen lái le* [a].

À [b]. Xiǎo Hóng, nǐ zěnmeyàng?

Wǒ hěn hǎo. Měi tiān dōu zài xué Yīngwén.

Xiǎo Hóng, nǐ měi tiān *liànxí Yīngwén liànxí duō cháng shíjiān* [3]?

Sān ge bàn *zhōngtóu* [c]. Hái kàn liǎng ge zhōngtóu de Yīngwén diànshì.

Āi, nǐmen liǎng ge *shì shénme shíhou dào de* [4]?

Gāng dào.

Bái Yīng'ài méi gēn nǐmen yìqǐ lái ma?

Tā *hái* [5] *méi lái? Wǒ yǐwéi* [d] tā yǐjīng lái le.

Wáng Péng, Lǐ Yǒu, lái, wǒ gěi nǐmen jièshào yí xià, zhè shì wǒ biǎojiě Hǎilún, zhè shì tā de érzi Tāngmǔ.

Nǐ hǎo, Hǎilún.

Nǐ hǎo, Wáng Péng. Wénzhōng hé Xiǎoyīn dōu shuō nǐ *yòu cōngming* [e] *yòu yònggōng* [6].

Nǎli, nǎli. Nǐ de Zhōngwén shuō de zhēn hǎo, shì zài nǎr xué de?

Zài shǔqī *bān* [f] xué de.

Āi, Tāngmǔ *zhǎng* [g] de zhēn kě'ài! Nǐmen kàn, tā xiào le. Tā jǐ suì le?

Gāng yí suì, shì qùnián shēng de, shǔ gǒu.

Nǐmen kàn, tā de liǎn yuán yuán de, yǎnjing dà dà de, bízi gāo gāo de, zuǐ bú dà yě bù xiǎo, zhǎng de hěn xiàng Hǎilún.

Māma zhème piàoliang, érzi zhǎng dà yídìng yě hěn shuài.

Lái, lái, lái, wǒmen chī dàngāo ba.

Děng děng Bái Yīng'ài ba. Tā zuì ài chī dàngāo.

Language Notes

a 你們來了。 *(Nǐmen lái le.)*

This sentence, equivalent to "You're here," not only acknowledges the visitors' arrival, but also serves as a casual greeting. [See also Cultural Literacy, Lesson 13.]

b 啊 *(a/à)*

Different from 啊 *(a)* in Dialogue 2 of Lesson 6, where it is pronounced in the neutral tone as a sentence-final particle, 啊 *(à)* here is pronounced in the fourth tone as an answer to someone else's greeting.

c 鐘頭 *(zhōngtóu)*

This is the colloquial equivalent of 小時 *(xiǎoshí)* (hour). [See also Vocabulary, Lesson 15.]

d 以為 *(yǐwéi)*

This is often used to signify an understanding or judgment that has proved to be erroneous, e.g.: 我以為你吃素 *(Wǒ yǐwéi nǐ chī sù)* (I thought you were vegetarian).

e 聰明 *(cōngming)*

聰 *(cōng)* literally means "able to hear well," and 明 *(míng)* means "able to see clearly," among other things. Therefore, 聰明 *(cōngming)* describes someone who is sharp or bright.

f 班 *(bān)* **vs.** 課 *(kè)*

These two words denote two different concepts that are represented by the same word, "class," in English. While 課 *(kè)* refers to an educational course or a meeting time for the course, 班 *(bān)* means a group of students taking a course together. Thus you would say 我今天有電腦課 *(Wǒ jīntiān yǒu diànnǎo kè)* (I have a computer class today), but 我的電腦班有二十個人 *(Wǒ de diànnǎo bān yǒu èrshí ge rén)* (There are twenty people in my computer class).

g 長 *(zhǎng/cháng)*

This character has two different meanings and pronunciations. As a verb, it is pronounced *"zhǎng,"* meaning "to grow." When used as an adjective, it is pronounced *cháng,* meaning "long."

Vocabulary

Audio

Flashcards

No.	Word	Pinyin	Part of Speech	Definition
1	鐘頭	zhōngtóu	n	hour
2	以為	yǐwéi	v	to assume erroneously
3	聰明	cōngming	adj	smart, bright, clever
4	用功	yònggōng	adj	hardworking, diligent, studious
5	暑期	shǔqī	n	summer term
6	班	bān	n	class
7	長	zhǎng	v	to grow, to appear
8	可愛	kě'ài	adj	cute, lovable
9	去年	qùnián	t	last year
10	屬	shǔ	v	to belong to
11	狗	gǒu	n	dog
12	臉	liǎn	n	face
13	圓	yuán	adj	round
14	眼睛	yǎnjing	n	eye
15	鼻子	bízi	n	nose
16	嘴	zuǐ	n	mouth
17	像	xiàng	v	to be like, to look like, to take after
18	長大	zhǎng dà	vc	to grow up
19	一定	yídìng	adj/adv	certain, definite; certainly, definitely
20	蛋糕	dàngāo	n	cake
21	最	zuì	adv	most, (of superlative degree) -est

蛋糕　蘋果　梨　西瓜

It's your birthday! You're having a party, and one of your friends has brought over a delicious selection of bubble tea (珍珠奶茶) (*zhēnzhū nǎichá*). What flavors did she bring?

GET Real WITH CHINESE

No.	Word	Pinyin	Part of Speech	Definition
22	海倫	*Hǎilún*	pn	Helen
23	湯姆	*Tāngmǔ*	pn	Tom

給朋友過生日開
舞會，你會準備
些什麼東西？

Gěi péngyou guò shēngrì kāi wǔhuì,
nǐ huì zhǔnbèi xiē shénme dōngxi?

What would you prepare for a friend's
birthday party?

How About You?

我會準備 ＿＿＿＿＿＿＿＿。
Wǒ huì zhǔnbèi ＿＿＿＿＿＿＿.

See index for corresponding vocabulary or research another term.

Grammar

Time duration (I)

To indicate the duration of an action, the following structure is used:

Subject + verb + (object + verb) + (了) *(le)* + duration of time

A　老高想在上海住一年。

Lǎo Gāo xiǎng zài Shànghǎi zhù yì nián.

Old Gao would like to live in Shanghai for a year.

B　我每天在書店工作三個鐘頭。

Wǒ měi tiān zài shūdiàn gōngzuò sān ge zhōngtóu.

I work at a bookstore for three hours every day.

C　昨天下雪下了一天。

Zuótiān xià xuě xià le yì tiān.

It snowed for a whole day yesterday.

D　你上暑期班上了多長時間？

Nǐ shàng shǔqī bān shàng le duō cháng shíjiān?

How long were you in summer school for?

Sentences in this pattern must be in the affirmative. If the verb takes an object, the verb has to be repeated, as in (C) and (D). If the verb has an object, the following alternative pattern can be used to express the same idea.

Subject + verb + (了) *(le)* + duration of time + (的) *(de)* + object

E　昨天下了一天（的）雪。

Zuótiān xià le yì tiān (de) xuě.

It snowed for a whole day yesterday.

F 我上了四個星期（的）暑期班。

Wǒ shàng le sì ge xīngqī (de) shǔqī bān.

I was at summer school for four weeks.

[✗ 我四個星期上了暑期班。]

The phrase for the length of time must not be put before the verb.

More exercises

EXERCISES

Complete the sentences with the phrases provided to indicate the duration of an action.
Use exercise 1 as an example.

1 我昨天上中文課   半個鐘頭

→ 我昨天上中文課上了半個鐘頭。/
   我昨天上了半個鐘頭的中文課。

2 我妹妹每天聽音樂   一個半鐘頭

3 我上個星期在圖書館工作   三天

---

4   Sentences with 是⋯的 *(shì...de)* **(I)**

To describe or inquire about the time, the place, the manner, or the initiator of an action that
we know already happened, use the 是⋯的 *(shì...de)* structure. The use of 是 *(shì)*, however,
is optional.

A Q: 你去過北京嗎？   A: 我去過北京。

Nǐ qù guo Běijīng ma?   *Wǒ qù guo Běijīng.*

Have you been to Beijing?   Yes, I've been to Beijing.

Having confirmed that the respondent has been to Beijing in the past, the questioner now
wants to find out when, how, and with whom the respondent went to Beijing:

Q: 你（是）跟誰一起去的？

Nǐ (shì) gēn shéi yìqǐ qù de?

With whom did you go?

A: 我（是）跟我表姐一起去的。

Wǒ (shì) gēn wǒ biǎojiě yìqǐ qù de.

I went with my cousin.

Q: 你們（是）什麼時候去的？

Nǐmen (shì) shénme shíhou qù de?

When did you go?

A: 我們（是）寒假去的。

Wǒmen (shì) hánjià qù de.

We went over winter break.

Q: 你們（是）怎麼去的？

Nǐmen (shì) zěnme qù de?

How did you get there?

A: 我們（是）坐飛機去的。

Wǒmen (shì) zuò fēijī qù de.

We flew.

B **Q:** 你看過這本書嗎？

Nǐ kàn guo zhè běn shū ma?

Have you read this book?

A: 看過。

Kàn guo.

Yes, I have.

Q: （是）什麼時候看的？

(Shì) shénme shíhou kàn de?

When did you read it?

[The questioner knows that the action 看 (kàn) already took place.]

A: （是）上個週末看的。

(Shì) shàng ge zhōumò kàn de.

I read it last weekend. (It was last weekend that I read it.)

C 你這條褲子真好看。（是）在哪兒買的？

Nǐ zhè tiáo kùzi zhēn hǎokàn. (Shì) zài nǎr mǎi de?

These pants of yours look great. Where did you get them?

[Most people buy pants (as opposed to making them at home, for example), so the action 買 *(mǎi)* is assumed.]

D Q: 你吃飯了嗎？

Nǐ chī fàn le ma?

Have you eaten yet?

A: 吃了。

Chī le.

Yes, I have.

[The action 吃 *(chī)* is now known.]

Q: （是）在哪兒吃的？

(Shì) zài nǎr chī de?

Where did you eat?

A: （是）在學生餐廳吃的。

(Shì) zài xuéshēng cāntīng chī de.

In the student cafeteria.

E Q: 你學過電腦嗎？

Nǐ xué guo diànnǎo ma?

Have you ever studied computer science?

A: 學過。

Xué guo.

Yes, I have.

Q: （是）跟誰學的？

(Shì) gēn shéi xué de?

Who did you study with?

A: （是）跟王老師學的。

(Shì) gēn Wáng lǎoshī xué de.

With Teacher Wang.

是 (shì) cannot be omitted in negative statements.

F Q: 你是在中國學的中文嗎？

Nǐ shì zài Zhōngguó xué de Zhōngwén ma?

Did you study Chinese in China?

A: 我不是在中國學的，是在美國學的。

Wǒ bú shì zài Zhōngguó xué de, shì zài Měiguó xué de.

No, I didn't study Chinese in China. I studied it in the U.S.

G Q: 小李是昨天走的嗎？

Xiǎo Lǐ shì zuótiān zǒu de ma?

Did Little Li leave yesterday?

A: 她不是昨天走的，好像是上个星期走的。

Tā bú shì zuótiān zǒu de, hǎoxiàng shì shàng ge xīngqī zǒu de.

No, she didn't leave yesterday. I think she left last week.

Characterize it!

What do the characters mean?

What is the common radical?

What does the radical mean?

How does the radical relate to the overall meaning of the characters?

① ② ③ ④

More characters

More exercises

EXERCISES

In pairs, form questions-and-answers by using the given question cue words and bracketed answers. Use 是…的 where appropriate. Use exercise 1 as an example.

1 你去紐約

去過嗎？（去過）　　　什麼時候？（去年）

跟誰一起？（同學）　　怎麼去？（坐飛機）

→ Q: 你去過紐約嗎？

A: 去過。

Q:（是）什麼時候去的？

A:（是）去年去的。

Q:（是）跟誰一起去的？

A:（是）跟同學一起去的。

Q:（是）怎麼去的？

A:（是）坐飛機去的。

2 你看中國電影

看過嗎？（看過）　　　在哪兒？（學校）

什麼時候？（上個星期）跟誰一起？（小王）

3 你吃紅燒牛肉

吃過嗎？（吃過）　　　在哪兒？（中國飯館）

什麼時候？（前天）　　跟誰一起？（弟弟）

---

5 | 還 (hái) (still)

還 (hái), as an adverb, can mean "still."

A 上午十一點了，他還在睡覺。

Shàngwǔ shíyī diǎn le, tā hái zài shuì jiào.

It's 11:00 a.m. He's still sleeping.

B　今天的功課我還沒寫完。

Jīntiān de gōngkè wǒ hái méi xiě wán.

I'm still not done with today's homework.

C　這個語法老師教了，可是我還不懂。

Zhè ge yǔfǎ lǎoshī jiāo le, kěshì wǒ hái bù dǒng.

The teacher went over this grammar point, but I still don't understand it.

EXERCISES

More exercises

Complete the sentences by inserting 還 where appropriate. Use exercise 1 as an example.

1　已經晚上十點了，弟弟沒回家

　　→　已經晚上十點了，弟弟還沒回家。

2　他在電話裡說了三次，我聽不清楚

3　這課的課文我看了一個鐘頭，　不懂

6　又⋯⋯又⋯⋯ *(yòu . . . yòu . . .)* **(both . . . and . . .)**

When two adjectives are joined in this structure, they must both be either positive or negative in meaning. For example, in 又聰明又用功 *(yòu cōngming yòu yònggōng)* (smart and hardworking) both adjectives are positive in meaning, while in 又多又難 *(yòu duō yòu nán)* (too much and difficult), both adjectives are negative in meaning.

EXERCISES

More exercises

Combine the adjectives by inserting 又⋯⋯又⋯⋯ where appropriate. Use exercise 1 as an example.

1　聰明　　用功　→　又聰明又用功

2　高　　　大

3　餓　　　累

Language Practice

Where did you get that?

INTERPERSONAL

You love something your classmate has or is wearing. You want to find out whether he/she bought it, and if so, where and when it was bought. Use the 是…的 *(shì . . . de)* structure when necessary, e.g.:

你的手機真酷……

Nǐ de shōujī zhēn kù . . .

（是）你買的還是別人送的？

(Shì) nǐ mǎi de háishi biérén sòng de?

（是）什麼時候買的？

(Shì) shénme shíhou mǎi de?

（是）在哪兒買的？

(Shì) zài nǎr mǎi de?

1   2   3

E   INTERPERSONAL   **Older or younger**   PRESENTATIONAL

Interview your classmates to find out everyone's birthplace, birth year, and Chinese zodiac sign. Then report to the class how many classmates are older than you, how many are younger than you, how many were born in the same state/province/city as you were, and which zodiac sign is most common in the class. Use the 是 · · · 的 *(shì . . . de)* structure when necessary.

1 你是在哪兒生的？

Nǐ shì zài nǎr shēng de?

3 你屬什麼？

Nǐ shǔ shénme?

2 你是哪一年生的？

Nǐ shì nǎ yì nián shēng de?

Wanderlust

In pairs, discuss where you have traveled. Take turns asking each other the questions below. Use the 是⋯的 (shì . . . de) structure when necessary.

1 你去過 (a city or country) 嗎？

Nǐ qù guo (a city or country) ma?

2 你（是）什麼時候去的？

Nǐ (shì) shénme shíhou qù de?

3 你（是）跟誰一起去的？

Nǐ (shì) gēn shéi yìqǐ qù de?

4 你（是）怎麼去的？

Nǐ (shì) zěnme qù de?

Tight schedule

Imagine that you've signed up to go on a whirlwind tour of China during summer break. You just got your itinerary, and the travel schedule looks very intense. The trip leaders have scheduled each day down to the minute. In pairs, form a question-and-answer about how much time you'll have for each activity, e.g.:

Q: 你每天洗澡洗多長時間？

Nǐ měi tiān xǐ zǎo xǐ duō cháng shíjiān?

7:30 a.m.–7:35 a.m.

A: 我每天洗澡洗五分鐘。

Wǒ měi tiān xǐ zǎo xǐ wǔ fēnzhōng.

1

1:30 p.m.–2:30 p.m.

2

5:30 p.m.–6:00 p.m.

3

11:00 p.m.–5:00 a.m.

Ask your partner about how much time he/she typically spends eating dinner every day.

INTERPERSONAL **Last night** **PRESENTATIONAL**

Survey your classmates about how they spent their time last night. Use the "subject + verb + (object + verb) + (了) + duration of time" or "subject + verb + (了) + duration of time + (的) + object" structure to indicate the duration of an action, e.g.:

Q: Emily, 你昨天晚上做什麼了？
Emily, nǐ zuótiān wǎnshang zuò shénme le?

A: 我昨天晚上看電視了。
Wǒ zuótiān wǎnshang kàn diànshì le.

Q: 你昨天晚上看電視看了多長時間？
Nǐ zuótiān wǎnshang kàn diànshì kàn le duō cháng shíjiān?

A: 我昨天晚上看電視看了半個鐘頭。 /
我昨天晚上看了半個鐘頭的電視。
Wǒ zuótiān wǎnshang kàn diànshì kàn le bàn ge zhōngtóu. /
Wǒ zuótiān wǎnshàng kàn le bàn gè zhōngtóu de diànshì.

Then share your findings with the class.

Emily 昨天晚上看電視看了半個鐘頭。
Emily zuótiān wǎnshang kàn diànshì kàn le bàn ge zhōngtóu.

INTERPERSONAL **Puppy love** **PRESENTATIONAL**

In pairs, describe this dog's features and comment on how cute it is.

Party planner

Find out among your classmates whose birthday is coming up by asking 誰的生日快到了？(*Shéi de shēngrì kuài dào le?*) (Whose birthday is coming up?). Everyone should take a turn asking that person what he/she likes to eat, drink, and do. Then work as a class to plan a birthday party together, and decide who will bring what to the party. In Chinese, note down the day of the party and the things you were assigned to bring.

Chinese Chat

On Facebook, Gao Wenzhong just posted about a party he's throwing. What are his friends going to bring?

高文中
November 12 at 12:50 pm

謝謝大家今天晚上來我家給我姐過生日！你們都準備帶些什麼呀？

👍 Like   💬 Comment   ➤ Share

👍❤ 52

王紅 我買了餃子。
November 12 at 12:52 pm · Like 👍 12 · Reply

王朋 我帶冰茶、可樂和花。
November 12 at 1:12 pm · Like 👍 10 · Reply

李友 水果和禮物！
November 12 at 1:31 pm · Like 👍 6 · Reply

海倫 我自己做的日本菜。
November 12 at 2:50 pm · Like 👍 15 · Reply

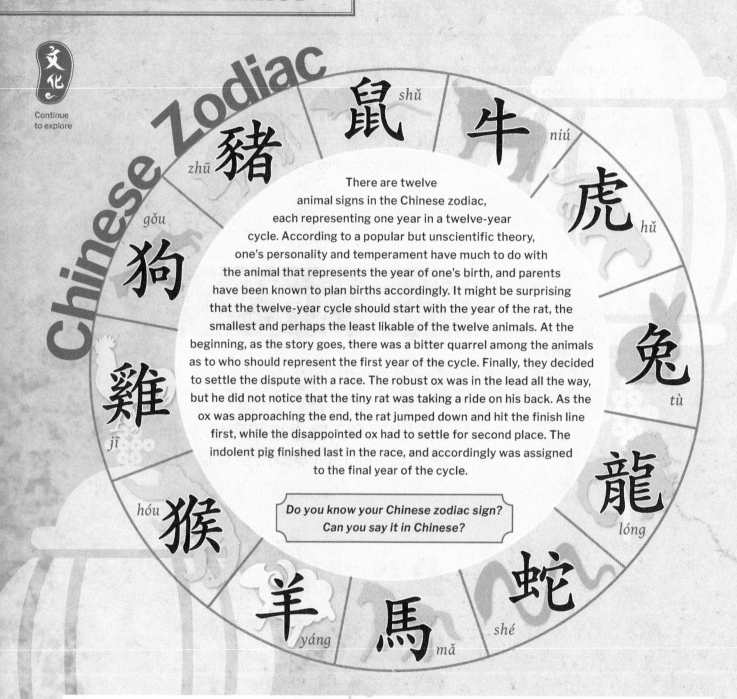

文化
Continue to explore

Chinese Zodiac

豬 zhū

鼠 shǔ

牛 niú

虎 hǔ

狗 gǒu

兔 tù

雞 jī

龍 lóng

猴 hóu

蛇 shé

羊 yáng

馬 mǎ

There are twelve animal signs in the Chinese zodiac, each representing one year in a twelve-year cycle. According to a popular but unscientific theory, one's personality and temperament have much to do with the animal that represents the year of one's birth, and parents have been known to plan births accordingly. It might be surprising that the twelve-year cycle should start with the year of the rat, the smallest and perhaps the least likable of the twelve animals. At the beginning, as the story goes, there was a bitter quarrel among the animals as to who should represent the first year of the cycle. Finally, they decided to settle the dispute with a race. The robust ox was in the lead all the way, but he did not notice that the tiny rat was taking a ride on his back. As the ox was approaching the end, the rat jumped down and hit the finish line first, while the disappointed ox had to settle for second place. The indolent pig finished last in the race, and accordingly was assigned to the final year of the cycle.

Do you know your Chinese zodiac sign? Can you say it in Chinese?

KARAOKE

Nowadays, when Chinese people sing for fun, they usually sing karaoke, 卡拉 OK (*kǎlā'OK*). Originally from Japan, karaoke has become a nightlife mainstay in Mainland China and Taiwan. Many young people regularly go to karaoke bars, known as KTVs or 歌廳 (*gētīng*), to have a good time or celebrate someone's birthday. They can order food and beverages and reserve private rooms for their parties. Some people even have karaoke equipment at home.

Gift Giving

The Chinese usually express their appreciation for gifts profusely, typically by saying 你太客氣了！(*Nǐ tài kèqi le!*) (You're too kind!). However, to avoid giving the impression of greediness, most Chinese people would refrain from opening a present immediately in front of the gift giver. Flowers can make good gifts, but on happy occasions, one should avoid bouquets of white flowers, which are typically for funerals. Another taboo is giving a clock to an elderly person as a present, because the phrase 送鐘 (*sòng zhōng*) (to give a clock as a present) sounds ominously like 送終 (*sòng zhōng*), which means to bid farewell to a deceased person.

COMPARE & CONTRAST

1 What would you say to a friend giving you a present? Would you open it right away? If you gave a present to a Chinese friend and he/she didn't open it right away, how would you feel? What would be culturally appropriate to say to him/her?

2 In the past, on a child's first birthday, his/her parents would organize a special ceremony called 抓周 (*zhuā zhōu*) (grabbing test). Various objects—a book, a writing brush, a carpenter's tool, cosmetics, etc. —would be spread out before the child, and parents, grandparents, and other relatives would wait with bated breath to see which object the child would pick up, as the child's choice was supposed to indicate his/her character and inclinations. Additionally, when a baby is one month old, many parents hold a special banquet called 滿月酒 (*mǎnyuèjiǔ*). What special milestone celebrations are held for children in your culture?

Potluck dinner parties are not common in China. Chinese hosts and hostesses typically prepare everything for their guests, and do not count on them to bring anything. However, visitors can still bring something as a token of appreciation, such as fruit.

Party Etiquette

Lesson Wrap-Up

Make It Flow!

The following sentences are arranged in a logical order. Combine the sentences into a coherent narrative. Substitute nouns with pronouns and change periods to commas where necessary. Avoid unnecessary repetitions of subject pronouns. Add the connective devices 只有 (zhǐyǒu), 先 (xiān), 然後 (ránhòu), 這個時候 (zhè ge shíhou), and 最後 (zuìhòu) where appropriate.

晚上王朋和李友到了高小音家。大家都來了。白英愛還沒來。大家祝小音生日快樂。大家一起聊天。王朋問妹妹小紅每天練習中文練習多長時間。王紅說每天練習中文練習三個半鐘頭。王紅說每天還看兩個鐘頭的英文電視。小音給王朋和李友介紹她的表姐海倫。海倫中文說得非常好。海倫是在暑期班學的中文。海倫有一個兒子。海倫的兒子叫湯姆。湯姆屬狗。湯姆剛一歲。湯姆長得很像海倫。湯姆很可愛。小音讓大家吃蛋糕。

Skit

Student A	Persuade your friend to go to a party with you. Tell him/her when and where the party is, who else will be there, and what kind of food and music he/she can expect.
Student B	You're not sure if you want to go. You have an exam next Monday and you didn't do well on the last one. You want to study and review. Are there other reasons for your lack of interest?
Student A	How can you get your friend to agree to go to the party with you?

Email

Tell a friend about the party you went to last weekend. Who was there? When did it start and what was it for? Describe somebody you met there. What did he/she look like? What did you talk about? How were the food and music? When did you get home? Did you have fun?

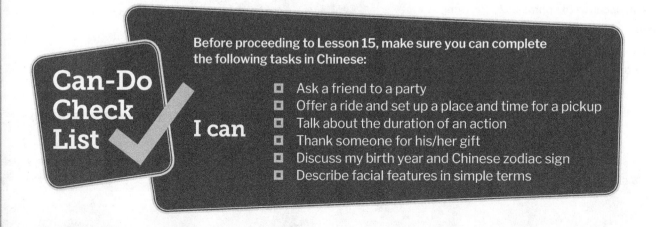

Can-Do Check List

I can

Before proceeding to Lesson 15, make sure you can complete the following tasks in Chinese:

- ☐ Ask a friend to a party
- ☐ Offer a ride and set up a place and time for a pickup
- ☐ Talk about the duration of an action
- ☐ Thank someone for his/her gift
- ☐ Discuss my birth year and Chinese zodiac sign
- ☐ Describe facial features in simple terms

第十五課

Dì shíwǔ kè

看病

Kàn bìng

SEEING A DOCTOR

Learning Objectives	Relate & Get Ready

In this lesson, you will learn to:

- Describe common cold and allergy symptoms
- Understand instructions on when and how often to take medications
- Talk about why you do or don't want to see the doctor
- Urge others to see a doctor when they are not feeling well

In your own culture/community:

- Can you see a doctor without an appointment?
- Do you have to pay an office visit fee before seeing a doctor?
- Is medication commonly prescribed and dispensed in the same place?
- Apart from medication, what other treatments might a doctor recommend?
- Is everyone covered by health insurance?

My Stomach Is Killing Me!

Dialogue 1

Audio

Video

（病人去醫院看病……）

醫生，我肚子疼死¹了。

你昨天吃什麼東西了？

我姐姐上個星期過生日，蛋糕沒吃完。昨天晚上我吃了幾口，夜裡肚子就疼起來²了，今天早上上了好幾次³廁所。

你把⁴蛋糕放在哪兒了？

放在冰箱裡了。

放了幾天了？

五、六天^a了。

發燒嗎？

不發燒。

你躺下。先檢查一下。

……

你吃蛋糕把肚子吃壞了。

得打針嗎？

不用打針，吃這種藥^b就可以。一天三次，一次兩片。

醫生，一天吃幾次？請您再說一遍。

一天三次，一次兩片。

好！飯前^c吃還是飯後吃？

飯前飯後都可以。不過，你最好二十四小時不要吃飯。

那我要餓死了。不行，這個辦法不好！

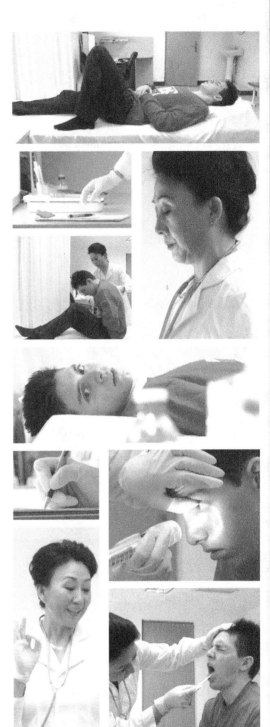

(Bìngrén qù yīyuàn kàn bìng . . .)

 Yīshēng, wǒ dùzi téng sǐ[1] le.

 Nǐ zuótiān chī shénme dōngxi le?

 Wǒ jiějie shàng ge xīngqī guò shēngrì, dàngāo méi

chī wán. Zuótiān wǎnshang wǒ chī le jǐ kǒu, yè li

dùzi jiù téng qǐ lái[2] le, jīntiān zǎoshang shàng le

hǎo jǐ cì[3] cèsuǒ.

 Nǐ bǎ[4] dàngāo fàng zài nǎr le?

 Fàng zài bīngxiāng lǐ le.

 Fàng le jǐ tiān le?

 Wǔ, liù tiān[a] le.

 Fā shāo ma?

 Bù fā shāo.

 Nǐ tǎng xia. Xiān jiǎnchá yí xià.

. . .

 Nǐ chī dàngāo bǎ dùzi chī huài le.

 Děi dǎ zhēn ma?

 Búyòng dǎ zhēn, chī zhè zhǒng yào[b] jiù kěyǐ.

Yì tiān sān cì, yí cì liǎng piàn.

 Yīshēng, yì tiān chī jǐ cì? Qǐng nín zài shuō

yí biàn.

 Yì tiān sān cì, yí cì liǎng piàn.

 Hǎo! Fàn qián[c] chī háishi fàn hòu chī?

 Fàn qián fàn hòu dōu kěyǐ. Búguò, nǐ zuìhǎo èrshí

sì xiǎoshí bú yào chī fàn.

 Nà wǒ yào è sǐ le. Bù xíng, zhè ge bànfǎ bù hǎo!

---

a 五、六天 *(wǔ, liù tiān)*

Approximate numbers can be expressed by two numbers in succession, e.g.: 五十六、七歲 *(wǔshí liù, qī suì)* (fifty-six or fifty-seven years old), 十八、九塊錢 *(shí bā, jiǔ kuài qián)* (eighteen or nineteen dollars), 三、四天 *(sān, sì tiān)* (three or four days), and 兩、三枝筆 *(liǎng, sān zhī bǐ)* (two or three pens). However, the numbers nine and ten cannot be used this way since in speech, it would be difficult to distinguish 九、十天 *(jiǔ, shí tiān)* from 九十天 *(jiǔshí tiān)* (ninety days).

b 吃藥 *(chī yào)*

"To take medicine" is 吃藥 *(chī yào)* (lit. to eat medicine). A more formal expression is 服藥 *(fú yào)*, which commonly appears in prescriptions and prescription instructions.

c 前 *(qián)* **and** 後 *(hòu)*

前 *(qián)* (before) in 飯前 *(fàn qián)* (before meals) and 後 *(hòu)* (after) in 飯後 *(fàn hòu)* (after meals) are the shortened forms of 以前 *(yǐqián)* (before) and 以後 *(yǐhòu)* (after), respectively.

Vocabulary

No.	Word	Pinyin	Part of Speech	Definition
1	病人	bìngrén	n	patient
	病	bìng	n/v	illness; to get sick
2	醫院	yīyuàn	n	hospital
3	看病	kàn bìng	vo	to see a doctor
4	肚子	dùzi	n	belly, abdomen, stomach
5	疼死	téng sǐ	adj + c	really painful [See Grammar 1.]
	疼	téng	adj	aching
	死	sǐ	v/c	to die; (a complement indicating an extreme degree)
6	夜裡	yè li	n	at night
7	好幾	hǎo jǐ		quite a few
8	廁所	cèsuǒ	n	restroom, toilet
9	把	bǎ	prep	(indicating disposition, arrangement, or settlement of something) [See Grammar 4.]
10	冰箱	bīngxiāng	n	refrigerator
11	發燒	fā shāo	vo	to have a fever
12	躺下	tǎng xia	vc	to lie down
	躺	tǎng	v	to lie, to recline
13	檢查	jiǎnchá	v	to examine
14	吃壞	chī huài	vc	to get sick because of bad food
	壞	huài	adj	bad
15	打針	dǎ zhēn	vo	to get an injection
	針	zhēn	n	needle

妈妈医生实用手册

儿童健康绝学系列

孩子发烧
怎么办

高亮 著

北京中医药大学博士
当归中医学堂特邀讲师

While browsing the bookstore at Beijing Capital International Airport, this title catches your eye. What do you think the book is about? Who is it written for?

GET
Real
WITH **CHINESE**

No.	Word	Pinyin	Part of Speech	Definition
16	藥	*yào*	n	medicine
17	片	*piàn*	m	(measure word for tablets, slices, etc.)
18	遍	*biàn*	m	(measure word for complete courses of an action or instances of an action)
19	最好	*zuìhǎo*	adv	had better
20	小時	*xiǎoshí*	n	hour
21	辦法	*bànfǎ*	n	method, way (of doing something)

你怎麼了？哪兒
不舒服？

Nǐ zěnme le? Nǎr bù shūfu?

What's wrong with you? Where's the discomfort?

我 ＿＿＿＿＿＿＿ 。

Wǒ ＿＿＿＿＿＿＿ .

See index for corresponding vocabulary or research another term.

How About You?

Grammar

1	Indicating an extreme degree using 死 (sǐ)

Placed after an adjective, 死 (sǐ) can serve as a complement to indicate an extreme degree of the condition described by the adjective.

A 打針疼死了。

Dǎ zhēn téng sǐ le.

Getting shots is extremely painful.

B 我餓死了。

Wǒ è sǐ le.

I'm starving.

C 今天熱死了。

Jīntiān rè sǐ le.

It's awfully hot today.

死 (sǐ) often follows adjectives with a pejorative meaning, and the combination carries a negative connotation, as shown in the examples above. However, 高興 (gàoxìng) (happy) 死了 (sǐ le) is one of few exceptions.

D 知道了這件事，他高興死了。

Zhīdào le zhè jiàn shì, tā gāoxìng sǐ le.

He was incredibly happy when he found out about this.

Most adjectives with a positive meaning cannot be followed by 死 (sǐ). People, therefore, seldom say:

[⊗ 他跟他的女朋友好死了。]

Note that when 死 (sǐ) is used as a resultative complement, it can literally mean "to die."

E　聽說那個地方有人餓死了。

Tīngshuō nà ge dìfang yǒu rén è sǐ le.

I heard people had died of hunger in that place.

More
exercises

EXERCISES

Complete the sentences by inserting 死了 where appropriate. Use exercise 1
as an example.

1　這兒的夏天　　　　　　　　熱

　　→ 這兒的夏天熱死了。

2　今天的考試　　　　　　難

3　我中午沒有時間吃飯　餓

---

2 | Indicating the beginning of an action using 起來 (qi lai)

起來 (qi lai) indicates the moment when something static becomes dynamic: that is, it
signifies the beginning of an action or state. Note that if there is an object when the 起來
(qi lai) structure is used, the object is placed between 起 (qi) and 來 (lai), as in (B) and (C).

A　我們一見面就聊起來了。

Wǒmen yí jiàn miàn jiù liáo qi lai le.

We started to chat as soon as we met.

B　他一回家就玩兒起手機來了。

Tā yì huí jiā jiù wánr qi shǒujī lai le.

He started to play with his cell phone as soon as he got home.

C　下了課以後，學生們打起球來。

Xià le kè yǐhòu, xuéshēng men dǎ qi qiú lai.

The students started playing ball once class was over.

EXERCISES

Complete the sentences with 起來. Use exercise 1 as an example.

1   小明上完課　就看電子郵件

　　→ 小明上完課，就看起電子郵件來了。

2   他剛吃完晚飯　就看書

3   弟弟一回到家　就打電話

<u>3</u>
> 次 (cì) **for frequency**

次 (cì) is the measure word most frequently used to express how many times an action is performed. The "number + 次 (cì)" combination follows the verb.

A　上午我打了兩次電話。/
　　　上午我打電話打了兩次。

Shàngwǔ wǒ dǎ le liǎng cì diànhuà./
Shàngwǔ wǒ dǎ diànhuà dǎ le liǎng cì.

I made two phone calls this morning.

B　我昨天吃了三次藥。

Wǒ zuótiān chī le sān cì yào.

I took medicine three times yesterday.

If the object represents a person or a place, 次 (cì) can go either between the verb and the object or after the object, as in (C) and (D).

C　去年我去了一次中國。/
　　　去年我去了中國一次。

Qùnián wǒ qù le yí cì Zhōngguó./Qùnián wǒ qù le Zhōngguó yí cì.

Last year I went to China once.

D　昨天我找了三次王醫生。/
　　昨天我找了王醫生三次。

Zuótiān wǒ zhǎo le sān cì Wáng yīshēng./Zuótiān wǒ zhǎo le Wáng yīshēng sān cì.

I went looking for Dr. Wang three times yesterday.

If the object is a personal pronoun, however, 次 (cì) must follow the object.

E　我昨天找了他兩次，他都不在。

Wǒ zuótiān zhǎo le tā liǎng cì, tā dōu bú zài.

Yesterday I went looking for him twice, but he wasn't around either time.

遍 (biàn) is another measure word for occurrences of actions, but it pertains to the entire course of an action from beginning to end.

F　請你念一遍課文。

Qǐng nǐ niàn yí biàn kèwén.

Please read the text (from beginning to end) once.

More
exercises

EXERCISES

Complete the sentences with 次 or 遍. Use exercise 1 as an example.

1　今天小明洗澡　　　　兩
　　→ 今天小明洗了兩次澡。/
　　　今天小明洗澡洗了兩次。

2　我每天念課文　　　　一

3　小明上個星期找老師　兩

The 把 (bǎ) construction (I)

Sentences with 把 (bǎ) are common in Chinese. The basic construction is as follows:

Subject + 把 (bǎ) + object + verb + other element (complement/ 了 [le], etc.)

In the 把 (bǎ) construction, what follows 把 (bǎ) and precedes the verb serves as both the object of 把 (bǎ) and the object of the verb. In general, a sentence with the 把 (bǎ) construction emphasizes the subject's disposition of or impact upon the object, with the result of the disposition or impact indicated by the element following the verb.

A 我把你要的書找到了。

Wǒ bǎ nǐ yào de shū zhǎo dào le.

I've found the books that you wanted.

[The resultative complement 到 (dào) serves as the "other element."]

In (A), the subject 我 (wǒ) exerts an impact on the book through the action of 找 (zhǎo), of which 到 (dào) is the result.

B 你把這個字寫錯了。

Nǐ bǎ zhè ge zì xiě cuò le.

You wrote this character wrong.

[The resultative complement 錯 (cuò) serves as the "other element."]

In (B), the subject 你 (nǐ) exerts an impact on the character through the action of 寫 (xiě), of which 錯 (cuò) is the result.

C 請把那條褲子給我。

Qǐng bǎ nà tiáo kùzi gěi wǒ.

Please pass me that pair of pants.

[The indirect object 我 (wǒ) serves as the "other element."]

D 你再把這篇課文看看。

Nǐ zài bǎ zhè piān kèwén kàn kan.

Would you take another look at this text?

[The reduplicated verb 看 (kàn) serves as the "other element."]

E 把這片藥吃了！

Bǎ zhè piàn yào chī le!

Take this tablet of medicine!

F 你怎麼把女朋友的生日忘了？

Nǐ zěnme bǎ nǚpéngyou de shēngrì wàng le?

How did you manage to forget your girlfriend's birthday?

[In (E) and (F), the particle 了 (*le*) serves as the "other element."]

(C), (D), and (E) suggest what the listener is requested to do to the objects (the pants, the text, and the medicine). The "other element" can be a complement as in (A) and (B), an indirect object as in (C), a reduplicated verb as in (D), or the particle 了 (*le*) as in (E) and (F).

In the 把 (*bǎ*) construction, the object is often something already known to both the speaker and the listener. For example, 你要的書 (*nǐ yào de shū*) in (A), 這個字 (*zhè ge zì*) in (B), 那條褲子 (*nà tiáo kùzi*) in (C), and 女朋友的生日 (*nǚpéngyou de shēngrì*) in (F) are all things that are already known. Compare the following two sentences:

G 老王給了小張一些錢。

Lǎo Wáng gěi le Xiǎo Zhāng yì xiē qián.

Old Wang gave Little Zhang some money.

H 老王把錢給小張了。

Lǎo Wáng bǎ qián gěi Xiǎo Zhāng le.

Old Wang gave the money to Little Zhang.

The object in (G), "some money," is unspecified. However, in (H), the speaker expects the listener to know what money is being referred to.

A sentence must use the 把 (*bǎ*) construction when the subject is given, the object is known to both the speaker and listener, and the verb is followed by a complement in the form of a prepositional phrase with 在 (*zài*) or 到 (*dào*).

I 你把筆放在桌子上。

Nǐ bǎ bǐ fàng zài zhuōzi shang.

Put the pen on the desk.

[❌ 你放筆在桌子上。]

J 請你把這個電腦送到律師的辦公室。

Qǐng nǐ bǎ zhè ge diàonǎo sòng dào lǜshī de bàngōngshì.

Please deliver this computer to the attorney's office.

[❌ 請你送這個電腦到律師的辦公室。]

EXERCISES

Rearrange these words to form new sentences with 把. Use exercise 1 as an example.

1 小明　放　杯子　在　　桌子上
　→ 小明把杯子放在桌子上。

2 請你　給　我　　看看　你家的照片

3 你　　給　老師　功課

⊕ More exercises

Characterize it!

| What do the characters mean? |
| What is the common radical? |
| What does the radical mean? |
| How does the radical relate to the overall meaning of the characters? |

❶ 病　❷ 疼　❸ 癢

⊞ More characters

Language Practice

Edge case `PRESENTATIONAL`

Based on the images given below, indicate an extreme degree of the condition by using
死 (sǐ), e.g.:

他渴死了。

Tā kě sǐ le.

 **1**

 **2**

 **3**

B **Routine inspection** `INTERPERSONAL`

In pairs, discuss your daily routine for studying Chinese and what happened yesterday.
Use the "number + 次/遍 (cì/biàn)" construction, e.g.:

聽錄音

tīng lùyīn

Q: 你每天聽幾遍/次錄音？or
你每天聽錄音聽幾遍/次？

Nǐ měi tiān tīng jǐ biàn/cì lùyīn? or Nǐ měi tiān tīng lùyīn tīng jǐ biàn/cì?

A: 我每天聽兩遍/兩次錄音。or
我每天聽錄音聽兩遍/兩次。

Wǒ měi tiān tīng liǎng biàn/liǎng cì lùyīn. or Wǒ měi tiān tīng lùyīn tīng liǎng biàn/liǎng cì.

Q: 昨天呢？

Zuótiān ne?

A: 我昨天聽了兩遍/兩次錄音。or
我昨天聽錄音聽了兩遍/兩次。

Wǒ zuótiān tīng le liǎng biàn/liǎng cì lùyīn. or Wǒ zuótiān tīng lùyīn tīng le liǎng biàn/liǎng cì.

1 念課文

niàn kèwén

2 復習生詞語法

fùxí shēngcí yǔfǎ

3 寫漢字

xiě Hànzì

Moving day	INTERPERSONAL

In pairs, role-play a friend helping another friend on moving day. Form a question-and-answer about where things should go by using the 把 *(bǎ)* construction, e.g.:

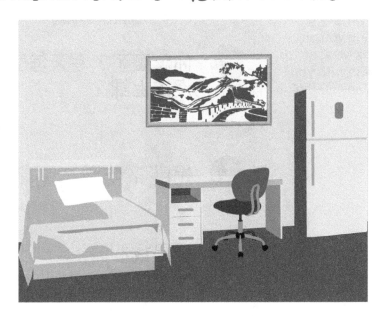

Q: 把紙和筆放在什麼地方？

Bǎ zhǐ hé bǐ fàng zài shénme dìfang?

A: 請把紙和筆放在桌子上。

Qǐng bǎ zhǐ hé bǐ fàng zài zhuōzi shang.

1

2

3

4

D | # You don't look well INTERPERSONAL

Your classmate is concerned about you and wants to know what's wrong. Based on the images, form a question-and-answer to discuss what's ailing you, e.g.:

Q: 你怎麼了？

Nǐ zěnme le?

A: 我頭疼。

Wǒ tóu téng.

1

2

3

Chinese Chat

Your friend is messaging you on Facebook Messenger to check in with you. How would you reply?

9:41 PM 85%

‹ Back   Ying Wang
Active Now • Messenger

你怎麼了？今天怎麼沒去上課？

是嗎？吃藥了嗎？

還是找個醫生給你檢查一下吧。

要不要我開車帶你去看病？

那你多喝水、早點兒睡。有事兒給我發短信。

Allergies

Dialogue 2

Audio

Video

（王朋這幾天好像生病了……）

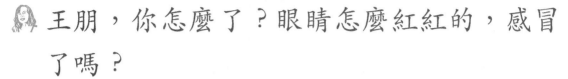 王朋，你怎麼了？眼睛怎麼紅紅的，感冒
了嗎？

沒感冒。我也不知道怎麼了，最近這幾天
身體很不舒服。眼睛又紅又癢。

你一定是對[5]什麼過敏了。

我想也是，所以去藥店買了一些藥。已經
吃了四、五種了，花了不少錢，都沒有用。

把你買的藥拿出來給我看看。

這些就是。

這些藥沒有用。為什麼不去看病？你沒有
健康保險嗎？

我有保險。可是我這個學期功課很多，
看病太花時間。

那你也得趕快去看病[a]。要不然病會越來越[6]重。

我想再吃點兒別的藥試試[b]。我上次生病，
沒去看醫生[a]，休息了兩天，最後也好了。

不行，不行，你太懶了。再說[7]，你不能
自己亂吃藥。走，我跟你看病去。

(Wáng Péng zhè jǐ tiān hǎoxiàng shēng bìng le . . .)

Wáng Péng, nǐ zěnme le? Yǎnjing zěnme hóng

hóng de, gǎnmào le ma?

Méi gǎnmào. Wǒ yě bù zhīdào zěnme le, zuìjìn zhè jǐ

tiān shēntǐ hěn bù shūfu. Yǎnjing yòu hóng yòu yǎng.

Nǐ yídìng shì duì⁵ shénme guòmǐn le.

Wǒ xiǎng yě shì, suǒyǐ qù yàodiàn mǎi le yì xiē

yào. Yǐjīng chī le sì, wǔ zhǒng le, huā le bù shǎo

qián, dōu méiyǒu yòng.

Bǎ nǐ mǎi de yào ná chū lai gěi wǒ kàn kan.

Zhè xiē jiù shì.

Zhè xiē yào méiyǒu yòng. Wèishénme bú qù kàn

bìng? Nǐ méiyǒu jiànkāng bǎoxiǎn ma?

Wǒ yǒu bǎoxiǎn. Kěshì wǒ zhè ge xuéqī gōngkè

hěn duō. Kàn bìng tài huā shíjiān.

Nà nǐ yě děi gǎnkuài qù kàn bìng[a]. Yàobùrán bìng

huì yuè lái yuè⁶ zhòng.

Wǒ xiǎng zài chī diǎnr bié de yào shì shi[b]. Wǒ

shàng cì shēng bìng, méi qù kàn yīshēng[a], xiūxi le

liǎng tiān, zuìhòu yě hǎo le.

Bù xíng, bù xíng, nǐ tài lǎn le. Zàishuō⁷, nǐ bù

néng zìjǐ luàn chī yào. Zǒu, wǒ gēn nǐ kàn bìng qu.

a 看病 (kàn bìng) vs. 看醫生 (kàn yīshēng)

The two phrases 看病 (kàn bìng) and 看醫生 (kàn yīshēng) are interchangeable, although in northern China, 看病 (kàn bìng) is much more common than 看醫生 (kàn yīshēng).

b 試試 (shì shi)

試試 (shì shi) can be used when trying most things. But when tasting or trying any food or drink, you say 我嚐嚐 (Wǒ cháng chang) (Let me taste it) instead of 我試試 (Wǒ shì shi) (Let me try it).

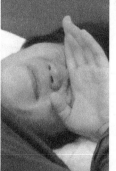

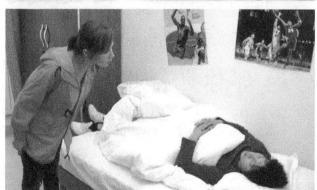

Vocabulary

No.	Word	Pinyin	Part of Speech	Definition
1	生病	shēng bìng	vo	to get sick
2	感冒	gǎnmào	v	to have a cold
3	身體	shēntǐ	n	body, health
4	癢	yǎng	adj	itchy
5	過敏	guòmǐn	v	to be allergic to
6	藥店	yàodiàn	n	pharmacy
7	健康	jiànkāng	adj/n	healthy; health
8	保險	bǎoxiǎn	n/adj	insurance; secure
9	趕快	gǎnkuài	adv	right away, quickly, in a hurry
10	要不然	yàobùrán	conj	otherwise
11	越來越	yuè lái yuè	adv	more and more [See Grammar 6.]
12	上次	shàng cì		last time
13	休息	xiūxi	v	to take a break, to rest
14	懶	lǎn	adj	lazy
15	再說	zàishuō	conj	moreover [See Grammar 7.]
16	亂	luàn	adv	randomly, arbitrarily, messily

Audio

Flashcards

你對什麼過敏？

Nǐ duì shénme guòmǐn?

What are you allergic to?

我對 ＿＿＿＿＿＿＿ 。

Wǒ duì ＿＿＿＿＿＿＿ .

See index for corresponding vocabulary or research another term.

GET Real WITH CHINESE

You see this thermometer inside a window in Qiqihar, one of the northernmost cities in China. What warning does it have for when the temperature dips below 18°C?

Grammar

---

5   **The preposition 對 (duì) (to, for)**

The preposition 對 (duì) (to, for) indicates a person or thing that is affected by someone or something else. Its English translation varies depending on the context.

A   這種藥對感冒很有用。

Zhè zhǒng yào duì gǎnmào hěn yǒu yòng.

This medicine is very effective for colds.

B   電腦對他練習發音很有用。

Diànnǎo duì tā liànxí fāyīn hěn yǒu yòng.

The computer is very useful for his pronunciation practice.

C   你一定（是）對什麼東西過敏了。

Nǐ yídìng (shì) duì shénme dōngxi guòmǐn le.

You must be allergic to something.

EXERCISES

Rearrange the words to form new sentences with 對. Use exercise 1 as an example.

More
exercises

1   這本書　很有用　找工作
　　→ 這本書對找工作很有用。

2   小王　　過敏　　　魚

3   這種藥　沒有用　感冒

越來越⋯ (yuè lái yuè . . .) (more and more . . .)

The structure 越來越⋯ (yuè lái yuè . . .) (more and more . . .) denotes a progressive change over time.

A 李友的中文越來越好。

Lǐ Yǒu de Zhōngwén yuè lái yuè hǎo.

Li You's Chinese is getting better and better.

B 天氣越來越暖和了。

Tiānqì yuè lái yuè nuǎnhuo le.

The weather is becoming warmer and warmer.

C 表姐考試考得越來越糟糕。

Biǎojiě kǎo shì kǎo de yuè lái yuè zāogāo.

My cousin is doing worse and worse on her exams.

More exercises

EXERCISES

Complete the sentences by inserting 越來越 where appropriate. Use exercise 1 as an example.

1 健康保險　　　貴

→ 健康保險越來越貴了。

2 老王的身體　　好

3 天氣　　　　　冷

The conjunction 再說 (zàishuō) (moreover)

The expression 再說 (zàishuō) (moreover) introduces an additional reason for an action taken or decision made. It is different from 再 + 說 (zài + shuō) (to say again).

A   Q: 你為什麼不去紐約？

Nǐ wèishénme bú qù Niǔyuē?

Why aren't you going to New York?

A: 我沒有時間，再說也沒有錢。

Wǒ méiyǒu shíjiān, zàishuō yě méiyǒu qián.

I don't have the time, and besides, I don't have the money.

B   我不喜歡今天晚上的舞會，音樂不好，再說人也太少。

Wǒ bù xǐhuan jīntiān wǎnshang de wǔhuì, yīnyuè bù hǎo, zàishuō rén yě tài shǎo.

I didn't like the dance party tonight. The music was lousy. Besides, there were too few people there.

Like 再說 (zàishuō), 而且 (érqiě) (moreover, in addition) also conveys the idea of "furthermore," "additionally," etc., but the clause that follows it may or may not be explanatory in nature. Compare the following sentences:

C   Q: 你為什麼不去紐約？

Nǐ wèishénme bú qù Niǔyuē?

Why aren't you going to New York?

A: 我沒有時間，而且也沒有錢。

Wǒ méiyǒu shíjiān, érqiě yě méiyǒu qián.

I don't have the time. Besides, I don't have the money.

Note: In (C), 而且 (érqiě) can be replaced with 再說 (zàishuō).

D 這是王先生，他不但是我的老師，
而且也是我的朋友。

Zhè shì Wáng xiānsheng, tā búdàn shì wǒ de lǎoshī, érqiě yě shì wǒ de péngyou.

This is Mr. Wang. He is not only my teacher but also my friend.

Note: In (D), 而且 (*érqiě*) cannot be replaced with 再說 (*zàishuō*).

[✗ 這是王先生，他不但是我的老師，
再說也是我的朋友。]

More
exercises

EXERCISES

Answer the questions with 再說. Use exercise 1 as an example.

1　Q: 你今天晚上為什麼不去看電影？
　　（我明天有考試）
　　（電影票賣完了）
　　A: 我明天有考試，再說電影票也賣完了。

2　Q: 你為什麼不去上你哥哥的那個大學？
　　（那個大學太遠）
　　（我不喜歡跟他在一個學校學習）
　　A: _____

3　Q: 你知道小王寒假為什麼不回家嗎？
　　（他說飛機票太貴）
　　（他父母去外國了）
　　A: _____

Language Practice

E [INTERPERSONAL] **Allergies! Allergies! Allergies!** [PRESENTATIONAL]

Survey your classmates about whether anyone is allergic to the following items.
Use 對 (duì)…過敏 (guòmǐn), e.g.:

Q: Dmitri, 你對味精過敏嗎？

Dmitri, nǐ duì wèijīng guòmǐn ma?

A: 我對味精過敏。／我對味精不過敏。

Wǒ duì wèijīng guòmǐn./Wǒ duì wèijīng bú guòmǐn.

 1

 2

 3

Then tally who's allergic to what, e.g.:

Dmitri 、 Maya 、……對味精過敏。

Dmitri, Maya, . . . , *duì wèijīng guòmǐn.*

F **Free advice** [PRESENTATIONAL]

How would you help incoming Chinese language students avoid falling into bad study habits?
Use 要不然 (yàobùrán) to give advice, e.g.:

你得多練習寫漢字，要不然你的漢字不好看。

Nǐ děi duō liànxí xiě Hànzì, yàobùrán nǐ de Hànzì bù hǎokàn.

Then use 要不然 (yàobùrán) to give incoming students some advice on how to take care
of themselves at college, e.g.:

如果身體不舒服，你就得去看病，要不然病會
越來越重。

Rúguǒ shēntǐ bù shūfu, nǐ jiù děi qù kàn bìng, yàobùrán bìng huì yuè lái yuè zhòng.

What's your take?

In pairs, form a question-and-answer about how your study of Chinese is progressing. Use 越來越 (yuè lái yuè) to indicate a progressive change, e.g.:

生詞　多 vs. 少

shēngcí　duō vs. *shǎo*

Q: 你覺得生詞越來越多還是越來越少？
Nǐ juéde shēngcí yuè lái yuè duō háishi yuè lái yuè shǎo?

A: 我覺得生詞越來越多 / 少。
Wǒ juéde shēngcí yuè lái yuè duō/shǎo.

1 功課　多 vs. 少
gōngkè　duō vs. *shǎo*

2 課文　長 vs. 短
kèwén　cháng vs. *duǎn*

3 考試　難 vs. 容易
kǎoshì　nán vs. *róngyì*

4 語法　難 vs. 容易
yǔfǎ　nán vs. *róngyì*

And not only that

In pairs, form a question-and-answer about why you didn't do certain things. Use 再說 (zàishuō) to introduce an additional reason, e.g.:

Q: 你今天為什麼沒吃早飯？
Nǐ jīntiān wèishénme méi chī zǎofàn?

A: 我沒時間，再說我也不餓。
Wǒ méi shíjiān, zàishuō wǒ yě bú è.

1 Q: 你為什麼不運動？
Nǐ wèishénme bú yùndòng?

A: _____

2 Q: 你為什麼寒假沒回家看爸爸媽媽？
Nǐ wèishénme hánjià méi huí jiā kàn bàba māma?

A: _____

3 Q: 你為什麼學中文？

Nǐ wèishénme xué Zhōngwén?

A: _____

4 Q: 你為什麼上這個學校？

Nǐ wèishénme shàng zhè ge xuéxiào?

A: _____

Chinese Chat

Your friend just published a post on haodf.com (好大夫在線) (Hǎo dàifu zàixiàn), a popular medical consultation and scheduling website in China. What's ailing him, and what does the doctor suggest?

李新
狀態：就診前

> 醫生，上週我眼睛特別紅，這幾天剛好，可是現在鼻子又特別癢 …… 吃了很多又貴又難吃的藥都沒用。我是感冒了還是過敏了？
>
> 來自好大夫APP（下載APP與醫生一對一免費溝通）

患

高朋 大夫

> 別亂吃藥，我得先給你檢查一下，快來醫院看病。

醫

Characterize it!

What do the characters mean?

What is the common radical?

What does the radical mean?

How does the radical relate to the overall meaning of the characters?

❶ 感

❷ 息

❸ 懶

More characters

文化e

Continue
to explore

Chinese Medicine

Before the seventeenth-century introduction of Western medicine (西醫) *(Xīyī)* by European missionaries, people in China had relied on traditional Chinese medicine (中醫) *(Zhōngyī)*. Its treatment modalities—acupuncture, herbal medicine, massage, etc.—remain well-respected options for treating various ailments in China, and many people opt for traditional medicine either in conjunction with or instead of Western medicine. Traditional Chinese medicine is by no means a panacea. However, some of its practices have found popularity in the West despite misgivings among medical professionals. Other practices have been confirmed by modern science: sweet wormwood *(Artemisia annua)* or 青蒿 *(qīnghāo)* has been used to treat fevers for more than two millennia. In the search for a drug to treat malaria, the Chinese chemist Tu Youyou consulted a text from the fourth century and succeeded in isolating the plant's active compound, artemisinin or 青蒿素 *(qīnghāosù)*, in the 1970s. Artemisinin is now one of the main drugs used in the treatment of malaria, and for her work, Tu was awarded the Nobel Prize in 2015.

COMPARE & CONTRAST

There are a variety of alternative medical treatments in China, including moxibustion (艾灸) *(ài jiǔ)*, in which dried mugwort is burned on the skin; acupuncture (針灸) *(zhēnjiǔ)*, in which specialized needles are inserted into the body at particular points; and cupping (拔罐) *(bá guàn)*, in which a vacuum is created on the skin with the use of glass cups. All of these practices are believed to facilitate the flow of qi through the body. Are alternative medical treatments used in your culture or community, and if so, how is their efficacy perceived?

Seeing *the* Doctor

In China, consulting a doctor requires the payment of a registration fee, 掛號費 (*guàhào fèi*), typically under twenty yuan (about three dollars). Consulting someone designated as a "senior expert," 專家 (*zhuānjiā*), however, can require a registration fee as high as several hundred yuan. Patients typically pay upfront for tests.

Injections, 打針 (*dǎ zhēn*), and intravenous infusions, which are 打點滴 (*dǎ diǎndī*) in Taiwan and 輸液 (*shū yè*) in Mainland China, are surprisingly common treatments in Chinese hospitals and clinics, even for ailments like colds.

Most outpatients in China pick up prescriptions from a pharmacy within the hospital itself. However, prescription medication can also be obtained from independent pharmacies.

Medical Care

Employees of all state-owned enterprises and institutions in China were entitled to free medical care until the 1980s. This became a huge financial burden on the government, and the practice was discontinued with the government's initiation of healthcare reform in the 1990s. China is currently in a transitional period toward a better-regulated system of medical insurance for all citizens. While almost everyone is now nominally under some kind of insurance coverage, there is a disparity in the quality of insurance programs in cities and those in rural areas, where healthcare facilities are inferior and ratios of out-of-pocket payments much higher.

Hua Tuo

Hua Tuo (華佗) (*Huà Tuó*), a famed physician who lived during the second century, is credited as the first in China to introduce anesthesia during surgery, using a concoction called 麻沸散 (*máfèisǎn*) before the operation. Following this, the modern Chinese term for anesthesia is 麻醉 (*mázuì*), literally "numb and inebriated." Hua Tuo also wrote a manual of qigong exercises, 五禽戲 (*Wǔ Qín Xì*) ("Games of Five Beasts"), based on his studies of the tiger, deer, bear, monkey, and crane. The pronunciation of Hua Tuo in ancient Chinese sounded similar to *gada*, Sanskrit for sickness and related to *Agada*, one of eight branches of Indian medicine. Some scholars have speculated that many stories of Hua Tuo's medical feats are in fact of Indian origin.

Lesson Wrap-Up

Make It Flow!

Rearrange the following sentences into a logical sequence. Then combine the sentences into a coherent narrative. Substitute nouns with pronouns and change periods to commas where appropriate. Avoid unnecessary repetitions of subject pronouns. Add the connective devices 就 (jiù), …以後 (…yǐhòu), and 還 (hái) where appropriate.

_____ 高文中昨天夜裡肚子疼起来了。

_____ 醫生說高文中吃蛋糕把肚子吃壞了。

_____ 醫生讓高文中吃一種藥。

_____ 高文中說二十四個小時不吃飯的辦法不好。

__1__ 高小音的生日蛋糕沒吃完。

_____ 高小音的生日蛋糕放在冰箱裡五、六天了。

_____ 醫生給高文中檢查了。

_____ 醫生說最好二十四個小時別吃飯。

_____ 今天高文中去醫院看病。

_____ 高文中昨天夜裡上了好幾次廁所。

_____ 高文中昨天晚上吃了幾口高小音的生日蛋糕。

Skit

You went to a friend's birthday party last Friday. You met a lot of interesting people. You liked the music and the food. You had a good time, but got sick. The doctor asks you what's wrong. You have a stomachache. The doctor wants to know what and how much you ate and drank last night. Depending on your answer, the doctor will examine you, see if you have a fever, and determine if you need injections or medication. If you need medicine, find out how many times a day you need to take it and whether you need to take it before or after you eat.

It's hay fever season. On a social media platform, post about allergy symptoms and remedies to help Chinese students on your campus deal. Explain how to distinguish allergy and cold symptoms, referring to the template below.

中國同學們，你們好！最近，你們是不是……？

過敏：

感冒：

怎麼辦：多……，多……，少……，少……

Can-Do Check List ✔ I can

Before proceeding to Lesson 16, make sure you can complete the following tasks in Chinese:

- ☐ Tell a doctor about my cold symptoms
- ☐ Ask a doctor if a shot or medicine is needed for treatment
- ☐ Follow and repeat a doctor's instructions on when and how often to take medicine
- ☐ Tell people about my allergies and briefly describe my symptoms

Keeping It Casual (Lessons 11–15)

Before you progress to the next half of the text, we'll review how some of the functional expressions from Lessons 11–15 are used in casual Chinese. After you complete the review, note any other casual expressions you would like to learn; then share the list with your teacher.

<u>1</u> | 在 *(zài)* **(to exist)**

When you think someone else might have something of yours, ask 我的⋯⋯在你那兒嗎? *(Wǒ de . . . zài nǐ nàr ma?)* instead of 你有我的⋯⋯嗎? *(Nǐ yǒu wǒ de . . . ma?).*

A   **Bai Ying'ai**

老師，我的功課在您那兒嗎？

Lǎoshī, wǒ de gōngkè zài nín nàr ma?

Teacher, do you have my homework?

Teacher Chang

我已經還給你了。

Wǒ yǐjīng huán gěi nǐ le.

I gave it to you already.

[還給 *(huán gěi)*, to return something (to someone)]

Bai Ying'ai

是嗎？對不起，我再找找。

Shì ma? Duìbuqǐ, wǒ zài zhǎo zhao.

Oh, you did? Sorry, I'll look for it again.

B   **Daughter**

媽，我的綠色襯衫在您那兒嗎？

Mā, wǒ de lǜ sè chènshān zài nín nàr ma?

Mom, do you have my green shirt?

Mother

在我這兒。給你吧。

Zài wǒ zhèr. Gěi nǐ ba.

Yes, I have it. Here you are.

C   **Wang Peng**   我的書還在你那兒嗎？昨天你拿去看了。

                                     Wǒ de shū hái zài nǐ nàr ma? Zuótiān nǐ ná qù kàn le.

                                     Do you still have my book? You took it to read yesterday.

       Gao Wenzhong   哦，還在我家，我回去拿。

                                     Ò, hái zài wǒ jiā, wǒ huí qu ná.

                                     Yeah, it's still at my place. I'll go get it.

2   Complimentary expressions

Note the different expressions that are used to compliment men, women, and children.

A   那個小孩真可愛。

Nà ge xiǎohái zhēn kě'ài.

That little kid is really cute.

B   她長得真好看！

Tā zhǎng de zhēn hǎokàn!

She's really beautiful!

C   李友長得很漂亮。

Lǐ Yǒu zhǎng de hěn piàoliang.

Li You looks very pretty.

D   王朋真帥。

Wáng Péng zhēn shuài.

Wang Peng is really handsome.

E   那個班的學生都很酷。

Nà ge bān de xuésheng dōu hěn kù.

The students in that class are all very cool.

3 | 怎麼了？(Zěnme le?) (What's the matter? What's wrong?)

You can ask 怎麼了？ *(Zěnme le?)* upon finding someone under unusual circumstances or showing signs of concern, anxiety, or pain.

A   **Little Gao**

你怎麼了？怎麼這麼不高興？

Nǐ zěnme le? Zěnme zhème bù gāoxìng?

What's the matter? Why are you so unhappy?

Mr. Fei

我的女朋友不愛我了。

Wǒ de nǚpéngyou bú ài wǒ le.

My girlfriend doesn't love me anymore.

B   **Li You**

怎麼了？眼睛怎麼這麼紅？

Zěnme le? Yǎnjīng zěnme zhème hóng?

What's wrong? Why are your eyes so red?

Wang Peng

沒什麼。我可能對什麼東西過敏了。

Méi shénme. Wǒ kěnéng duì shénme dōngxi guòmǐn le.

It's nothing. I may be allergic to something.

4 | 糟糕 (zāogāo) ([it's] awful/what a mess)

Say this when you realize you've forgotten something important or something consequential has gone wrong.

A   **Gao Wenzhong**

糟糕，我的信用卡不見了。

Zāogāo, wǒ de xìnyòngkǎ bú jiàn le.

Shoot! My credit card has disappeared.

Wang Peng

快給你爸爸打電話吧。

Kuài gěi nǐ bàba dǎ diànhuà ba.

Hurry, call your dad.

B   **Li You**

糟糕，快要考試了，我還沒準備好。

Zāogāo, kuài yào kǎo shì le, wǒ hái méi zhǔnbèi hǎo.

Drat. It's almost time for the test. I am not ready yet.

Bai Ying'ai

你沒聽說嗎？今天不考試了。

Nǐ méi tīngshuō ma? Jīntiān bù kǎo shì le.

Didn't you hear? There's no test today.

Li You

是嗎？那太好了！……為什麼？

Shì ma? Nà tài hǎo le! . . . Wèishénme?

Really? That's great! . . . How come?

Bai Ying'ai

老師病了。

Lǎoshī bìng le.

The teacher is sick.

約會

Yuēhuì

DATING

In this lesson, you will learn to:

- Describe how long you've known someone
- Ask someone out on a date
- Make arrangements to go out with friends
- Accept or gently decline a date
- End a phone conversation politely

In your own culture/community:

- Is it socially acceptable to call a person you only met once and whose phone number you obtained indirectly?
- Is it impolite to decline a date without providing an excuse?
- How do you end a phone conversation without being rude?

Seeing a Movie

Dialogue 1

Audio

Video

王朋跟李友在同^a一個學校學習，他們認識已經快半年了。王朋常常幫李友練習說中文。他們也常常一起出去玩兒，每次都玩兒得¹很高興。李友對王朋的印象^b很好，王朋也很喜歡李友，他們成了好朋友。

這個週末學校演一個中國電影^c，我們一起去看，好嗎？

好啊！不過，聽說看電影的人很多，買得到²票嗎？

票已經買好了，我費了很大的力氣才買到。

好極了！我早^d就想看中國電影了。還有別人跟我們一起去嗎？

沒有，就³我們倆^e。

好。什麼時候？

後天晚上八點。

看電影以前，我請你吃晚飯。

太好了！一言為定^f。

Wáng Péng gēn Lǐ Yǒu zài tóng ^a *yí ge xuéxiào xuéxí, tāmen rènshi yǐjīng kuài bàn nián le. Wáng Péng chángcháng bāng Lǐ Yǒu liànxí shuō Zhōngwén. Tāmen yě chángcháng yìqǐ chū qu wánr, měi cì dōu wánr de* [1] *hěn gāoxìng. Lǐ Yǒu duì Wáng Péng de yìnxiàng* ^b *hěn hǎo, Wáng Péng yě hěn xǐhuan Lǐ Yǒu, tāmen chéng le hǎo péngyou.*

Zhè ge zhōumò xuéxiào yǎn yí ge Zhōngguó diànyǐng ^c *, wǒmen yìqǐ qù kàn, hǎo ma?*

Hǎo a! Búguò, tīngshuō kàn diànyǐng de rén hěn duō, mǎi de dào [2] *piào ma?*

Piào yǐjīng mǎi hǎo le, wǒ fèi le hěn dà de lìqi cái mǎi dào.

Hǎo jí le! Wǒ zǎo ^d *jiù xiǎng kàn Zhōngguó diànyǐng le. Hái yǒu bié rén gēn wǒmen yìqǐ qù ma?*

Méiyǒu, jiù [3] *wǒmen liǎ* ^e *.*

Hǎo. Shénme shíhou?

Hòutiān wǎnshang bā diǎn.

Kàn diànyǐng yǐqián, wǒ qǐng nǐ chī wǎnfàn.

Tài hǎo le! Yì yán wéi dìng ^f *.*

Language Notes

a 同 *(tóng)*
This word cannot be used as a predicate. Even as an attributive, its usage is very limited.

b 印象 *(yìnxiàng)*
Compare 李友對王朋的印象很好 *(Lǐ Yǒu duì Wáng Péng de yìnxiàng hěn hǎo)* (Li You has a very good impression of Wang Peng) and 李友給王朋的印象很好 *(Lǐ Yǒu gěi Wáng Péng de yìnxiàng hěn hǎo)* (Li You made a very good impression on Wang Peng).

c 演電影 *(yǎn diànyǐng)*
The phrase 演電影 *(yǎn diànyǐng)* (to show a film) is interchangeable with 放電影 *(fàng diànyǐng)*. In addition, 演電影 *(yǎn diànyǐng)* can also mean "to act in a film."

d 早 *(zǎo)*
The primary meaning of 早 *(zǎo)* is "early," but in an extended sense it can also mean "a long time ago" or "early on."

e 倆 *(liǎ)*
This is a colloquial equivalent of 兩個 *(liǎng ge)*.

f 一言為定 *(yì yán wéi dìng)*
This phrase literally means "achieving certainty with one word" and is one of many four-character idioms that have their origins in classical Chinese and continue to be used by many native speakers of the language.

Vocabulary

Audio

Flashcards

No.	Word	Pinyin	Part of Speech	Definition
1	同	*tóng*	adj	same
2	印象	*yìnxiàng*	n	impression
3	成	*chéng*	v	to become
4	演	*yǎn*	v	to show (a film), to perform
5	費	*fèi*	v	to spend, to take (effort)
6	力氣	*lìqi*	n	strength, effort
7	就	*jiù*	adv	just, only (indicating a small number)
8	倆	*liǎ*	nu+m	(coll.) two
9	後天	*hòutiān*	t	the day after tomorrow
10	一言為定	*yì yán wéi dìng*		that settles it, that's settled, it's decided

How About You?

週末你想約朋友
出去做什麼？

*Zhōumò nǐ xiǎng yuē péngyou chūqu
zuò shénme?*

What would you like to ask your friends
to do over the weekend?

我想約朋友去 _____ 。

Wǒ xiǎng yuē péngyou _____ .

See index for corresponding vocabulary or research another term.

Grammar

| 1 | **Descriptive complements (II)** |

The subject of a sentence can be described by a complement following 得 (*de*).

A　我們玩兒得很高興。

Wǒmen wánr de hěn gāoxìng.

We had a happy time playing.

(We played, and we were very happy.)

B　孩子笑得很可愛。

Háizi xiào de hěn kě'ài.

The kid gave a very cute smile.

(The child smiled, and the child looked cute.)

C　他打球打得很累。

Tā dǎ qiú dǎ de hěn lèi.

He was worn out from playing ball.

(He played ball, and he was worn out.)

D　他高興得又唱又跳。

Tā gāoxìng de yòu chàng yòu tiào.

He was so happy that he ended up singing and dancing.

(He was happy, and he was singing and dancing.)

In these examples, the verbs 玩 (*wán*) and 笑 (*xiào*), the verb phrase 打球 (*dǎ qiú*), and the adjective 高興 (*gāoxìng*) give the causes, while the complements 高興 (*gāoxìng*), 可愛 (*kě'ài*), 累 (*lèi*), and 又唱又跳 (*yòu chàng yòu tiào*) describe the effects on the subject.

As shown in (A), (B), and (C), when an adjective serves as a descriptive complement, it is often preceded by the adverb 很 (*hěn*), just like a predicate adjective.

A complement describing the subject seldom appears in the negative.

[⊗ 他高興得沒有又唱又跳。]

EXERCISES

Complete the sentences with a descriptive complement. Use exercise 1 as an example.

1 妹妹　　　　　唱歌　　高興

　→　妹妹唱歌唱得很高興。

2 我　　　　　　寫漢字　累

3 小高的妹妹　長　　　　高

---

2 | **Potential complements (I)**

得 (de) or 不 (bu) is placed between a verb and a resultative or directional complement to indicate whether a certain result can be realized or not.

A　Student A　你能學會跳舞嗎？

Nǐ néng xué huì tiào wǔ ma?

Can you learn to dance?

Student B　跳舞太難，我學不會。

Tiàowǔ tài nán, wǒ xué bu huì.

Dancing is too difficult. I can't learn it.

B　Student A　你晚上六點半能回來嗎？
我等你吃晚飯。

Nǐ wǎnshang liù diǎn bàn néng huí lai ma? Wǒ děng nǐ chī wǎnfàn.

Can you be back by 6:30 tonight? I'll wait for you for dinner.

Student B　我得開會，六點半回不來。

Wǒ děi kāi huì, liù diǎn bàn huí bu lái.

I have to go to a meeting and won't make it back by 6:30.

C Student A 這本書我考試要用，你今天看得完嗎？

Zhè běn shū wǒ kǎoshì yào yòng, nǐ jīntiān kàn de wán ma?

I need this book for an exam. Can you finish reading this book today?

Student B 這本書我今天看不完，你先用吧，
我以後再看。

Zhè běn shū wǒ jīntiān kàn bu wán, nǐ xiān yòng ba, wǒ yǐhòu zài kàn.

I can't finish this book today. You use it first; I'll read it later.

D 那個字怎麼寫，我想不起來了。

Nà ge zì zěnme xiě, wǒ xiǎng bu qǐ lái le.

I can't remember how to write that character.
[See Dialogue 2 for 想不起來 (xiǎng bu qǐ lái).]

E 健康保險太貴，我買不起。

Jiànkāng bǎoxiǎn tài guì, wǒ mǎi bu qǐ.

Health insurance is too expensive. I can't afford it.

Potential complements usually appear in negative sentences. They are used in affirmative sentences much less often. In affirmative sentences, we normally use the "能 (néng) + verb + resultative/directional complement" structure:

F 今天的功課不多，我很快就能做完。

Jīntiān de gōngkè bù duō, wǒ hěn kuài jiù néng zuò wán.

There isn't much homework today. I can finish it very quickly.

G 這個中國電影的中文不難，我能看懂。

Zhè ge Zhōngguó diànyǐng de Zhōngwén bù nán, wǒ néng kàn dǒng.

The language in this Chinese movie isn't difficult. I can understand it.

Potential complements can be used to ask questions. In these situations, we can answer affirmatively using potential complements.

H Q: 這條中文短信你看得懂嗎？

Zhè tiáo Zhōngwén duǎnxìn nǐ *kàn de dǒng* ma?

Can you understand this Chinese text message?

A: 我看得懂。

Wǒ *kàn de dǒng*.

Yes, I can understand it.

I Q: 二十個餃子你吃得完吃不完？

Èrshí ge jiǎozi nǐ *chī de wán chī bu wán*?

Can you eat twenty dumplings or not?

A: 我吃得完。

Wǒ *chī de wán*.

Yes, I can.

Potential complements are an important feature of Chinese. They are often the only way to convey the idea that the absence of certain conditions prevents a result from being achieved. Potential complements have a unique function that cannot be fulfilled by the "不能 (bù néng) + verb + resultative/directional complement" construction. Sometimes we have to use potential complements in negative sentences. If we used the "不能 (bù néng) + verb + resultative/directional complements" construction, the sentence would be incorrect.

[✗ 老師說得太快，我不能聽清楚。]

Sometimes the meaning would change:

J 門太小，我進不去。

Mén tài xiǎo, wǒ *jìn bu qù*.

The door is too narrow. I can't go in.

K 裡面正在開會，你不能進去！

Lǐmiàn zhèngzài kāi huì, nǐ *bù néng jìnqu!*

They are having a meeting inside. You can't go in.

A potential complement cannot be used in a 把 (bǎ) sentence, either.

[✗ 我把今天的功課做不完。]

EXERCISES

Answer the questions in the negative with a potential complement. Use exercise 1 as an example.

More exercises

1　你下午三點能回來/回得來嗎？

　　→ 我下午有課，三點回不來。

2　你能看懂/看得懂這本中文書嗎？

3　你今天能寫完/寫得完一百個漢字嗎？

SHANGHAI SYMPHONY HALL
上海交响乐团音乐厅

"回味肖邦"
肖邦音乐套曲中国首演及钢琴作品音乐会

剧场	主厅	区域	H区 双号
日期	2016-11-04	座位	1排 8座
时间	19:30	票价	280元

SSOS161030000004

上海交响乐团音乐厅 SHANGHAI SYMPHONY HALL 上海市复兴中路1380号 NO. 1380 MIDDLE FUXING ROAD, SHANGHAI

GET Real WITH CHINESE

You bought this ticket for someone special. What kind of event is it for? What other information can you identify?

就 (jiù) (only, just)

When used before a noun, pronoun, or verb, 就 (jiù) means "only" or "just." Often, the noun, pronoun, or verb can be modified by a numeral-measure word combination.

A 我們班人很少，就七個學生。

Wǒmen bān rén hěn shǎo, jiù qī ge xuésheng.

Our class is small, with just seven students.

B 今天功課很少，就寫五個漢字。

Jīntiān gōngkè hěn shǎo, jiù xiě wǔ ge Hànzì.

There's little homework today. We only have to write five characters.

C 我們一家五口，就我對味精過敏。

Wǒmen yì jiā wǔ kǒu, jiù wǒ duì wèijīng guòmǐn.

There are five people in our family. Only I am allergic to MSG.

D 今天我就有一節課。

Jīntiān wǒ jiù yǒu yì jié kè.

Today I have only one class.

More exercises

EXERCISES

Complete the sentences by inserting 就 where appropriate. Use exercise 1 as an example.

1 我們的電腦班很小　　　　　二十個學生

→ 我們的電腦班很小，就二十個學生。

2 這個城市的中國飯館很多　　我去過兩家

3 弟弟這個月沒花很多錢　　　兩百塊

Chinese Chat

A friend is messaging you on Facebook Messenger to make plans. How would you respond?

Language Practice

How did you feel?

In pairs, ask each other questions about how the following activities affect or affected you, e.g.:

Student A　你昨天晚上寫漢字寫得累不累？

Nǐ zuótiān wǎnshang xiě Hànzì xiě de lèi bu lèi?

Student B　我昨天晚上寫漢字寫得很累／不累。你呢？

Wǒ zuótiān wǎnshang xiě Hànzì xiě de hěn lèi/bú lèi. Nǐ ne?

1　你每天上課上得累不累？

Nǐ měi tiān shàng kè shàng de lèi bu lèi?

2　你昨天晚上睡覺睡得舒服不舒服？

Nǐ zuótiān wǎnshang shuì jiào shuì de shūfu bu shūfu?

3　你上個週末玩兒得高興不高興？

Nǐ shàng ge zhōumò wánr de gāoxìng bu gāoxìng?

First day

In pairs, form a question-and-answer about your partner's first day of school. Use 得 *(de)* or 不 *(bu)* to indicate whether you achieved the desired result or not, e.g.:

Q:　你找得到找不到你的教室？

Nǐ zhǎo de dào zhǎo bu dào nǐ de jiàoshì?

A:　我找得到我的教室。／我找不到我的教室。

Wǒ zhǎo de dào wǒ de jiàoshì./Wǒ zhǎo bu dào wǒ de jiàoshì.

1 你買得到買不到你要的書？

Nǐ mǎi de dào mǎi bu dào nǐ yào de shū?

2 你聽得懂聽不懂中文老師說的話？

Nǐ tīng de dǒng tīng bu dǒng Zhōngwén lǎoshī shuō de huà?

3 你看得清楚看不清楚老師寫的字？

Nǐ kàn de qīngchu kàn bu qīngchu lǎoshī xiě de zì?

---

c | **Bring it on** | INTERPERSONAL

In pairs, form a question-and-answer about whether you and your partner would be up to the challenge of an eating or drinking competition involving the following items and quantities. Use 得 *(de)* or 不 *(bu)*, e.g.:

 x30

Q: 你吃得完吃不完三十個熱狗？

Nǐ chī de wán chī bu wán sānshí ge règǒu?

A: 我吃得完三十個熱狗。／

我吃不完三十個熱狗。

Wǒ chī de wán sānshí ge règǒu./Wǒ chī bu wán sānshí ge règǒu.

1  x100   **2**  x10   **3** x15   **4**  x20   **5** x25

| How do you pronounce the characters? |
| What is the common component? |
| How do you pronounce the common component? |
| How does the component relate to the pronunciation of the characters? |

Characterize it!

❶   ❷   ❸

嗎　媽　碼

More characters

IC fan quiz

In pairs, form a question-and-answer to test how much of an IC fan you are. Use 就 *(jiù)* to indicate exceptions, e.g.:

Q: 他們都有弟弟嗎？

Tāmen dōu yǒu dìdi ma?

A: 不，就高小音一個人有弟弟。

Bù, jiù Gāo Xiǎoyīn yí ge rén yǒu dìdi.

1 他們都會滑冰嗎？

Tāmen dōu huì huá bīng ma?

2 他們都吃素嗎？

Tāmen dōu chī sù ma?

3 他們都愛吃蛋糕嗎？

Tāmen dōu ài chī dàngāo ma?

4 他們都不會說英文嗎？

Tāmen dōu bú huì shuō Yīngwén ma?

Turning Down an Invitation

Dialogue 2

Audio

Video

（費先生給李友打電話……）

喂，請問李友小姐在嗎？

我就是。請問你是哪一位？

我姓費，你還記得[a]我嗎？

姓費？

你還記得上個月高小音的生日舞會嗎？
我就是最後請你跳舞的那個人。你再想
想。想起來了嗎？

對不起，我想不起來。

我是高小音的中學同學。

是嗎？你是怎麼知道我的電話號碼的？

是小音告訴我的。

費先生，你有事嗎？

這個週末你有空兒嗎？我想請你去跳舞。

這個週末不行，下個星期我有三個考試。

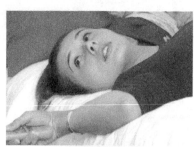

沒關係，下個週末怎麼樣？你考完試，我們好好兒[b]玩兒玩兒。

下個週末也不行，我要從宿舍搬出去[4]，得打掃、整理房間。

你看下下個週末，好不好？

對不起，下下個週末更不行了，我要跟我的男朋友去紐約旅行。

……那……

費先生，對不起，我的手機沒電了。再見！

喂……喂……

(Fèi xiānsheng gěi Lǐ Yǒu dǎ diànhuà . . .)

Wéi, qǐng wèn Lǐ Yǒu xiǎojiě zài ma?

Wǒ jiù shì. Qǐng wèn nǐ shì nǎ yí wèi?

Wǒ xìng Fèi, nǐ hái jìde^a *wǒ ma?*

Xìng Fèi?

Nǐ hái jìde shàng ge yuè Gāo Xiǎoyīn de shēngrì

wǔhuì ma? Wǒ jiù shì zuìhòu qǐng nǐ tiào wǔ de

nà ge rén. Nǐ zài xiǎng xiang. Xiǎng qi lai le ma?

Duìbuqǐ, wǒ xiǎng bu qǐ lái.

Wǒ shì Gāo Xiǎoyīn de zhōngxué tóngxué.

Shì ma? Nǐ shì zěnme zhīdào wǒ de diànhuà

hàomǎ de?

Shì Xiǎoyīn gàosu wǒ de.

Fèi xiānsheng, nǐ yǒu shì ma?

Zhè ge zhōumò nǐ yǒu kòngr ma? Wǒ xiǎng qǐng

nǐ qù tiào wǔ.

Zhè ge zhōumò bù xíng, xià ge xīngqī wǒ yǒu sān

ge kǎoshì.

Méi guānxi, xià gè zhōumò zěnmeyàng? Nǐ kǎo

wán shì, wǒmen hǎohāor^b *wánr wanr.*

Xià ge zhōumò yě bù xíng, wǒ yào cóng sùshè

*bān chu qu*⁴*, děi dǎsǎo, zhěnglǐ fángjiān.*

Nǐ kàn xià xià ge zhōumò, hǎo bu hǎo?

Duìbuqǐ, xià xià ge zhōumò gèng bù xíng le, wǒ

yào gēn wǒ de nánpéngyou qù Niǔyuē lǚxíng.

. . . Nà . . .

Fèi xiānsheng, duìbuqǐ, wǒ de shǒujī méi diàn le.

Zàijiàn!

Wéi . . . wéi . . .

a 記得 (jìde)

While 記得 (jìde) pertains to the continuous state of remembering, 想起來 (xiǎng qi lai) refers to the mental act of retrieving information from your memory. Thus you can say: 我記得他上過我的課，可是我想不起來他叫什麼名字。 (Wǒ jìde tā shàng guo wǒ de kè, kěshì wǒ xiǎng bu qi lai tā jiào shénme míngzi) (I remember that he took my class, but I can't recall his name at the moment).

b 好好兒 (hǎohāor)

This colloquial expression means "all out, to one's heart's content" and often precedes a verb to serve as an adverbial, e.g.: 考試以後我要去紐約好好兒玩兒玩兒 (Kǎo shì yǐhòu wǒ yào qù Niǔyuē hǎohāor wánr wanr) (After the test I want to go to New York and have a great time). Note the different tone for the reduplicated syllable 好 (hǎo).

Vocabulary

Audio

Flashcards

No.	Word	Pinyin	Part of Speech	Definition
1	記得	jìde	v	to remember
	記	jì	v	to record
2	想	xiǎng	v	to think
3	想起來	xiǎng qi lai	vc	to remember, to recall
4	號碼	hàomǎ	n	number
5	搬	bān	v	to move
6	打掃	dǎsǎo	v	to clean up (a room, apartment or house)
	掃	sǎo	v	to sweep
7	整理	zhěnglǐ	v	to put in order
8	房間	fángjiān	n	room
9	旅行	lǚxíng	v	to travel
10	電	diàn	n	electricity

週末我想請你去
跳舞，有空嗎？

*Zhōumò wǒ xiǎng qǐng nǐ qù tiào wǔ,
yǒu kòng ma?*

I'd like to take you dancing this weekend.
Are you free?

對不起，週末不行，
我得 _____ 。

*Duìbuqǐ, zhōumò bù xíng,
wǒ děi _____ .*

How About You?

See index for corresponding vocabulary or research another term.

Grammar

4	**Directional complements (II)**

Directional complements indicate the direction in which a person or an object moves. A directional verb such as 上 *(shang)* (to go up), 下 *(xia)* (to go down), 進 *(jin)* (to go in), 出 *(chu)* (to go out), 回 *(hui)* (to return), 過 *(guo)* (to go over, to pass), 起 *(qi)* (to rise), 開 *(kai)* (to part from), 到 *(dao)* (to arrive), 來 *(lai)* (to come), and 去 *(qu)* (to go) can be placed after another verb to become what is known as a "simple directional complement."

Simple directional complements:

Pattern A1
Subject + verb + place word/noun (phrase) + 來/去
(lai/qu)

A 她下樓來。

Tā xià lóu lai.

She comes downstairs.

B 她上樓去。

Tā shàng lóu qu.

She goes upstairs.

C 請你買一些水果來。

Qǐng nǐ mǎi yì xiē shuǐguǒ lai.

Please buy some fruit (and bring it) here. (anticipated action)

D 你給他送一點兒吃的東西去。

Nǐ gěi tā sòng yì diǎnr chī de dōngxi qu.

Take some food to him. (anticipated action)

E 妹妹給爸爸拿了一杯咖啡來。

Mèimei gěi bàba ná le yì bēi kāfēi lai.

My younger sister brought Dad a cup of coffee. (completed action)

Pattern A2
Subject + verb + 來/去 + noun
(lai/qu)

F 他買來了一些水果。

Tā mǎi lai le yì xiē shuǐguǒ.

He bought and brought over some fruit. (completed action)

G 他給朋友送去了一些花。

Tā gěi péngyou sòng qu le yì xiē huā.

He sent some flowers to his friend. (completed action)

When the object of the verb is a location word as in (A) and (B), the sentence can only appear in Pattern A1. When the object is a regular noun and the action is not completed, the sentence often appears in Pattern A1 as well, as in (C) and (D). If the action is completed, the sentence can appear either in Pattern A1 or in Pattern A2. It is, therefore, a good idea to memorize Pattern A1 as the failsafe form.

Pattern B
Subject + verb + 上/下/進/出/回/過/起/開/到/來/去 + place word/noun
(shang / xia / jin / chu / hui / guo / qi / kai / dao / lai / qu)

H 他走上樓。

Tā zǒu shang lóu.

He walks upstairs.

[The sentence doesn't indicate whether the speaker is upstairs or downstairs.]

I 老師走進教室。

Lǎoshī zǒu jin jiàoshì.

The teacher walks into the classroom.

[The sentence doesn't indicate whether the speaker is in the classroom or not.]

J 請你拿出一張紙。

Qǐng nǐ ná chu yì zhāng zhǐ.

Please take out a piece of paper. (anticipated action)

K 媽媽買回了一些水果。

Māma mǎi hui le yì xiē shuíguǒ.

Mom bought some fruit. (completed action)

In Pattern B, note that when the directional complement is 上/下/進/出/回/過/起/開/到 (shang/xia/jin/chu/hui/guo/qi/kai/dao), regardless if the object is a place word or an ordinary noun, if the action is completed or not, the object comes after the directional complement.

When a simple directional complement—上/下/進/出/回/過/起/到 (shang/xia/jin/chu/hui/guo/qi/dao)—is combined with 來(lai) or 去 (qu), we have what is called a "compound directional complement," again with two basic patterns.

Compound directional complements:

Pattern A
Subject + verb + 上/下/進/出/回/過/起/到 + place word/noun + 來/去
(shang/xia/jin/chu/hui/guo/qi/dao)   (lai/qu)

L 她走下樓來。

Tā zǒu xia lóu lai.

She walks downstairs.

[The speaker is downstairs.]

M 老師走進教室來/去。

Lǎoshī zǒu jin jiàoshì lai/qu.

The teacher walks into the classroom.

[With 來 (lai), the speaker is in the classroom; with 去 (qu), the speaker is outside the classroom.]

N 弟弟跳上床來/去。

Dìdi tiào shang chuáng lai/qu.

My little brother jumps onto the bed.

[With 來 (lai), the speaker is on the bed; with 去 (qu), the speaker is not on the bed.]

O 請你買回一些梨來。

Qǐng nǐ mǎi hui yì xiē lí lai.

Please buy some pears and bring them back here. (anticipated action)

P 請大家都拿起筆來。

Qǐng dàjiā dōu ná qi bǐ lai.

Everyone, please pick up a pen. (anticipated action)

Q 他拿出了一張紙來。

Tā ná chu le yì zhāng zhǐ lai.

He took out a piece of paper. (completed action)

Pattern B
Subject + verb + 上／下／進／出／回／過／起 + 來／去 + noun
(shang/xia/jin/chu/hui/guo/qi)   (lai/qu)

R 他買回來了一些水果。

Tā mǎi hui lai le yì xiē shuǐguǒ.

He bought some fruit (and brought it back here). (completed action)

S 妹妹拿出來一件新買的衣服。

Mèimei ná chu lai yí jiàn xīn mǎi de yīfu.

My younger sister took out a jacket she just bought.

As in the case of the simple directional compounds, when the object is a location word, the sentence appears only in Pattern A, as in (L), (M), and (N). If the object is a regular noun and the action is not completed, the sentence often appears in Pattern A as well, as in (O) and (P). If the action is completed, the sentence can appear either in Pattern A or in Pattern B as in (Q), (R), and (S). Again, it is not a bad idea to memorize Pattern A as the failsafe form.

EXERCISES

Reference the parenthetical information to complete the sentences with a directional complement. Use exercise 1 as an example.

More exercises

1　他很快地　　走下樓　　（說話人在樓下）
　　→ 他很快地走下樓來。

2　你快一點兒　跑上樓　　（說話人在樓下）

3　我看見他剛才 走進你的房間
　　（說話人在房間外邊）

Characterize it!

What do the characters mean?
What is the common radical?
What does the radical mean?
How does the radical relate to the overall meaning of the characters?

❶ 搬　❷ 打　❸ 掃

More characters

请勿打扰

请打扫房间

GET Real WITH CHINESE

You're staying at a hotel in Xi'an, and would like to get your room cleaned while you head out for some sightseeing. Which of these door hangers should you use?

Language Practice

<u>E</u>

What do you think?

PRESENTATIONAL

Having bought or done something, you want to get your friends' opinions, e.g.:

  這是我剛買的鞋，你看看怎麼樣？

Zhè shì wǒ gāng mǎi de xié, nǐ kàn kan zěnmeyàng?

1

2

3    [See also Language Note b, Dialogue 2, Lesson 15.]

4  [See also Language Note b, Dialogue 2, Lesson 15.]

<u>F</u>

Charades

PRESENTATIONAL

Choose a classmate you admire, then have the rest of your class guess who it is by saying things like 她／他就是⋯⋯的那個人 (*Tā jiù shì . . . de nà ge rén*). See how many such sentences are required before someone guesses correctly.

By any chance, could I . . .

Try to soften your tone by repeating the verb.

1   You would like to see your partner's family picture.

2   You want your partner to have a look at the characters you have written.

3   You want to listen to your partner's recording.

4   You want to use your partner's cell phone.

5   You want your partner to help you look for your book.

6   You hope your partner will practice Chinese with you.

Chinese Chat

Li You just updated her status on Weibo and Mr. Fei left some comments. What do you think Li You is hinting at?

9:48 PM   85%

李友   ☆
01-22 16:20 來自 華為 Mate 9

雖然今天很冷，但是我心裡暖暖的。

轉發 2   **評論 4**   讚 8

小費   👍 2   💬
01-22 16:28

為什麼啊？

李友：因為和朋友看了一個非常好
　　　看的中國電影……

小費：那下週我們也一起去看電影
　　　吧？

李友：糟糕，今天的功課又多又難，
　　　可能做不完……不聊了……

　🔗 轉發　｜　評論　｜　👍 讚

文化
Continue
to explore

Marriage

Until the first half of the twentieth century, arranged marriages were the norm in China, and divorces were rare. Love marriages are now the ideal. People are free to date, marry, and divorce. Nevertheless, upon finding that their children have reached a certain age without having acquired a boyfriend or girlfriend, some parents opt to take matters into their own hands and arrange a few blind dates, 相親 *(xiāng qīn)*, for their offspring. In premodern China, intimate contact between unmarried young men and women was strictly prohibited. Traditionally, Chinese people shied away from public displays of affection, and even as recently as the 1980s, one seldom saw couples holding hands on the street. Today, although there has been debate over what counts as appropriate public behavior, public displays of affection have become much more common.

COMPARE & CONTRAST

1 In China and elsewhere, a tendency toward avoiding direct, blunt language in the context of dating can result in white lies to avoid hurting people's feelings. In one common scenario in Chinese romantic comedies, a girl calls a boy for help with her computer as a way to get to know him better. In another scenario, a girl arranges to get a call in the middle of a bad date, and then leaves in a hurry on the pretext of an emergency. In your culture/community, how common are white lies in the context of dating? In your opinion, are white lies essential or detrimental to ensuring that things with your date are on an even keel?

2 *If You Are the One*, 非誠勿擾 (*Fēi Chéng Wù Rǎo*), is a popular Chinese dating show that first aired on Chinese TV in January 2010. It broke ratings records and attracted attention from the international press. The format of the program is based on the Australian dating show *Take Me Out*. Episodes of *If You Are the One* with English subtitles can be found on the Internet. Watch an episode and check out the English-language coverage of the success and controversy of the show. How does the episode compare with similar programs in your country?

Dates

Seeing movies is part of the nightlife in Chinese cities, especially for people going out on dates. Karaoke clubs, upscale restaurants, theme parks, and game centers are also top spots for couples to visit.

SAVING FACE

Chinese people are typically very concerned about face, 面子 (*miànzi*)—both for themselves and others. Consequently, excuses are often provided when turning down requests and offers, and blunt rejections are avoided.

MATCHMAKING
CORNERS

Some Chinese parents anxious to find love matches for their children congregate in parks on weekends. People's Park in Shanghai, for instance, is famous for having a matchmaking corner (相親角) (*xiāngqīnjiǎo*). On pieces of paper suspended from long strings, parents advertise their eligible children. Visitors to the park will find swarms of parents scrutinizing descriptions of age, height, job, income, personality, and so on in hopes of identifying a suitable mate for their son or daughter. For a fee, parents can advertise their children for five months. Sociologists cite the gender imbalance and high-achieving young women's difficulty in finding spouses as some of the reasons for parents' taking the matter into their own hands.

The matchmaking corner in People's Park, Shanghai

Lesson Wrap-Up

Rearrange the sentences into a logical sequence. Then combine the sentences into a coherent narrative. Avoid repeating unnecessarily identical elements. Substitute nouns with pronouns and change periods to commas where appropriate. Add the connective devices 已經 (yǐjīng), 也 (yě), 才 (cái), 早就…了 (zǎo jiù … le), and 還 (hái) where appropriate.

_____王朋和李友常常一起出去玩兒。

_____王朋很喜歡李友。

_____這個週末學校演一個中國電影。

__1__王朋和李友在同一個學校學習。

_____王朋費了很大力氣買到兩張票。

_____李友說想看中國電影。

_____王朋說"好極了，一言為定"。

_____王朋和李友在同一个學校學習快半年了。

_____李友對王朋的印象很好。

_____李友很高興。

_____李友說看電影以前請王朋吃飯。

_____王朋常常幫助李友練習中文。

_____王朋要請李友去看電影。

Skit

You want to ask a classmate out. Find out if he/she would like to have lunch or go to a movie or concert with you. How would you start? The direct approach: I like you. Would you like to . . . ? The indirect approach: There is a very interesting film/concert/great new restaurant. Let your schoolmate know why he/she would enjoy the film/concert/new restaurant. Find out if he/she would like to go with you. You know he/she is free. Hopefully, the answer is yes!

Dating Profile

Your best friend is too busy to date, so you decide to help him/her out. Create a profile for your friend. Describe his/her personality, hobbies, background, and goals. Share the profile in class and see if you can make a connection for your friend.

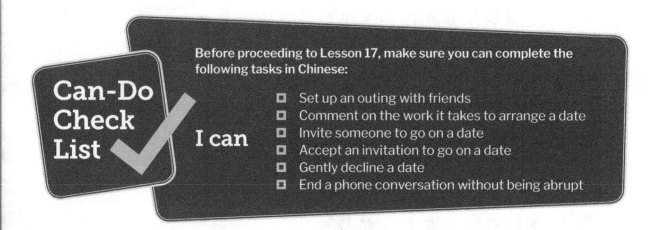

Can-Do Check List

I can

Before proceeding to Lesson 17, make sure you can complete the following tasks in Chinese:

- ☐ Set up an outing with friends
- ☐ Comment on the work it takes to arrange a date
- ☐ Invite someone to go on a date
- ☐ Accept an invitation to go on a date
- ☐ Gently decline a date
- ☐ End a phone conversation without being abrupt

租房子

Zū fángzi

RENTING AN APARTMENT

Learning Objectives	**Relate & Get Ready**

In this lesson, you will learn to:

- Describe your current and ideal dwellings
- Name common pieces of furniture
- State how long you have been living at your current residence
- Explain why a place is or isn't right for someone
- Discuss and negotiate rent, utilities, and security deposits

In your own culture/community:

- How do you find an apartment to rent?
- What are typical living arrangements for young adults?
- What are the pros and cons of living in a dorm vs. in an apartment?
- Do leases include clauses for security deposits and pets? What other issues do leases cover?

Finding a Better Place

Narrative

Audio

Video

王朋在學校的宿舍住了兩個學期了[1]。他覺得宿舍太吵，睡不好覺，房間太小，連電腦都[2]放不下[3]，再說也沒有地方可以做飯，很不方便，所以準備下個學期搬出去住。他找房子找了一個多[4]月了，可是還沒有找到合適的。剛才他在報紙上看到了一個廣告，說學校附近有一套公寓出租，離學校很近，走路只要五分鐘，很方便。公寓有一個[a]臥室，一個廚房，一個衛生間[b]，一個客廳，還帶傢俱。王朋覺得這套公寓可能對他很合適。

Wáng Péng zài xuéxiào de sùshè zhù le liǎng ge xuéqī le¹. *Tā juéde sùshè tài chǎo, shuì bu hǎo jiào, fángjiān tài xiǎo,* lián diànnǎo dōu² fàng bu xià³, *zàishuō yě méi-yǒu dìfang kěyǐ zuò fàn, hěn bù fāngbiàn, suǒyǐ zhǔnbèi xià ge xuéqī bān chu qu zhù. Tā zhǎo fángzi zhǎo le yí ge* duō⁴ *yuè le, kěshì hái méiyǒu zhǎo dào héshì de. Gāng-cái tā zài bàozhǐ shang kàn dào le yí ge guǎnggào, shuō xuéxiào fùjìn yǒu yí tào gōngyù chūzū, lí xuéxiào hěn jìn, zǒu lù zhǐ yào wǔ fēnzhōng, hěn fāngbiàn. Gōngyù yǒu yí ge*ᵃ *wòshì, yí ge chúfáng, yí ge* wèishēngjiānᵇ*, yí ge kètīng, hái dài jiājù. Wáng Péng juéde zhè tào gōngyù kěnéng duì tā hěn héshì.*

a 個 *(gè)* **vs.** 間 *(jiān)*

When speaking more formally, people prefer 間 *(jiān)* as the measure word for rooms, e.g.: 一間臥室 *(yì jiān wòshì)*, 一間廚房 *(yì jiān chúfáng)*, 一間衛生間 *(yì jiān wèishēngjiān)*, 一間客廳 *(yì jiān kètīng)*, and 一間教室 *(yì jiān jiàoshì)*.

b 衛生間 *(wèishēngjiān)*

衛生間 *(wèishēngjiān)* (lit. hygiene room) is the most frequently used term for the bathroom in Mainland China. In public places 衛生間 *(wèishēngjiān)* simply means "restroom." Other Chinese terms for "bathroom" and "restroom" include 浴室 *(yùshì)* (bathroom with a shower or bathtub); 廁所 *(cèsuǒ)* (toilet, public restroom with no bathing facilities); 洗手間 *(xǐshǒujiān)* (restroom or bathroom); and 化粧室 *(huàzhuāngshì)* (bathroom) (lit. powder room), which is used mainly in Taiwan, especially for bathrooms in restaurants and department stores. Occasionally, some Chinese speakers refer to the restroom euphemistically as 一號 *(yī hào)* (lit. Number One).

Vocabulary

Audio

Flashcards

No.	Word	Pinyin	Part of Speech	Definition
1	吵	chǎo	v/adj	to quarrel; noisy
2	連	lián	prep	even
3	做飯	zuò fàn	vo	to cook, to prepare a meal
4	報紙	bàozhǐ	n	newspaper
5	廣告	guǎnggào	n	advertisement
6	附近	fùjìn	n	vicinity, neighborhood, nearby area
7	套	tào	m	(measure word for things that come in a set/sets)
8	公寓	gōngyù	n	apartment
9	出租	chūzū	v	to rent out
10	走路	zǒu lù	vo	to walk
11	分鐘	fēnzhōng	n	minute
12	臥室	wòshì	n	bedroom
13	廚房	chúfáng	n	kitchen
14	衛生間	wèishēngjiān	n	bathroom
15	客廳	kètīng	n	living room
16	傢俱	jiājù	n	furniture
17	可能	kěnéng	mv/adj	may; possible

浏览以下页面了解更多信息！

单人房分租

只限女性，不养宠物。不抽烟，无不良嗜好。
公寓位于莲湖区劳动路。房间干净、安静，
交通便利。月租1200元（水、电、网费全包）。

感兴趣请加我QQ2345xxxxx。

GET Real WITH CHINESE

你希望你的客廳裡有什麼傢俱？

Nǐ xīwàng nǐ de kètīng lǐ yǒu shénme jiājù?

What furniture do you hope to have in your living room?

我希望我的客廳
裡有 _____ 。

Wǒ xīwàng wǒ de kètīng lǐ yǒu _____ .

How About You?

See index for corresponding vocabulary or research another term.

Grammar

---

1 | Verb + 了 *(le)* + numeral + measure word + noun + 了 *(le)*

This structure usually implies that the action has been continuing for some time and will likely last into the future. For example, 王朋在學校的宿舍住了兩個學期了 (*Wáng Péng zài xuéxiào de sùshè zhù le liǎng ge xuéqī le*) means that Wang Peng has been living on campus for two semesters up to this moment and will continue to live there.

A | Q: 你開出租汽車開了幾年了？

Nǐ kāi chūzū qìchē kāi le jǐ nián le?

How many years have you been driving a cab for?

A: 一年半了。

Yì nián bàn le.

For a year and a half now.

B | 弟弟寫電子郵件寫了半個鐘頭了，不知道還要寫多長時間。

Dìdi xiě diànzǐ yóujiàn xiě le bàn ge zhōngtóu le, bù zhīdào hái yào xiě duō cháng shíjiān.

My younger brother has been writing emails for half an hour. Who knows how much longer he'll be at it.

The following two sentences differ in meaning:

C | 他病了三天了。

Tā bìng le sān tiān le.

He has been sick for three days.

[His illness has continued for three days and he currently remains sick.]

D 他病了三天。

Tā bìng le sān tiān.

He was sick for three days.

[He recovered from the illness on the fourth day.]

However, the new sentence pattern with the additional sentence-final 了 (le) can be followed by another clause that suggests that the action will likely cease.

E 這本書我已經看了兩遍了，不想再看了。

Zhè běn shū wǒ yǐjīng kàn le liǎng biàn le, bù xiǎng zài kàn le.

I've read this book twice already and don't want to read it again.

This structure can be used in reference to both time and quantity:

F 衣服我已經買了三件了，再買兩件就夠了。

Yīfu wǒ yǐjīng mǎi le sān jiàn le, zài mǎi liǎng jiàn jiù gòu le.

I've already bought three pieces of clothing. I'll buy two more and that'll be plenty.

G 我打掃房子打掃了一上午了，想休息一下。

Wǒ dǎsǎo fángzi dǎsǎo le yí shàngwǔ le, xiǎng xiūxi yí xià.

I've been cleaning the house all morning. I'd like to take a break.

EXERCISES

Paraphrase the sentences to describe the time duration using the ⋯ 了 ⋯ 了 structure where appropriate. Use exercise 1 as an example.

More exercises

1 小高八點開始吃早飯。
　現在九點，他還在吃早飯。
　→ 小高吃早飯吃了一個小時了。

2 老李昨天晚上十點睡覺。
　現在上午十點，他還在睡覺。

3 小王五月開始找房子。
　現在是七月，他還在找房子。

連…都/也… (lián … dōu/yě …)

連 (lián) is an intensifier which is always used in conjunction with 都/也 (dōu/yě).

A 我姐姐的孩子很聰明，連日語都會說。

Wǒ jiějie de háizi hěn cōngming, lián Rìyǔ dōu huì shuō.

My sister's child is really smart. She can even speak Japanese.

B 我弟弟的公寓裡連一件傢俱也沒有。

Wǒ dìdi de gōngyù lǐ lián yí jiàn jiājù yě méiyǒu.

There isn't even a single piece of furniture in my younger brother's apartment.

C 你怎麼連藥都忘了吃？

Nǐ zěnme lián yào dōu wàng le chī?

How could you even forget to take your medicine?

D 昨天學的生詞我連一個也不記得了。

Zuótiān xué de shēngcí wǒ lián yí ge yě bú jìde le.

I can't recall even a single new word we learned yesterday.

What follows 連 (lián) usually represents an extreme case: the biggest or smallest, the best or worst, the most difficult or easiest, etc. (A), for instance, implies that Japanese is very difficult. If a child can speak such a difficult language as Japanese, then the child must be very intelligent. Similarly, if my younger brother doesn't have a single piece of furniture in his apartment, it must look very bare.

More exercises

EXERCISES

Rewrite the sentences to intensify the information in parentheses using the 連…都/也… structure where appropriate. Use exercise 1 as an example.

1　小白的公寓沒有（廚房）。

　　→ 小白的公寓連廚房都沒有。

2　我妹妹（星期天）去圖書館看書。

3　小王忘了（女朋友的電話號碼）。

Potential complements (II)

The "verb + 不下 *(bu xià)*" structure suggests that a location or container in question does not have the capacity to accommodate a certain number of people or things.

A 這個客廳大是大，不過坐不下二十個人。

Zhè ge kètīng dà shi dà, búguò zuò bu xià èrshí ge rén.

This living room is pretty spacious, but it still isn't large enough to seat twenty people.

B 這張紙寫不下八百個字。

Zhè zhāng zhǐ xiě bu xià bābǎi ge zì.

This piece of paper isn't big enough to write eight hundred characters on.

C 這個冰箱放不下兩個西瓜。

Zhè ge bīngxiāng fàng bu xià liǎng ge xīgua.

This refrigerator isn't big enough for two watermelons.

EXERCISES

More exercises

In pairs, form a question-and-answer about the capacity of a space using 得下 and 不下 where appropriate. Use exercise 1 as an example.

1　這個教室　　　　　坐三十個學生
　→　Q: 這個教室坐得下三十個學生嗎？
　　　A: 這個教室坐得下/坐不下三十個學生。

2　小高　　　　　　　喝五瓶可樂

3　這套公寓　　　　　住六個人

多 *(duō)* can be placed after a number to indicate an approximate number. The combination indicates not an exact number but a general numeric range, e.g., 十多個 *(shí duō ge)* means more than ten but fewer than twenty; it could be eleven, twelve, thirteen, etc.

If the concept represented by the noun is not divisible into smaller units, and the number is ten or a multiple of ten, 多 *(duō)* precedes the measure word.

A   二十多個人

       èrshí duō ge rén

       more than twenty people

B   三十多個學生

       sānshí duō ge xuésheng

       more than thirty students

C   一百多張紙

       yì bǎi duō zhāng zhǐ

       more than one hundred sheets of paper

However, if the concept represented by the noun can be divided into smaller units (e.g., 一塊錢 = 十毛, 一個星期 = 七天 *[yí kuài qián = shí máo, yí ge xīngqī = qī tiān]*), there are two possibilities. If the number is not ten or a multiple of ten, 多 *(duō)* should be used after the measure word, e.g., 七塊多錢 *(qī kuài duō qián)* (more than seven dollars but less than eight), 一個多星期 *(yí ge duō xīngqī)* (more than one week but less than two). If the number is ten or a multiple of ten, 多 *(duō)* can be used either before the measure word, e.g., 十多塊錢 *(shí duō kuài qián)* (more than ten dollars but less than twenty) or after the measure word, e.g., 十塊多錢 *(shí kuài duō qián)* (more than ten dollars but less than eleven), but these two options represent different numeric ranges.

D   這枝筆一塊多錢。

       Zhè zhī bǐ yí kuài duō qián.

       This pen is one dollar something.

       (The price is more than one dollar but less than two.)

E 我們班有二十多個學生。

Wǒmen bān yǒu èrshí duō ge xuéshēng.

There are over twenty students in our class.

(There are more than twenty students but fewer than thirty.)

F 妹妹感冒十多天了。

Mèimei gǎnmào shí duō tiān le.

My younger sister has had a cold for more than ten days.

(The number of days is between ten and twenty.)

G 他昨天買了四十多個梨。

Tā zuótiān mǎi le sìshí duō ge lí.

He bought over forty pears yesterday.

(The number is between forty and fifty.)

H 他昨天買禮物花了一百多塊錢。

Tā zuótiān mǎi lǐwù huā le yìbǎi duō kuài qián.

He bought over one hundred dollars' worth of gifts yesterday.

(He spent more than one hundred dollars but less than two hundred.)

I Student A 這雙黑鞋十多塊錢。

Zhè shuāng hēi xié shí duō kuài qián.

This pair of black shoes is over ten dollars.

(The price is more than ten dollars but less than twenty.)

Student B 這雙咖啡色的鞋十塊多錢。

Zhè shuāng kāfēi sè de xié shí kuài duō qián.

This pair of brown shoes is a little bit over ten dollars.

(The price is more than ten dollars but less than eleven.)

J **Student A** 這家飯館兒的師傅和服務員認識十年多了。

Zhè jiā fànguǎnr de shīfu hé fúwùyuán rènshi shí nián duō le.

The chef and the waiter at this restaurant have known each other for ten years and some months.

(The length of time is longer than ten years but shorter than eleven.)

Student B 我以為他們認識十多年了。

Wǒ yǐwéi tāmen rènshi shí duō nián le.

I thought they had known each other for a dozen years or so.

(The length of time is between ten and twenty years.)

More exercises

EXERCISES

Translate the approximate number using 多 where appropriate. Use exercise 1 as an example.

1 over one hundred books

→ 一百多本書

2 more than fifty students

3 over two hundred and fifty Chinese characters but fewer than two hundred and sixty

Chinese Chat

Bai Ying'ai just posted a review on Airbnb. Would you consider staying at the same place after reading her review?

65條評價 ★★★★⯪   搜索評價

概述   準確性   ★★★★★   位置   ★★★★⯪
             溝通交流   ★★★★★   入住   ★★★★★
             清潔度   ★★★★★   性價比   ★★★★⯪

白英愛

我在這個公寓住了兩天了。公寓帶傢俱；離公園、商店、地鐵站都很近，做什麼都非常方便。冰箱裡每天都有水果和飲料，這樣連早飯都不用出去吃了！

👍 有用

Language Practice

Time flies

INTERPERSONAL

In pairs, ask a partner the following questions.

1 你學中文學了多長時間了？

Nǐ xué Zhōngwén xué le duō cháng shíjiān le?

2 你在這個學校學習了多長時間了？

Nǐ zài zhè ge xuéxiào xuéxí le duō cháng shíjiān le?

3 你在你現在住的地方住了多長時間了？

Nǐ zài nǐ xiànzài zhù de dìfang zhù le duō cháng shíjiān le?

Based on your partner's situation, you may also want to ask how long he/she has been working, involved in his/her hobbies, etc.

Space cadet

PRESENTATIONAL

Little Bai is absent-minded and often forgetful. Based on the statements given below, recap what he forgot to do using 連···都/也··· *(lián ... dōu/yě ...)*, e.g.:

He even forgot to bring a pen with him when he had to take a test.

考試的時候，他連筆都/也忘了帶了。

Kǎo shì de shíhòu, tā lián bǐ dōu/yě wàng le dài le.

1 He even forgot his mother's birthday.

2 He didn't even remember his own phone number.

3 He even forgot to bring money when he was treating his friends to dinner.

Little Bai just moved, and is getting fed up with his new apartment. Describe what his apartment is like using 連…都/也… (lián … dōu/yě …), e.g.:

The apartment doesn't even have a kitchen.

公寓連廚房都/也沒有。

Gōngyù lián chúfáng dōu/yě méiyǒu.

4 His bathroom doesn't even have (running) water.

5 His bedroom is so tiny that even a bed cannot be placed in it.

6 His living room is so small that it cannot even seat five people.

Little Bai is also behind the times. Describe what he doesn't know using 連…都/也… (lián … dōu/yě …), e.g.:

He doesn't even know how to use a computer.

小白連電腦都/也不會用。

Xiǎo Bái lián diànnǎo dōu/yě bú huì yòng.

7 He doesn't know how to use a cell phone.

8 He doesn't know how to send email.

9 He doesn't know how to use a credit card.

C | **Sizing up** | INTERPERSONAL

In pairs, ask a partner how spacious his/her apartment/room, living room, classroom, refrigerator, desk, etc. are. Use the proper verb for each question, e.g.:

Q: 你的公寓/房間住得下多少/幾個人？

Nǐ de gōngyù/fángjiān zhù de xià duōshao/jǐ ge rén?

A: 我的公寓/房間住得下兩個人。

Wǒ de gōngyù/fángjiān zhù de xià liǎng ge rén.

1

2

3

4

5

Calling about an Apartment for Rent

Dialogue

Audio

Video

（王朋打電話問租房子的事兒……）

喂，請問你們是不是^a有公寓出租？

有啊，一房一廳^b，非常乾淨，還帶傢俱。

有什麼傢俱？

客廳裡有一套沙發、一張飯桌跟四把椅子。臥室裡有一張床、一張書桌和一個書架。

你們那裡安靜不安靜？

非常安靜。

每個月房租多少錢？

八百五十元。

八百五十美元？人民幣差不多是……有一點兒貴，能不能便宜點兒？

那你不用付水電費。

要不要付押金？

要多付一個月的房租當押金，搬出去的時候還給你。另外，我們公寓不准養寵物。

沒關係，我對養寵物沒有興趣^c，什麼寵物都⁵不養。

那太好了。你今天下午來看看吧。

好。

Language Notes

a 是不是··· *(shì bu shì . . .)*

Here, this means "Is it true that . . ."

b 一房一廳 *(yì fáng yì tīng)* / 一室一廳 *(yí shì yì tīng)*

Both expressions refer to an apartment with one bedroom and one living room. By the same token, you may refer to a two-bedroom apartment with a living room as 兩房一廳 *(liǎng fáng yì tīng)* or 兩室一廳 *(liǎng shì yì tīng)*.

c 有興趣 *(yǒu xìngqù)* vs. 有意思 *(yǒu yìsi)*

Do not confuse 有興趣 *(yǒu xìngqù)* with 有意思 *(yǒu yìsi)*. While 有興趣 *(yǒu xìngqù)* is a verb phrase that describes someone who is interested (in something), 有意思 *(yǒu yìsi)* is an adjective describing someone or something that is interesting.

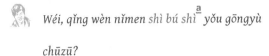

(Wáng Péng dǎ diànhuà wèn zū fángzi de shìr . . .)

Wéi, qǐng wèn nǐmen shì bú shì[a] yǒu gōngyù chūzū?

Yǒu a, yì fáng yì tīng[b], fēicháng gānjìng, hái dài jiājù.

Yǒu shénme jiājù?

Kètīng li yǒu yí tào shāfā, yì zhāng fànzhuō gēn sì bǎ yǐzi. Wòshì li yǒu yì zhāng chuáng, yì zhāng shūzhuō hé yí ge shūjià.

Nǐmen nàlǐ ānjìng bu ānjìng?

Fēicháng ānjìng.

Měi ge yuè fángzū duōshao qián?

Bābǎi wǔshí yuán.

Bābǎi wǔshí Měiyuán? Rénmínbì chàbuduō shì . . . Yǒu yì diǎnr guì, néng bu néng piányi diǎnr?

Nà nǐ búyòng fù shuǐ diàn fèi.

Yào bu yào fù yājīn?

Yào duō fù yí ge yuè de fángzū dāng yājīn, bān chu qu de shíhou huán gěi nǐ. Lìngwài, wǒmen gōngyù bù zhǔn yǎng chǒngwù.

Méi guānxi, wǒ duì yǎng chǒngwù méiyǒu xìngqù[c], shénme chǒngwù dōu[5] bù yǎng.

Nà tài hǎo le. Nǐ jīntiān xiàwǔ lái kàn kan ba.

Hǎo.

Vocabulary

Audio

Flashcards

No.	Word	Pinyin	Part of Speech	Definition
1	一房一廳	yì fáng yì tīng		one bedroom and one living room
2	乾淨	gānjìng	adj	clean
3	沙發	shāfā	n	sofa
4	飯桌	fànzhuō	n	dining table
5	椅子	yǐzi	n	chair
6	書桌	shūzhuō	n	desk
7	書架	shūjià	n	bookcase, bookshelf
8	那裡	nàli	pr	there
9	安靜	ānjìng	adj	quiet
10	房租	fángzū	n	rent
11	元	yuán	m	(measure word for the basic Chinese monetary unit), yuan
12	美元	Měiyuán	n	American dollar (USD)
13	人民幣	Rénmínbì	n	renminbi (RMB, Chinese currency)
	人民	rénmín	n	the people
	幣	bì	n	currency
14	差不多	chàbuduō	adv/adj	almost, nearly; similar
15	費	fèi	n	fee, expenses
16	押金	yājīn	n	security deposit
17	當	dāng	v	to serve as, to be

No.	Word	Pinyin	Part of Speech	Definition
18	還	*huán*	v	to return (something)
19	另外	*lìngwài*	conj	furthermore, in addition
20	准	*zhǔn*	v	to allow, to be allowed
21	養	*yǎng*	v	to raise
22	寵物	*chǒngwù*	n	pet
23	興趣	*xìngqù*	n	interest

你（想）養什麼寵物？

Nǐ (xiǎng) yǎng shénme chǒngwù?

What pets do you (want to) raise?

我（想）養  。

Wǒ (xiǎng) yǎng _____ .

See index for corresponding vocabulary or research another term.

Characterize it!

What do the characters mean?		
What is the common radical?		
What does the radical mean?		
How does the radical relate to the overall meaning of the characters?		

❶ ❷ ❸

More characters

Grammar

Question pronouns using 都/也 (dōu/yě)

A question pronoun can appear in a statement. When it is followed by 都/也 (dōu/yě), it simply means "all" or "none" in the sense that everything in question is either included or excluded.

A Q: 你想喝點兒什麼飲料？

Nǐ xiǎng hē diǎnr shénme yǐnliào?

What beverage would you like to drink?

A: 謝謝，我不渴，什麼都不想喝。

Xièxie, wǒ bù kě, shénme dōu bù xiǎng hē.

Thanks. I'm not thirsty. I don't feel like drinking anything.

B 這些公寓我哪套都不租。

Zhè xiē gōngyù wǒ nǎ tào dōu bù zū.

I'm not renting any of these apartments.

C 中國我什麼地方都沒去過。

Zhōngguó wǒ shénme dìfang dōu méi qù guo.

I haven't been anywhere in China.

D 我什麼寵物都不養。養寵物太麻煩了！

Wǒ shénme chǒngwù dōu bù yǎng. Yǎng chǒngwù tài máfan le!

I don't keep any pets. Keeping pets is too much trouble!

E 在這個城市，哪兒也吃不到糖醋魚。

Zài zhè ge chéngshì, nǎr yě chī bu dào tángcùyú.

You can't find sweet-and-sour fish anywhere in this city.

F Q: 在舞會上你認識了誰？

Zài wǔhuì shang nǐ rènshi le shéi?

Who did you get to know at the dance party?

A: 我誰都沒認識。

Wǒ shéi dōu méi rènshi.

I didn't get to know anybody.

G 你明天幾點跟我見面都行。

Nǐ míngtiān jǐ diǎn gēn wǒ jiàn miàn dōu xíng.

You can meet with me anytime tomorrow.

H 這些藥我哪種都試過，對我的過敏都沒有用。

Zhè xiē yào wǒ nǎ zhǒng dōu shì guo, duì wǒ de guòmǐn dōu méiyǒu yòng.

I've tried all of these medicines; none are effective for my allergies.

EXERCISES

Rewrite the sentences to intensify the statement using the "interrogative pronoun + 都／也" structure where appropriate. Use exercise 1 as an example.

More exercises

1   我不養寵物。 (not any)

→ 我什麼寵物都不養。

2   我昨天沒有買衣服。 (not any)

3   小高不認識這裡的人。 (not anyone)

Language Practice

<u>D</u>

Polar extremes

PRESENTATIONAL

Aisha and Mona are twins, but they couldn't be more different: Aisha is easygoing and Mona is difficult. Describe how they differ from each other using 都/也 (dōu/yě), e.g.:

Aisha likes all colors. Mona hates all colors.

Aisha 什麼顏色都喜歡。Mona 什麼顏色都不喜歡。

Aisha *shénme yánsè dōu xǐhuan.* Mona *shénme yánsè dōu bù xǐhuan.*

1 Aisha eats all sorts of fruits and vegetables. Mona eats no fruits and vegetables at all.

2 Aisha has been to all kinds of places. Mona hasn't been anywhere.

3 Aisha is happy all the time. Mona is unhappy all the time.

4 Everyone thinks Aisha is cool. Everyone thinks Mona is no fun.

GET Real WITH CHINESE

You're looking to rent an apartment in Quincy, a Massachusetts city with a large Chinese population. You want an apartment near Quincy Center. Which apartment has the best location?

室及醫療服務.

新公室及醫療服務.

近大學. 現

校, 閒

房屋出租

月租

Quincy: 2房1廳, 1廚房, 近巴士站 $1,450

2房1廳, 1廚房, 有車位, 近地鐵 $1,500

排屋, 2房大廳, 有後院, 1.5浴, 有車位, 近地鐵.. $1,700

全新, 750方呎, 2房1廳, 近地鐵 $1,900

4房2廳, 1廚房, 有車位, 近市中心 $2,000

Waltham: 公寓, 2房2廳, 2全浴. 新廚房, 有車位......... $1,800

Weymouth: 翻新2房, 1廚房, 700方呎, 有車位, 近巴士站..$1,300

Somerville: 3房1廳, 1廚房, 近地鐵 $2,300

$369,000
全浴, 有車房, 3200
2個車位

57 Mar
地皮
可以建地3C
Hawkes Pon

1241B S.
複式公寓
全海景, 不用水
房, 廚房, 客廳
大睡房, 大浴室

Behind the façade

Take a look at the floor plan of this apartment. Name the rooms and describe what's in each of them.

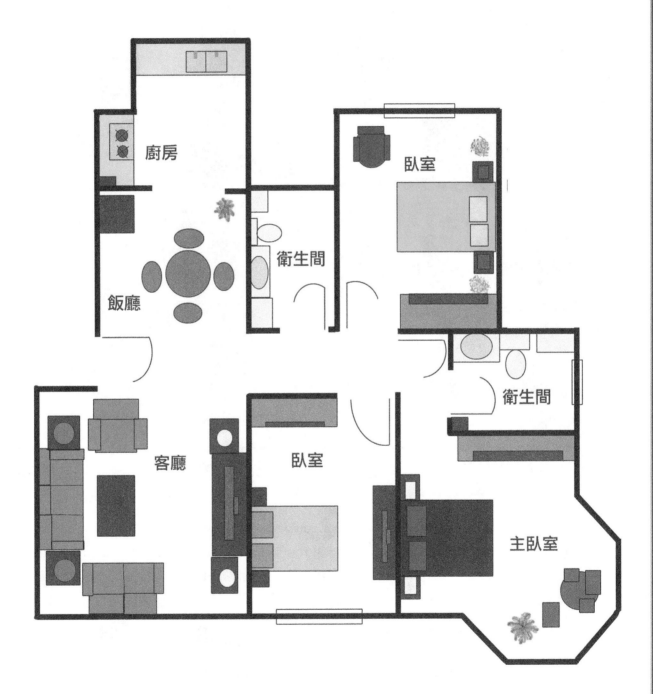

F   **In my room**

In pairs, describe the room in the picture, i.e., what's in it and how things are positioned.
Don't forget the person and the dog.

G   **On campus or off?**

As a journalist for the student newspaper, you've been tasked with surveying the student
body about the pros and cons of living in the dorms or off campus. Find an interviewee and
report back to the class on what he/she thinks about where they live and whether they want
to stay or move, e.g.:

Carlos 覺得他的公寓/宿舍對他很/不合適。
所以他不想/想搬出去。因為⋯⋯

Carlos *juéde tā de gōngyù/ sùshè duì tā hěn/bù héshì.*

Suǒyǐ tā bù xiǎng/xiǎng bān chu qu. Yīnwèi . . .

| What do the characters mean? |
| What is the common radical? |
| What does the radical mean? |
| How does the radical relate to the overall meaning of the characters? |

❶ 安 ❷ 客 ❸ 室 ❹ 寓

More characters

< Messages　　**李明**　　Contact

您好！我叫李明。我朋友小張告訴我您有公寓出租，讓我給您發短信。

...

請問公寓裡有幾個臥室？有沒有自己的衛生間和廚房？帶不帶傢俱？

...

離地鐵站或者公共汽車站近嗎？

...

好，謝謝您。您告訴我在哪兒，我下午去看看。

...

📷 | iMessage　　　　　Send

Chinese Chat

A prospective tenant is texting you on iMessage to inquire about your apartment for rent. How would you reply?

文化

Continue
to explore

DORMS

Until the late 1990s, college students in China were required to live in dorms on campus, with six or seven to a room and possibly dozens sharing a common bathroom at the end of the hallway. Because there was no place to cook in the dorms, everyone ate in the on-campus student dining halls, 學生餐廳 *(xuéshēng cāntīng)*. Living conditions for students have improved substantially since the late 1990s. At some colleges, students who can afford it now have the option of renting apartments off campus. Foreign students generally live in special dorms, two to a room, but some choose to live with host families or rent their own apartments.

Apartments

Renting an apartment in a Chinese city is not difficult. Listings can be found online and in local newspapers. You can also call or stop by one of the many intermediary companies, 仲介公司 *(zhòngjiè gōngsī)*—agencies that match apartment owners with potential tenants.

Housing development has been a pillar of the Chinese economy for the last two decades, and living conditions for a significant portion of the urban population have improved enormously. However, while some have profited dramatically from the real estate market, skyrocketing prices in many cities have made housing prohibitively expensive for those of average means, leading to a widening gap between rich and poor. Many middle-class people feel crushed by heavy mortgages and refer to themselves as "slaves to houses," 房奴 *(fángnú)*. Meanwhile, in other areas, growth in the housing market has outpaced demand, leading to entire neighborhoods of finished but empty buildings. One example of this "ghost city" phenomenon is Ordos in Inner Mongolia, where thousands of newly built apartments go unlit at night.

Pets

Traditionally, people in China have had a special love for keeping songbirds as pets, in addition to cats and dogs. In 1983, amid fears of rabies, Beijing officially banned non-working dogs, as well as six other animals, from within city limits; this ban was only lifted in the early 1990s. Even in the present, only dogs under thirty-five centimeters (about fourteen inches) in length are permitted in the city. Nevertheless, dogs are now extremely popular and have become much-loved members of many urban households. In the countryside, the most popular household pets are cats, at least partly for the practical purpose of keeping the mouse population under control.

COMPARE & CONTRAST

1 Landlords in China often ask for a deposit and several months' rent in advance. Therefore, phrases like 押一付三 (*yā yī fù sān*) and 押一付二 (*yā yī fù èr*) are often seen in rental ads. What do they mean? Are there similar practices in your country?

2 Among the large population of pet owners closely bonded with their pets, the term 毛小孩（兒）(*máo xiǎohái[r]*) (lit. furry kid) is catching on. There are now pet-friendly hotels and restaurants, as well as tour packages tailored to the needs of pet owners. How pet-friendly is your community? How do people feel about pets in stores and restaurants?

3 With the rise of home ownership as a symbol of financial security, many parents of daughters have come to believe in home ownership as a prerequisite for prospective sons-in-law. For such parents, the notion of a married couple living in rented accommodation is unacceptable. Hence, many grooms, with or without family help, feel obligated to purchase homes before getting married. Although this pressure is intended to ensure security for the couple, it can be a terrible burden. In your culture/community, is there a relationship between housing and marriage? Is the bride's or the groom's family typically responsible for paying for the wedding? How are owning and renting perceived by most people?

Lesson Wrap-Up

Make It Flow!

The following sentences are in a logical sequence. Combine them into a coherent narrative. Avoid repeating unnecessarily identical elements. Substitute the nouns with designated pronouns such as 那個人 (nà ge rén) and change periods to commas where appropriate. Add the adverb 還 (hái) and the conjunction 不過 (búguò) where appropriate.

王朋給出租房子的人打電話。王朋問出租房子的人有沒有公寓出租。出租房子的人說有公寓出租。出租房子的人說公寓一室一廳。出租房子的人說公寓非常乾淨。出租房子的人說公寓帶傢俱。王朋問公寓帶什麼傢俱。出租房子的人告訴王朋公寓帶什麼傢俱。出租房子的人告訴王朋公寓房租多少錢。出租房子的人告訴王朋公寓不能養寵物。王朋聽了以後覺得公寓好像不錯。王朋下午想去看看公寓。

Skit

You need to find an affordable apartment in New York City this summer, so you decide to check out Chinatown. You look through the ads in the Chinese-language newspapers and write down several phone numbers. The first landlord that you call has a furnished apartment on Mercer Street. You want to find out how you can get to work from the apartment by subway or by bus (you'll be working on Manhattan's west side), how the apartment is furnished, the noise level, how much the deposit and rent are, whether utilities are included, etc.

Advertisement

You're studying in China and looking for a roommate. Based on this lesson's Chinese rental ads, write an ad for your apartment. Where is it located? How many bedrooms does it have? Is it furnished? Are pets allowed? Is it near a university or sports center? What type of roommate are you looking for? Don't forget to include your contact information. Your teacher will circulate or "publish" all the ads submitted. Which ad would attract your attention?

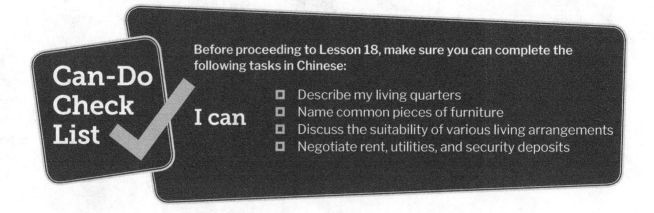

Can-Do Check List

I can

Before proceeding to Lesson 18, make sure you can complete the following tasks in Chinese:

- ☐ Describe my living quarters
- ☐ Name common pieces of furniture
- ☐ Discuss the suitability of various living arrangements
- ☐ Negotiate rent, utilities, and security deposits

Lesson 18

第十八課

Dì shíbā kè

運動

Yùndòng

SPORTS

Learning Objectives

In this lesson, you will learn to:

- Name and discuss some popular sports
- Talk about your exercise habits
- Compare soccer and American football in simple terms

Relate and Get Ready

In your own culture/community:

- Do people exercise regularly?
- Are most people sports fans?
- Which sports are most popular?
- Are there many sports programs on TV?
- Which is more popular, American football or soccer?

Getting in Shape

Dialogue 1

Audio

Video

（高文中跟王朋聊天兒……）

你看，我的肚子越來越大了。

你平常吃得那麼多，又[a]不運動，當然越來越胖了。

那怎麼辦呢？

如果怕胖，你一個星期運動兩、三次，每次半個小時，肚子就會小了。

我兩年沒運動了[1]，做什麼運動呢？

最簡單的運動是跑步。

冬天那麼冷，夏天那麼熱，跑步太難受[2]了。

你打網球吧。

打網球得買網球拍、網球鞋，你知道，網球拍、網球鞋貴極了！

找幾個人打籃球吧。買個籃球很便宜。

那每次都得打電話約人，麻煩死了。

你去游泳吧。不用找人，也不用花很多錢，什麼時候去都可以。

游泳？我怕水，太危險了，淹死了怎麼辦？

我也沒辦法了。你不願意運動，那就胖下去[3]吧。

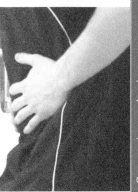

(Gāo Wénzhōng gēn Wáng Péng liáo tiānr . . .)

Nǐ kàn, wǒ de dùzi yuè lái yuè dà le.

Nǐ píngcháng chī de nàme duō, yòu[a] bú yùndòng,

dāngrán yuè lái yuè pàng le.

Nà zěnme bàn ne?

Rúguǒ pà pàng, nǐ yí ge xīngqī yùndòng liǎng, sān

cì, měi cì bàn ge xiǎoshí, dùzi jiù huì xiǎo le.

Wǒ liǎng nián méi yùndòng le[1], zuò shénme

yùndòng ne?

Zuì jiǎndān de yùndòng shì pǎo bù.

Dōngtiān nàme lěng, xiàtiān nàme rè, pǎo bù tài

nánshòu[2] le.

Nǐ dǎ wǎngqiú ba.

Dǎ wǎngqiú děi mǎi wǎngqiú pāi, wǎngqiú xié, nǐ

zhīdao wǎngqiú pāi, wǎngqiú xié guì jí le!

Zhǎo jǐ ge rén dǎ lánqiú ba. Mǎi ge lánqiú hěn piányi.

Nà měi cì dōu děi dǎ diànhuà yuē rén, máfan sǐ le.

Nǐ qù yóu yǒng ba. Búyòng zhǎo rén, yě búyòng huā

hěn duō qián, shénme shíhou qù dōu kěyǐ.

Yóu yǒng? Wǒ pà shuǐ, tài wēixiǎn le, yān sǐ le

zěnme bàn?

Wǒ yě méi bànfǎ le. Nǐ bú yuànyì yùndòng, nà jiù

pàng xia qu[3] ba.

a 又 (yòu)

又 (yòu) can indicate a recurrence of an action or a state over the course of time, e.g.: 我昨天看了一個電影，今天又看了一個 (*Wǒ zuótiān kàn le yí ge diànyǐng, jīntiān yòu kàn le yí ge*) (I watched a movie yesterday, and I watched another one today). 又 (yòu) can also suggest the augmentation or exacerbation of certain conditions or circumstances, as in this excerpt from the dialogue: 你平常吃得那麼多，又不運動，當然越來越胖了 (*Nǐ píngcháng chī de nàme duō, yòu bú yùndòng, dāngrán yuè lái yuè pàng le*) (You usually eat so much, and on top of that you don't exercise; no wonder you're putting on more and more weight).

Vocabulary

No.	Word	Pinyin	Part of Speech	Definition
1	當然	dāngrán	adv	of course
2	胖	pàng	adj	fat
3	怕	pà	v	to fear, to be afraid of
4	簡單	jiǎndān	adj	simple
5	跑步	pǎo bù	vo	to jog
	跑	pǎo	v	to run
6	難受	nánshòu	adj	hard to bear, uncomfortable [See Grammar 2.]
7	網球	wǎngqiú	n	tennis
8	拍	pāi	n	racket
9	籃球	lánqiú	n	basketball
10	游泳	yóu yǒng	vo	to swim
11	危險	wēixiǎn	adj	dangerous
12	淹死	yān sǐ	vc	to drown
13	願意	yuànyì	mv	to be willing

Audio

Flashcards

你喜歡做什麼
運動？

Nǐ xǐhuan zuò shénme yùndòng?
What sports do you like to play?

我喜歡 ＿＿＿＿＿＿ 。
Wǒ xǐhuan ＿＿＿＿＿＿ .

See index for corresponding vocabulary or research another term.

GET
Real
WITH **CHINESE**

As you walk along
the edge of a river
in Hangzhou, you
see this sign. What
is its message?

河内危险
禁止游泳

Grammar

| **1** | **Duration of inactivity** |

Time expression + 沒 *(méi)* + verb + (了) *(le)*

This structure indicates that an action has not been or was not performed for a certain period of time.

A　他三天沒上網了。

Tā sān tiān méi shàng wǎng le.

He hasn't been online for three days.

[✕ 他沒上網三天了。]

B　我兩年沒檢查身體了。

Wǒ liǎng nián méi jiǎnchá shēntǐ le.

I haven't had a check-up in two years.

C　我的狗病了，一天沒吃東西了。

Wǒ de gǒu bìng le, yì tiān méi chī dōngxi le.

My dog is sick; she hasn't eaten anything for a day.

D　妹妹上個月特別忙，三個星期沒回家。

Mèimei shàng ge yuè tèbié máng, sān ge xīngqī méi huí jiā.

My younger sister was especially busy last month, and she didn't come home for three weeks.

E　去年寒假我去英國旅行，一個月沒吃中國菜。

Qùnián hánjià wǒ qù Yīngguó lǚxíng, yí ge yuè méi chī Zhōngguó cài.

I went on a trip to the UK over winter break last year, and didn't eat any Chinese food for a month.

Note that there is a difference between this construction and its affirmative counterpart. Compare:

F   **Student A**   我學了兩年中文了。

Wǒ xué le liǎng nián Zhōngwén le.

I have been studying Chinese for two years.

Student B   是嗎？我兩年沒學中文了。

Shì ma? Wǒ liǎng nián méi xué Zhōngwén le.

Really? I haven't studied Chinese for two years.

More
exercises

EXERCISES

Complete the sentences to indicate the duration of inactivity, using the "Time expression +
沒 + verb + (了)" structure where appropriate. Use exercise 1 as an example.

1   小李付房租   兩個月

       →   小李兩個月沒付房租了。

2   小王買衣服   半年

3   王朋打球   三個星期

---

2 | 好/難 *(hǎo/nán)* **+ verb** |

Some verbs can be preceded by 好 *(hǎo)* (fine, good, nice) or 難 *(nán)* (difficult); the resulting
compounds become adjectives. In this case, 好 *(hǎo)* usually means "easy" while 難 *(nán)*
means "difficult."

A   好受   難受   **C**   好走   難走

     hǎoshòu   *nánshòu*   *hǎozǒu*   *nánzǒu*

     easy to bear   hard to bear   easy to walk on   hard to walk on

B   好寫   難寫   **D**   好說   難說

     hǎoxiě   *nánxiě*   *hǎoshuō*   *nánshuō*

     easy to write   hard to write   easy to say   difficult to say

E 好懂　　難懂

hǎodǒng　　*nándǒng*

easy to understand　　hard to understand

F 好唱　　難唱

hǎochàng　　*nánchàng*

easy to sing　　hard to sing

In other compounds, however, 好 (*hǎo*) suggests that the action represented by the verb is pleasant, while 難 (*nán*) means the opposite.

G 好吃　　難吃

hǎochī　　*nánchī*

delicious　　unappetizing

I 好聽　　難聽

hǎotīng　　*nántīng*

pleasant to listen to　　unpleasant to listen to

H 好看　　難看

hǎokàn　　*nánkàn*

pretty　　ugly

EXERCISES

Fill in the blanks using the "好/難 + verb" structure. The verbs are in parentheses. Use exercise 1 as an example.

More exercises

1 我喜歡媽媽做的菜，因為媽媽做的菜都很 _____。（吃）

→ 我喜歡媽媽做的菜，因為媽媽做的菜都很好吃。

2 弟弟買的襯衫很便宜，可是很 _____。（看）

3 這種咖啡雖然貴，可是真的非常 _____。（喝）

Indicating continuation using 下去 (xia qu)

下去 (*xia qu*) signifies the continuation of an action that is in progress.

A 說下去。

Shuō xia qu.

Go on speaking.

B 你別念下去了，我一點兒也不喜歡聽。

Nǐ bié niàn xia qu le, wǒ yì diǎnr yě bù xǐhuan tīng.

Please stop reading. I don't like listening to that at all.

C 中文很有意思，我想學下去。

Zhōngwén hěn yǒu yìsi, wǒ xiǎng xué xia qu.

Chinese is very interesting. I'd like to continue learning it.

D 你已經跑了一個多小時了，再跑下去，
要累死了。

Nǐ yǐjīng pǎo le yí ge duō xiǎoshí le, zài pǎo xia qu, yào lèi sǐ le.

You've already been running for more than an hour; if you keep running, you'll be exhausted.

More exercises

EXERCISES

Fill in the blanks to indicate the continuation of an action or situation using the verbs in the parentheses and 下去. Use exercise 1 as an example.

1 你唱歌真好聽，＿＿＿＿＿＿吧。（唱）

→ 你唱歌真好聽，唱下去吧。

2 我很喜歡我的公寓，
想在這兒＿＿＿＿＿＿。（住）

3 你跑步跑了兩個小時了，
不能再＿＿＿＿＿＿了。（跑）

Language Practice

What's the matter?

PRESENTATIONAL

Gao Wenzhong is not feeling well. Describe what he has been through using the structure "time expression + 沒 (méi) + V + 了 (le)," e.g.:

睡覺 ⊗ 三天

shuì jiào ⊗ *sān tiān*

高文中三天沒睡覺了。

Gāo Wénzhōng sān tiān méi shuì jiào le.

1 吃東西 ⊗ 兩天

   chī dōngxi ⊗ *liǎng tiān*

2 喝東西 ⊗ 一天

   hē dōngxi ⊗ *yì tiān*

3 上課 ⊗ 一個星期

   shàng kè ⊗ *yí ge xīngqī*

| What do the characters mean? |
| What is the common radical? |
| What does the radical mean? |
| How does the radical relate to the overall meaning of the characters? |

Characterize it!

❶ 游 ❷ 泳 ❸ 淹

More characters

Silent treatment

Wang Peng and Li You had a fight. The two of them haven't seen each other, called, texted, or chatted online for a while now. In pairs, form a question-and-answer about their strained relationship based on the images, e.g.:

a week

Q: 李友多長時間沒跟王朋見面了？

Lǐ Yǒu duō cháng shíjiān méi gēn Wáng Péng jiàn miàn le?

A: 李友一個星期沒跟王朋見面了。

Lǐ Yǒu yí ge xīngqī méi gēn Wáng Péng jiàn miàn le.

1 5 days

2 6 days

3 7 days

Chinese Chat

Gao Wenzhong is chatting with Wang Peng on LINE. Describe Gao Wenzhong's future exercise plans.

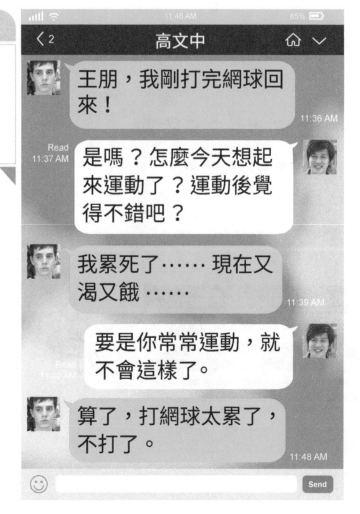

高文中

王朋，我剛打完網球回來！
11:36 AM

Read 11:37 AM

是嗎？怎麼今天想起來運動了？運動後覺得不錯吧？

我累死了⋯⋯ 現在又渴又餓⋯⋯
11:39 AM

要是你常常運動，就不會這樣了。

算了，打網球太累了，不打了。
11:48 AM

Open for comment

In pairs, use the "好／難 *(hǎo/nán)* + verb" structure to discuss with your partner and find out whether you have similar or different opinions based on the images, e.g.:

Q:　你覺得哪種茶好喝，哪種茶難喝？

Nǐ juéde nǎ zhǒng chá hǎohē, nǎ zhǒng chá nánhē?

A:　我覺得 (name of a tea) 很好喝。

我覺得 (name of a tea) 很難喝。

Wǒ juéde (name of a tea) hěn hǎohē. Wǒ juéde (name of a tea) hěn nánhē.

1

2

3

Then report your findings to the class. If the two of you share the same opinion, you can say:

Anya 跟我一樣，我們都覺得⋯⋯

Anya *gēn wǒ yíyàng, wǒmen dōu juéde . . .*

If you don't share the same opinion, then you can say:

Anya 跟我不一樣，她覺得⋯⋯我覺得⋯⋯

Anya *gēn wǒ bù yíyàng, tā juéde . . . wǒ juéde . . .*

Watching American Football

Dialogue 2

王朋的妹妹王紅剛從北京來，要在美國上[a]大學，現在住在高小音家裡學英文。為了[b]提高英文水平，她每天都看兩個小時的電視[4]。

快把電視打開，足球比賽開始了。

是嗎？我也喜歡看足球賽[c]。……這是什麼足球[d]啊？怎麼不是圓的？

這不是國際[e]足球，這是美式足球。

足球應該用腳踢，為什麼那個人用手抱著[5]跑呢？

美式足球可以用手。

你看，你看，那麼多人都壓在一起，下面的人不是要被[6]壓壞[f]了嗎？

別擔心，他們的身體都很棒，而且還穿特別的運動服，沒問題。

我看了半天[g]也看不懂。還是看別的吧。

你在美國住半年就會喜歡了。我男朋友看美式足球的時候，常常連飯都忘了吃。

Pinyin Dialogue

(Wáng Péng de mèimei Wáng Hóng gāng cóng Běijīng lái, yào zài Měiguó shàng[a] dàxué, xiànzài zhù zài Gāo Xiǎoyīn jiā li xué Yīngwén. Wèile[b] tígāo Yīngwén shuǐpíng, tā měi tiān dōu kàn liǎng ge xiǎoshí de diànshì[4].)

 Kuài bǎ diànshì dǎ kāi, zúqiú bǐsài kāishǐ le.

 Shì ma? Wǒ yě xǐhuan kàn zúqiú sài[c]... Zhè shì shénme zúqiú[d] a? Zěnme bú shì yuán de?

 Zhè bú shì guójì[e] zúqiú, zhè shì Měishì zúqiú.

 Zúqiú yīnggāi yòng jiǎo tī, wèishénme nà ge rén yòng shǒu bào zhe[5] pǎo ne?

 Měishì zúqiú kěyǐ yòng shǒu.

 Nǐ kàn, nǐ kàn, nàme duō rén dōu yā zài yìqǐ, xiàmiàn de rén bú shì yào bèi[6] yā huài[f] le ma?

 Bié dān xīn, tāmen de shēntǐ dōu hěn bàng, érqiě hái chuān tèbié de yùndòngfú, méi wèntí.

 Wǒ kàn le bàntiān[g] yě kàn bu dǒng. Háishi kàn bié de ba.

 Nǐ zài Měiguó zhù bànnián jiù huì xǐhuan le. Wǒ nánpéngyou kàn Měishì zúqiú de shíhou, chángcháng lián fàn dōu wàng le chī.

Language Notes

a 上 *(shàng)*

This is a versatile verb. To board a car or plane is 上車／飛機 *(shàng chē/fēijī)*, and to go to the bathroom is 上廁所 *(shàng cèsuǒ)*. In this lesson, 上學 *(shàng xué)* means "to go to school" in colloquial Mandarin, so you can say 上小學／中學／大學 *(shàng xiǎoxué/zhōngxué/dàxué)* for attending elementary school/middle school/college.

b 為了 *(wèile)*

This usually appears in the first clause of a complex sentence, e.g.: 為了學好中文，他每天聽兩個小時錄音 *(Wèile xué hǎo Zhōngwén, tā měi tiān tīng liǎng ge xiǎoshí lùyīn)* (In order to learn Chinese well, he listens to recordings for two hours every day).

c 賽 *(sài)*

This is short for 比賽 *(bǐsài)*.

d 足球 *(zúqiú)*

This term literally means "football" and refers to soccer, not American football. To avoid confusion, Chinese speakers refer to American football as 美式足球 *(Měishì zúqiú)* (American-style football) or 美式橄欖球 *(Měishì gǎnlǎn qiú)* (lit. American-style olive ball). Rugby is known as 英式橄欖球 *(Yīngshì gǎnlǎn qiú)*.

e **Adjectives as attributes**

Certain adjectives, such as 國際 *(guójì)*, 男 *(nán)*, 女 *(nǚ)*, and 黑白 *(hēibái)*, can only function as attributives and not as predicates.

f 壓壞 *(yā huài)*

壓壞 *(yā huài)* in this context means "to be crushed and injured." 壞 *(huài)* indicates the result of 壓 *(yā)*.

g 半天 *(bàntiān)*

This does not always mean exactly "a half day" as the word literally suggests. Rather, it often denotes a comparatively long stretch of time.

Vocabulary

Audio

Flashcards

No.	Word	Pinyin	Part of Speech	Definition
1	上大學	shàng dàxué	vo	to attend college/university
2	為了	wèile	prep	for the sake of
3	提高	tígāo	v	to improve, to raise, to heighten
4	水平	shuǐpíng	n	level, standard
5	足球	zúqiú	n	soccer, football
6	比賽	bǐsài	n/v	game, match, competition; to compete
7	國際	guójì	adj	international
8	美式	Měishì	adj	American-style
9	應該	yīnggāi	mv	should, ought to
10	腳	jiǎo	n	foot
11	踢	tī	v	to kick
12	手	shǒu	n	hand
13	抱	bào	v	to hold or carry in the arms
14	壓	yā	v	to press, to hold down, to weigh down
15	被	bèi	prep	by [See Grammar 6.]
16	擔心	dān xīn	vo	to worry
17	棒	bàng	adj	fantastic, super [colloq.]

You see this TV drama being advertised in the Taipei Metro. What do you think it's about?

GET **Real** WITH CHINESE

No.	Word	Pinyin	Part of Speech	Definition
18	運動服	*yùndòngfú*	n	sportswear, athletic clothing
19	半天	*bàntiān*		half a day, a long time

你喜歡看什麼
運動比賽？

Nǐ xǐhuan kàn shénme yùndòng bǐsài?

What sports games do you enjoy watching?

我喜歡看 _____ 。

Wǒ xǐhuan kàn _____ .

See index for corresponding vocabulary or research another term.

Grammar

<table>
<tr><td>4</td><td>Duration of activity (II)</td></tr>
</table>

As we learned in Grammar 3, Lesson 14, when a sentence contains both a time expression indicating the duration of an action and an object, it needs to be formed in one of these two patterns: repetition of the verb (*) or placement of the time expression before the object, often with 的 (de) (**). Let's look at some more examples and see how they differ from those in Grammar 1 of this lesson.

A　她每天聽錄音聽一個小時。*

Tā měi tiān tīng lùyīn tīng yí ge xiǎoshí.

她每天聽一個小時（的）錄音。**

Tā měi tiān tīng yí ge xiǎoshí (de) lùyīn.

She listens to the audio for an hour every day.

B　她每天下午游泳游四十分鐘。*

Tā měi tiān xiàwǔ yóu yǒng yóu sìshí fēnzhōng.

她每天下午游四十分鐘（的）泳。**

Tā měi tiān xiàwǔ yóu sìshí fēnzhōng (de) yǒng.

She swims for forty minutes every afternoon.

C　她每天看英文報紙看兩個小時，所以英文越來越好了。*

Tā měi tiān kàn Yīngwén bàozhǐ kàn liǎng ge xiǎoshí, suǒyǐ Yīngwén yuè lái yuè hǎo le.

她每天看兩個小時（的）英文報紙，所以英文越來越好了。**

Tā měi tiān kàn liǎng ge xiǎoshí (de) Yīngwén bàozhǐ, suǒyǐ Yīngwén yuè lái yuè hǎo le.

She reads English-language newspapers for two hours every day, so her English is getting better and better.

EXERCISES

Indicate the time duration of the action by repeating the verbs or placing the time expression before the object. Use exercise 1 as an example.

1 　我昨天跳舞　　　　　　　　　　兩個小時

　→ 我昨天跳舞跳了兩個小時。/

　我昨天跳了兩個小時（的）舞。

2 　她每天看中文書　　　　　　　　三個小時

3 　老王昨天下午睡覺　　　　　　　四十分鐘

---

5 | **The particle 著** *(zhe)*

著 *(zhe)* signifies the continuation of an action or a state. Its function is descriptive. When 著 *(zhe)* is used between two verbs, the one that precedes 著 *(zhe)* signifies the accompanying action, while the second verb signifies the main action.

A 　老師站著教課，學生坐著聽課。

　Lǎoshī zhàn zhe jiāo kè, xuésheng zuò zhe tīng kè.

　While the teacher stood lecturing, the students sat listening.

B 　我喜歡躺著聽音樂。

　Wǒ xǐhuan tǎng zhe tīng yīnyuè.

　I like to listen to music while lying down.

C 　美式足球可以抱著球跑。

　Měishì zúqiú kěyǐ bào zhe qiú pǎo.

　In American football, you can run while holding the ball in your hands.

著 *(zhe)* is normally used after a verb to indicate a continuing action or a state. 在 *(zài)* is normally used before a verb to indicate an ongoing action.

D Q: 學生們在做什麼呢？

Xuésheng men zài zuò shénme ne?

What are the students doing?

A: 在運動。

Zài yùndòng.

They're exercising.

在 (zài) in (D) cannot be replaced with 著 (zhe). Likewise, 著 (zhe) in the earlier sentences cannot be replaced with 在 (zài).

More exercises

EXERCISES

Form sentences to signify the accompanying action by using 著. Use exercise 1 as an example.

1　老王　看　電視　坐

　　→ 老王坐著看電視。

2　弟弟　吃　飯　站

3　老師　上　課　坐

6　**Passive-voice sentences using 被/叫/讓 (bèi/jiào/ràng)**

A sentence in the passive voice can be constructed with 被 (bèi), 叫 (jiào), or 讓 (ràng), using the following structure:

> Receiver of the action + 被 (bèi)/叫 (jiào)/讓 (ràng) + agent of the action + verb + other element (complement/ 了 [le], etc.)

A 我的功課被/叫/讓狗吃了。

Wǒ de gōngkè bèi/jiào/ràng gǒu chī le.

My homework was eaten by my dog.

B　你買的那些書被/叫/讓你的女朋友
　　拿去了。

Nǐ mǎi de nà xiē shū bèi/jiào/ràng nǐ de nǚpéngyou ná qù le.

The books that you bought were taken away by your girlfriend.

C　糟糕，你的網球拍被/叫/讓我壓壞了。

Zāogāo, nǐ de wǎngqiú pāi bèi/jiào/ràng wǒ yā huài le.

Oh gosh, your tennis racket was crushed into pieces [by me].

D　你看，我的梨被/叫/讓你的西瓜
　　壓壞了。

Nǐ kàn, wǒ de lí bèi/jiào/ràng nǐ de xīgua yā huài le.

Take a look. My pears were crushed by your watermelon.

In Chinese, the passive voice is not used as often as it is in English. It often carries a negative connotation, and is typically used in situations that are unpleasant for the receiver of the action or in situations where something is lost. As in the 把 *(bǎ)* structure (see Lesson 13), the verb is usually followed by another element, such as a complement or 了 *(le)*.

In a passive-voice sentence with 被 *(bèi)*/叫 *(jiào)*/讓 *(ràng)*, the agent of the action does not always have to be specified. If the agent of the action is someone that is not identifiable or need not be identified, the agent can simply be referred to as 人 *(rén)* (someone, people).

E　我的信用卡被/叫/讓人拿走了。

Wǒ de xìnyòngkǎ bèi/jiào/ràng rén ná zǒu le.

My credit card was taken away by someone.

With 被 *(bèi)*, the agent of the action can be omitted from the sentence:

F　同學們在教室裡又唱又跳，他快被
　　吵死了。

Tóngxué men zài jiàoshì li yòu chàng yòu tiào, tā kuài bèi chǎo sǐ le.

His classmates are singing and dancing in the classroom.
He is being driven to distraction by the noise.

被 *(bèi)* sometimes can be used in a positive sense, but we will not discuss this in detail here.

EXERCISES

Form sentences in the passive voice using 被/叫/讓 and 了.

Use exercise 1 as an example.

1   他的車　　　女朋友開回家

→ 他的車被女朋友開回家了。

2   她買的水果　她妹妹吃完

3   小李的書　　小高拿到教室去

246   Integrated Chinese 2 | Textbook

Language Practice

Packed schedule

PRESENTATIONAL

Based on the prompts, summarize who did what for how long yesterday. Repeat the verb or place the time expression before the object to indicate the duration of the action, e.g.:

費先生昨天跳舞跳了三個小時。/
費先生昨天跳了三個小時（的）舞。

Fèi xiānsheng zuótiān tiào wǔ tiào le sān ge xiǎoshí./

Fèi xiānsheng zuótiān tiào le sān ge xiǎoshí (de) wǔ.

1  7:00 a.m.–8:00 a.m.

2  7:30 a.m.–8:15 a.m.

3   11:00 a.m.–12:00 p.m.

4   10:00 a.m.–12:30 p.m.

5   4:00 p.m.–6:30 p.m.

All in the technique

In groups, discuss traditional or innovative ways you can think of to improve Chinese proficiency. Then present each group's study strategies to the class, e.g.:

Q: 怎麼才能提高中文水平？

Zěnme cái néng tígāo Zhōngwén shuǐpíng?

A: 為了提高中文水平，你應該每天聽兩個小時（的）錄音。/ 為了提高中文水平，你應該每天聽錄音聽兩個小時。

Wèile tígāo Zhōngwén shuǐpíng, nǐ yīnggāi měi tiān tīng liǎng ge xiǎoshí (de) lùyīn. /
Wèile tígāo Zhōngwén shuǐpíng, nǐ yīnggāi měi tiān tīng lùyīn tīng liǎng ge xiǎoshí.

1   **2**  **3**

F **What's going on?**

Describe what the IC characters are doing using the "verb + 著 (zhe)" structure, e.g.:

王朋和李友站著聊天兒。
高文中坐著看電視。

Wáng Péng hé Lǐ Yǒu zhàn zhe liáo tiānr.

Gāo Wénzhōng zuò zhe kàn diànshì.

1  **2**

3  **4**

That's unfortunate

Use the 被 (bèi)/叫 (jiào)/讓 (ràng) structure to describe what happened to Little Gao yesterday.

1 His homework was eaten by his dog.

2 His coffee was drunk by his sister.

3 His credit card was taken away from him by his mother.

4 His car was driven to school by his brother.

5 The birthday gift that he was going to give to his friend was crushed by the sofa.

Have any of these ever happened to you? Do you have any similar experiences that you could share with your class?

INTERPERSONAL

Fitness queen/king!

PRESENTATIONAL

Survey your class for a research project about physical activity.

1 Do you exercise?

2 If so, how often do you exercise? If not, how long have you not been exercising?

3 If so, how long do you exercise each time? If not, when do you plan to start exercising, if ever?

4 What sports do you play, if any, and why do you like them?

5 Are there sports that you don't like to play? Why not?

Compare each other's information and report to the class who the fitness queen/king is.

Possible sentence patterns include: _____ 運動得最多，是我們的 運動天王！(_____ yùndòng de zuì duō, shì wǒmen de yùndòng tiānwáng!)

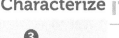

What do the characters mean?

What is the common radical?

What does the radical mean?

How does the radical relate to the overall meaning of the characters?

Characterize it!

❶   ❷   ❸

More characters

文化

Co...
to explo...

POPULAR SPORTS

In recent decades, China has consolidated its status as the leading sports power in Asia. In some sports, such as table tennis and diving, China has enjoyed a dominant position in the world. By far the most popular sport in China, as in many other countries, is soccer, but ironically, China's national soccer team is second-rate at best. What Chinese speakers call "football," 足球 (zúqiú), is actually soccer in American English. American football is not played there. In fact, not many people in China would understand the frenzy and exhilaration of American fans watching what can seem to be little more than a group scuffling on grass.

COMPARE & CONTRAST

1 Chinese athletics have been a national success story, and sports victories in China have been emotionally viewed as symbols of Chinese modernization. Chinese athletes began to "win glory for the country," 為國爭光 (wèi guó zhēng guāng), in the 1950s. In step with development, China has emerged as an athletic powerhouse, particularly at the Olympic Games. In your view, what common desires are satisfied by identification with a local or national sports team? Are there similar ties between sports and pride in your community/country?

2 China's athletic prowess is fueled by the country's extensive network of sports schools, which supply a steady stream of highly trained gymnasts, divers, and swimmers, as well as ping-pong, badminton, volleyball, basketball, and soccer players, to the national teams through a system based on that used in the former Soviet Union. Each year, gifted children are recruited into state-sponsored schools focused on athletic performance rather than academics. How similar or different is the path to becoming a star athlete in your country?

MORNING
exercises

In every Chinese city, with the early morning comes the spectacular sight of dozens, even hundreds, of men and women gathering in parks to practice t'ai chi ch'uan, 太極拳 (tàijíquán), and other forms of exercise. Most practitioners are older people and retirees.

A recent phenomenon is "public-square dancing," 廣場舞 (guǎngchǎng wǔ), which typically takes place in the early morning or early evening in neighborhood parks or squares. Its participants, mostly middle-aged and retired women, believe in the health benefits of their practice, but the loud music they play has been controversial.

Women engaged in public-square dancing

Cuju (蹴鞠) (cùjū), a game played as early as the Han dynasty (202 BCE–220 CE), is recognized as the earliest precursor of the modern sport of soccer. Cuju was initially played with a ball filled with feathers, then later played with an inflated ball. During the Tang (618–907 CE) and Song (960–1279 CE) dynasties, cuju was popular among all social classes and among both men and women; fields for playing cuju were reportedly numerous in the Tang and Song capitals of Chang'an and Bianliang. As in soccer, players were not allowed to touch the ball with their hands. Gao Qiu, a hooligan in the classic Chinese novel *Outlaws of the Marsh*, becomes a favorite of the emperor because of his extraordinary skills as a cuju player and goes on to perpetrate all sorts of nefarious deeds. As a result, one of the novel's heroes, who falls victim to Gao, is forced into becoming an outlaw.

Cuju

Gao Qiu showing off his footwork

diet

&WEIGHT

With the improvement in living standards in China over recent decades, the consumption of calorie-rich foods, especially meat, has been on the rise. Obesity has quietly become a problem for many people in urban areas, especially children. The transformation in people's lifestyles has affected language as well: before the 1970s, one could say 你胖了 (*Nǐ pàng le*) (You've put on weight) as a compliment, but this is no longer the case.

Lesson Wrap-Up

The following sentences are arranged in a logical order. Combine the sentences into a coherent narrative. Substitute nouns with pronouns and change periods to commas where necessary. Avoid unnecessary repetitions of subject pronouns. Add the connective devices 又 (yòu), 所以 (suǒyǐ), 如果 (rúguǒ), and 可是 (kěshì) where appropriate.

高文中兩年沒運動了。高文中平常吃得很多。高文中越來越胖。

高文中問王朋怎麼辦。王朋說一個星期運動兩三次，每次半個小時，肚子就會小了。高文中不知道做什麼運動好。王朋告訴高文中可以跑步。王朋告訴高文中可以打網球。王朋告訴高文中可以打籃球。王朋告訴高文中可以游泳。高文中覺得，跑步冬天太冷。高文中覺得，跑步夏天太熱。高文中覺得，跑步太難受。高文中覺得，打網球買網球拍太貴。高文中覺得，打網球買網球鞋太貴。高文中覺得，打籃球每次都得打電話約人，太麻煩。高文中覺得，游泳太危險。高文中怕淹死。

王朋沒有辦法了。高文中可能還得胖下去。

You're a freshman who has been enjoying college life. You love your classes, professors, and new friends, but your hectic, unhealthy lifestyle has meant that you've put on fifteen pounds (磅) (bàng). You've been staying up late, helping yourself to multiple slices of pizza, and avoiding the gym. You decide to go to a wellness coach. The coach tries to find out about your habits and recommends various kinds of exercise. Respond to his/her suggestions: Do you like the recommendations? Will you able to follow them? You will jointly decide on a plan to get you back in shape.

Make a short video introducing American football to a Chinese audience. What is the biggest difference between American football and soccer? How do the clothes and equipment for each sport compare? Are players allowed to manipulate the ball with their hands? How long is a game? Is football more popular among men or women? Do you have a favorite team? Who are some of the most famous players?

Can-Do Check List ✓

I can

Before proceeding to Lesson 19, make sure you can complete the following tasks in Chinese:

- ☐ Briefly explain the appeal, or lack thereof, of certain sports
- ☐ Describe the frequency and duration of my exercise routine, or how long I haven't exercised
- ☐ Make a simple comparison between soccer and American football

第十九課

Dì shíjiǔ kè

旅行

Lǚxíng

TRAVEL

Learning Objectives

In this lesson, you will learn to:

- Talk about your plans for summer break
- Describe what kind of city Beijing is
- Describe your travel itinerary
- Ask for discounts, compare airfares and routes, and book airplane tickets
- Ask about seat assignments and request meal accommodations based on your dietary restrictions or preferences

Relate & Get Ready

In your own culture/community:

- How do students normally spend the summer?
- What town or city is the nearest cultural or political center? What are its special attractions?
- Where can people get good deals on airline tickets?
- How are discounts expressed and advertised?

Traveling to Beijing

Dialogue 1

Audio

Video

（暑假快要到了……）

李友，時間過得真快，馬上就要放假了，我們的同學，有的去暑期班學習，有的去公司實習，有的回家打工，你有什麼計劃？

我還沒有想好。你呢，王朋？

我暑假打算[a]回北京去看父母。

是嗎？我聽說北京這個城市很有意思。

當然。北京是中國的首都，也是中國的政治、文化中心，有很多名勝古蹟。

對啊，長城很有名。

還有，北京的好飯館多得不得了[1]。

真的？我去過香港、台北，還沒去過北京，要是能去北京就好了。

那你跟我一起回去吧，我當你的導遊。

真的嗎？那太好了！護照我已經有了，我得趕快辦[b]簽證。

那我馬上給旅行社打電話訂飛機票。

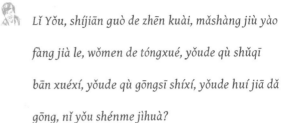

(Shǔjià kuài yào dào le . . .)

Lǐ Yǒu, shíjiān guò de zhēn kuài, mǎshàng jiù yào fàng jià le, wǒmen de tóngxué, yǒude qù shǔqī bān xuéxí, yǒude qù gōngsī shíxí, yǒude huí jiā dǎ gōng, nǐ yǒu shénme jìhuà?

Wǒ hái méiyǒu xiǎng hǎo. Nǐ ne, Wáng Péng?

Wǒ shǔjià dǎsuàn[a] huí Běijīng qù kàn fùmǔ.

Shì ma? Wǒ tīngshuō Běijīng zhè ge chéngshì hěn yǒu yìsi.

Dāngrán. Běijīng shì Zhōngguó de shǒudū, yě shì Zhōngguó de zhèngzhì, wénhuà zhōngxīn, yǒu hěn duō míngshèng gǔjì.

Duì a, Chángchéng hěn yǒumíng.

Hái yǒu, Běijīng de hǎo fànguǎn duō de bùdéliǎo[1].

Zhēn de? Wǒ qù guo Xiānggǎng, Táiběi, hái méi qù guo Běijīng, yàoshi néng qù Běijīng jiù hǎo le.

Nà nǐ gēn wǒ yìqǐ huí qu ba, wǒ dāng nǐ de dǎoyóu.

Zhēn de ma? Nà tài hǎo le! Hùzhào wǒ yǐjīng yǒu le. Wǒ děi gǎnkuài bàn[b] qiānzhèng.

Nà wǒ mǎshàng gěi lǚxíngshè dǎ diànhuà dìng fēijī piào.

Language Notes

[a] 打算 (dǎsuàn) vs. 計劃 (jìhuà)

打算 (dǎsuàn) is synonymous with 計劃 (jìhuà), but the former is more colloquial.

[b] 辦 (bàn)

To apply for a certificate or an official document, you can use this verb, especially in spoken Chinese, e.g.: 辦護照 (bàn hùzhào) (to apply for a passport), 辦簽證 (bàn qiānzhèng) (to apply for a visa), 辦學生證 (bàn xuéshēng zhèng) (to apply for a student ID), 辦手續 (bàn shǒuxù) (to do paperwork), and 辦結婚證 (bàn jiéhūn zhèng) (to apply for a marriage license).

Vocabulary

Audio

Flashcards

No.	Word	Pinyin	Part of Speech	Definition
1	馬上	*mǎshàng*	adv	immediately, right away
2	放假	*fàng jià*	vo	go on vacation, have time off
	放	*fàng*	v	to let go, to set free
	假	*jià*	n	vacation, holiday
3	公司	*gōngsī*	n	company
4	實習	*shíxí*	v	to intern
5	打工	*dǎ gōng*	vo	to work at a temporary job (often part time)
6	計劃	*jìhuà*	n/v	plan; to plan
7	暑假	*shǔjià*	n	summer vacation
8	打算	*dǎsuàn*	v/n	to plan; plan
9	父母	*fùmǔ*	n	parents, father and mother
10	首都	*shǒudū*	n	capital city
11	政治	*zhèngzhì*	n	politics
12	文化	*wénhuà*	n	culture
13	名勝古蹟	*míngshèng gǔjì*		famous scenic spots and historic sites
14	有名	*yǒumíng*	adj	famous, well-known
15	導遊	*dǎoyóu*	n	tour guide
16	護照	*hùzhào*	n	passport
17	簽證	*qiānzhèng*	n	visa

Your friend wore this shirt to school after a study-abroad semester. What does it tell you about his trip to China?

我登上了万里长城

No.	Word	Pinyin	Part of Speech	Definition
18	旅行社	lǚxíngshè	n	travel agency
19	訂	dìng	v	to reserve, to book (a ticket, a hotel room, etc.)
20	長城	Chángchéng	pn	the Great Wall
21	香港	Xiānggǎng	pn	Hong Kong
22	台北	Táiběi	pn	Taipei

你暑假打算去什麼
地方旅行？

Nǐ shǔjià dǎsuàn qù shénme dìfang lǚxíng?

Where do you plan to travel over summer break?

AFRICA

ASIA

EUROPE

我打算去 ＿＿＿＿＿＿＿ 。

Wǒ dǎsuàn qù ＿＿＿＿＿＿.

See index for corresponding vocabulary or research another term.

How About You?

Grammar

1

不得了 *(bùdéliǎo)* **(extremely)**

The expression 不得了 *(bùdéliǎo)* (extremely), which often follows the structure "adjective + 得 *(de)*," indicates a high degree, in the speaker's judgment, of the attribute signified by the adjective. For example, if one cannot stand the summer heat in a certain place, one can say:

A　那個地方夏天熱得不得了。

Nà ge dìfang xiàtiān rè de bùdéliǎo.

Summer is unbearably hot in that place.

If the Great Wall was extremely crowded, you could say:

B　長城上的人多得不得了。

Chángchéng shàng de rén duō de bùdéliǎo.

There were an incredible number of people on the Great Wall.

Verbs like 想 *(xiǎng)*, 喜歡 *(xǐhuan)*, and 愛 *(ài)* can also be followed by "得 *(de)* + 不得了 *(bùdéliǎo)*."

C　海倫的孩子真可愛，大家喜歡得不得了。

Hǎilún de háizi zhēn kě'ài, dàjiā xǐhuan de bùdéliǎo.

Helen's kid is so adorable. Everyone just loves him.

More
exercises

EXERCISES

Rewrite the sentences by replacing 極了 with 不得了 and adding 得 where appropriate. Use exercise 1 as an example.

1　在高速公路上開車讓小高緊張極了。

　　→ 在高速公路上開車讓小高緊張得不得了。

2　那個商店的傢俱貴極了。

3　有的人覺得國際足球比賽好看極了。

Language Practice

Planning ahead	INTERPERSONAL

In pairs, form a question-and-answer about each other's plans for a particular time, e.g.:

tonight

你今天晚上打算做什麼？

Nǐ jīntiān wǎnshang dǎsuàn zuò shénme?

1 the coming weekend
2 summer break
3 next semester
4 next year

B	INTERPERSONAL	**Survey says**	PRESENTATIONAL

Interview your classmates to find out more about their opinions and experiences. Then report the results of your survey to the class by using "我的同學有的人⋯⋯，有的人⋯⋯" (*Wǒ de tóngxué yǒude rén . . . , yǒude rén . . .*). Each student should choose a different topic to inquire about. Possible topics include: your classmates' thoughts on Chinese pronunciation, Chinese grammar, or Chinese characters; their allergies, living arrangements, or travel plans; or their favorite cuisines, fruits, colors, sports, or beverages, e.g.:

我的同學有的人喜歡喝可樂，有的人
喜歡喝咖啡。

Wǒ de tóngxué yǒude rén xǐhuan hē kělè, yǒude rén xǐhuan hē kāfēi.

Geography buff

In pairs, form a question-and-answer to quiz each other about the capitals of different countries, e.g.:

Q: 中國的首都是哪一個城市？

Zhōngguó de shǒudū shì nǎ yí ge chéngshì?

A: 中國的首都是北京。

Zhōngguó de shǒudū shì Běijīng.

1 美國
Měiguó

3 日本
Rìběn

5 加拿大
Jiā'nádà
(Canada)

7 澳大利亞
Àodàlìyà
(Australia)

2 英國
Yīngguó

4 韓國
Hánguó
(South Korea)

6 墨西哥
Mòxīgē
(Mexico)

Places to go, people to meet

You must have people that you adore or dislike. Share your sentiments with the class.

可愛
kě'ài

海倫的兒子可愛得不得了。
Hǎilún de érzi kě'ài de bùdéliǎo.

1 帥
shuài

3 漂亮
piàoliang

5 酷
kù

7 懶
lǎn

2 聰明
cōngming

4 用功
yònggōng

6 壞
huài

What about places? Where do you like and dislike visiting?

1	漂亮 *piàoliang*	4	乾淨 *gānjìng*	7	冷 *lěng*
2	好玩（兒） *hǎowán(r)*	5	人多 *rén duō*	8	危險 *wēixiǎn*
3	安靜 *ānjìng*	6	熱 *rè*	9	吵 *chǎo*

E
When I get older
INTERPERSONAL

Survey your classmates to find out their aspirations for the future.

你以後想當什麼？老師、導遊、律師，
還是醫生？

Nǐ yǐhòu xiǎng dāng shénme? Lǎoshī, dǎoyóu, lǜshī, háishi yīshēng?

F
INTERPERSONAL
Globetrotter
PRESENTATIONAL

In pairs, recap what you know about Beijing, then find one or two other cities in the world that are similar to it in certain ways. What do they have in common? If you could travel to any city in the world during your next vacation, where would you go? Why? What attractions would you especially want to see? Present your choice of destination and your reasons for selecting it to your class, either in writing on a poster or in a video shared on social media.

Planning an Itinerary

Dialogue 2

Audio

Video

（王朋給旅行社打電話訂機票……）

天一旅行社，你好。

你好。請問六月初[a]到北京的機票多少錢？

您要買單程票還是往返票？

我要買兩張往返票。

你想買哪家航空公司的？

哪家的便宜，就買哪[2]家的。

請等等，我查一下……好幾家航空公司
都有航班[b]。中國國際航空公司，一千五[3]，
直飛。西北航空公司正在打折[c]，差不多
一千四百六十，可是要轉機。

西北只比國航[d]便宜四十幾塊錢[4]，我還是
買國航吧。

哪一天走[e]？哪一天回來？

六月十號走，七月十五號回來。現在可以
訂位子嗎？

可以。你們喜歡靠窗戶的還是靠走道的？

靠走道的。對了[f]，我朋友吃素，麻煩幫她
訂一份素餐。

沒問題……您在北京要訂旅館、租車嗎？

不用，謝謝！

(Wáng Péng gěi lǚxíngshè dǎ diànhuà dìng jīpiào . . .)

Tiān Yī lǚxíngshè, nǐ hǎo.

Nǐ hǎo. Qǐng wèn liùyuè chū^a dào Běijīng de jīpiào

duōshao qián?

Nín yào mǎi dānchéng piào háishi wǎngfǎn piào?

Wǒ yào mǎi liǎng zhāng wǎngfǎn piào.

Nǐ xiǎng mǎi nǎ jiā hángkōng gōngsī de?

Nǎ jiā de piányi, jiù mǎi nǎ² jiā de.

Qǐng děng deng, wǒ chá yixià . . . Hǎo jǐ jiā

hángkōng gōngsī dōu yǒu hángbān^b. Zhōngguó

Guójì Hángkōng Gōngsī, yì qiān wǔ³, zhífēi. Xīběi

Hángkōng Gōngsī zhèngzài dǎ zhé^c, chàbuduō yì

qiān sì bǎi liùshí, kěshì yào zhuǎn jī.

Xīběi zhǐ bǐ Guóháng^d piányi sìshí jǐ kuài qián⁴,

wǒ háishi mǎi Guóháng ba.

Nǎ yì tiān zǒu^e? Nǎ yì tiān huí lai?

Liùyuè shí hào zǒu, qīyuè shíwǔ hào huí lai.

Xiànzài kěyǐ dìng wèizi ma?

Kěyǐ. Nǐmen xǐhuan kào chuānghu de háishi kào

zǒudào de?

Kào zǒudào de. Duì le^f, wǒ péngyou chī sù, máfan

bāng tā dìng yí fèn sùcān.

Méi wèntí . . . Nín zài Běijīng yào dìng lǚguǎn,

zū chē ma?

Búyòng, xièxie!

a 初 (chū), 中 (zhōng), and 底 (dǐ)

月初 (yuè chū) is the first few days of the month, 月中 (yuè zhōng) is the middle of the month, and 月底 (yuè dǐ) is the final days of the month. You can also say 年初 (nián chū) (beginning of the year), 年中 (nián zhōng) (middle of the year), and 年底 (nián dǐ) (end of the year). The words 初 (chū) (beginning), 中 (zhōng) (middle), and 底 (dǐ) (end, bottom) compound with 月 (yuè) or 年 (nián), but are never used with 星期 (xīngqī).

b 航班 (hángbān) vs. 班機 (bānjī)

In Mainland China, people use 航班 (hángbān), whereas in Taiwan, people say 班機 (bānjī).

c 打折 (dǎ zhé)

Discounts are expressed differently in Chinese from English. In English the emphasis is on the amount that is given as a discount, e.g., ten percent off. In Chinese, however, the emphasis is on the post-discount amount. Therefore, ten percent off in Chinese would be rendered as 打九折 (dǎ jiǔ zhé), or ninety percent of the original price, and twenty-five percent off would be 打七五折 (dǎ qī wǔ zhé), or seventy-five percent of the original price. 打對折 (dǎ duì zhé) means that the discounted price is fifty percent of the original price.

d 國航 (Guóháng)

中國國際航空公司 (Zhōngguó Guójì Hángkōng Gōngsī) (Air China, lit. China International Airlines) is often shortened to 國航 (Guóháng).

e 走 (zǒu)

As you learned in Lesson 10, the basic meaning of 走 (zǒu) is "to walk." Here, 走 (zǒu) means to leave or to depart.

f 對了 (duì le)

This term is often used when one suddenly thinks of something. For instance, if a student is saying goodbye to his classmate, and all of a sudden it occurs to him that they need to study for a test the next day, the student can say: 明天見。……對了，明天考試，別忘了復習。 (Míngtiān jiàn … Duì le, míngtiān kǎo shì, bié wàng le fùxí) (See you tomorrow … Oh right, we have a test tomorrow. Don't forget to review.)

你去旅行的時候會帶些什麼東西？

Nǐ qù lǚxíng de shíhou huì dài xiē shénme dōngxi?

What would you bring with you when traveling?

How About You?

我會帶 ＿＿＿＿＿＿＿＿ 。
Wǒ huì dài ＿＿＿＿＿＿＿＿ .

See index for corresponding vocabulary or research another term.

Vocabulary

No.	Word	Pinyin	Part of Speech	Definition
1	初	*chū*	n	beginning
2	單程	*dānchéng*	n	one-way trip
3	往返	*wǎngfǎn*	v	make a round trip, go there and back
4	航空	*hángkōng*	n	aviation
5	查	*chá*	v	to check, to look into
6	航班	*hángbān*	n	scheduled flight
7	千	*qiān*	nu	thousand
8	直飛	*zhí fēi*		fly directly
9	打折	*dǎ zhé*	vo	to sell at a discount, to give a discount
10	轉機	*zhuǎn jī*	vo	change planes
11	靠	*kào*	v	to lean on, to lean against, to be next to
12	窗戶	*chuānghu*	n	window
13	走道	*zǒudào*	n	aisle
14	份	*fèn*	m	(measure word for meal orders, jobs)
15	素餐	*sùcān*	n	vegetarian meal
16	旅館	*lǚguǎn*	n	hotel
17	租	*zū*	v	to rent
18	中國國際航空公司	*Zhōngguó Guójì Hángkōng Gōngsī*	pn	Air China
19	西北航空公司	*Xīběi Hángkōng Gōngsī*	pn	Northwest Airlines

Audio

Flashcards

You decide to bypass the travel agent and book your trip from Beijing to Shanghai using an app. What flight options are available?

Chinese Chat

You're exchanging WeChat messages with a friend about the upcoming summer break. How would you complete the conversation?

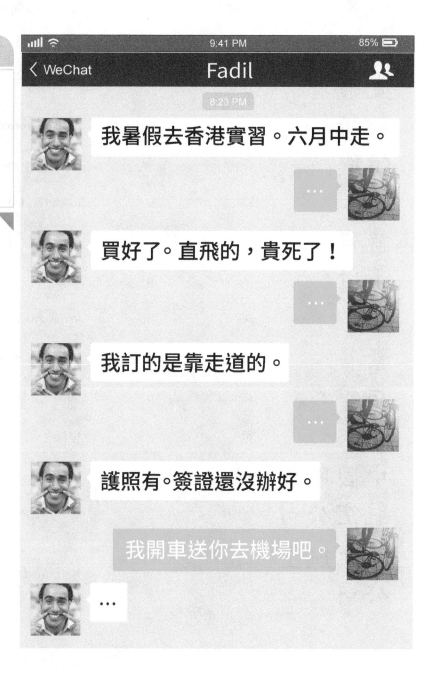

Grammar

Question pronouns as indefinite references
(whoever, whatever, etc.)

The equivalent of the "question pronoun + -ever" expression in English is formed by repeating a question pronoun in two separate but related clauses in the same sentence. The first occurrence refers to an indefinite person, object, time, place, etc. The second occurrence then refers to that same person, object, time, place, etc.

A 誰想去，誰就去。

Shéi xiǎng qù, shéi jiù qù.

Whoever wants to go can go.

B 你吃什麼，我就吃什麼。

Nǐ chī shénme, wǒ jiù chī shénme.

I'll have whatever you're having.

C 哪雙鞋便宜，就買哪雙。

Nǎ shuāng xié piányi, jiù mǎi nǎ shuāng.

Buy whichever pair of shoes is the cheapest.

D Q: 你想怎麼走？

Ní xiǎng zěnme zǒu?

Which way do you want to take?

A: 怎麼近，怎麼走。

Zěnme jìn, zěnme zǒu.

Let's take whichever's the shortest.

In this kind of sentence, sometimes the two occurrences of the question pronoun play the same grammatical role, i.e, both are subjects, as in (A); or both are objects, as in (B). Sometimes the two occurrences of the question pronoun perform different grammatical functions. In (C), for example, the first 哪雙 (nǎ shuāng) is the subject whereas the second 哪雙 (nǎ shuāng) is the object. The adverb 就 (jiù) often precedes the verb in the second clause, but not always, as in (E) and (F) below.

E 哪兒安靜，我住哪兒。

Nǎr ānjìng, wǒ zhù nǎr.

I'll live wherever it's quiet.

F Q: 他找誰幫他搬傢俱？

Tā zhǎo shéi bāng tā bān jiājù?

Who's he going to ask to help him move his furniture?

A: 誰身體棒，他找誰。

Shéi shēntǐ bàng, tā zhǎo shéi.

He'll ask whoever is strong.

EXERCISES

More exercises

In pairs, form a question-and answer and use the question pronouns as indefinite references to show you're being flexible or accommodating. Use exercise 1 as an example.

1 下個週末　　　去哪兒

→ Student A 下個週末我們去哪兒？

Student B 你想去哪兒，我們就去哪兒。

2 今天晚飯　　　吃什麼

3 明年暑假　　　做什麼

More characters

① 計 ② 訂 ③ 證

What do the characters mean?

What is the common radical?

What does the radical mean?

How does the radical relate to the overall meaning of the characters?

Numbers over one thousand

You have already learned how to count in Chinese up to a thousand.

一	十	百	千
yī	*shí*	*bǎi*	*qiān*
1	**10**	**100**	**1,000**
one	ten	hundred	thousand

In Chinese, the next-largest unit after a thousand is not ⊗ 十千, but 萬 *(wàn)*. Even though long Arabic numbers are segmented into three-digit sets in writing and in print, such numbers have to be expressed in four-digit sets. The four-digit set of 萬 *(wàn)* starts at the fifth digit from the right; the next four-digit set is that of 億 *(yì)*. In the examples below, we have indicated such divisions as an aid.

Chinese	Pinyin	Chinese Mental Division	Arabic Number	English
（一）千	*(yì) qiān*	1000	1,000	thousand
（一）萬	*(yí) wàn*	1:0000	10,000	ten thousand
十萬	*shí wàn*	10:0000	100,000	hundred thousand
（一）百萬	*(yì) bǎi wàn*	100:0000	1,000,000	million
（一）千萬	*(yì) qiān wàn*	1000:0000	10,000,000	ten million
（一）億/ （一）萬萬	*(yí) yì/ (yí) wànwàn*	1:0000:0000	100,000,000	hundred million
十億	*shí yì*	10:0000:0000	1,000,000,000	billion

A 12,345 (1｜2345)

一萬兩千三百四十五

yí wàn liǎng qiān sān bǎi sìshíwǔ

B 25,000 (2｜5000)

兩萬五千

liǎng wàn wǔ qiān

C 340,876 (34｜0876)

三十四萬〇八百七十六

sānshísì wàn líng bā bǎi qīshíliù

D 1,000,900,000 (10｜0090｜0000)

十億〇九十萬

shí yì líng jiǔshí wàn

More exercises

EXERCISES

Say the following amounts of money in Chinese. Use exercise 1 as an example.

1 $1111.11

→ 一千一百一十一塊一毛一分錢

2 $2202.59

3 $34560.05

---

4 | **Comparative sentences using 比 (bǐ) (II)**

In a sentence where 比 (bǐ) is used, a numeral + measure word combination can be placed after the adjective to indicate a disparity in numerical terms. [See also Grammar 1, Lesson 11.]

> X + 比 (bǐ) + Y + adjective + numeral + measure word + noun

A 我們班比你們班多四個學生。

Wǒmen bān bǐ nǐmen bān duō sì ge xuésheng.

Our class is larger than yours by four students.

B　這件襯衫比那件襯衫貴二十塊錢。

Zhè jiàn chènshān bǐ nà jiàn chènshān guì èrshí kuài qián.

This shirt is twenty dollars more expensive than that shirt.

C　我的房租比你的便宜五百塊。

Wǒ de fángzū bǐ nǐ de piányi wǔ bǎi kuài.

My rent is five hundred dollars cheaper than yours.

D　我表弟比我小三歲。

Wǒ biǎodì bǐ wǒ xiǎo sān suì.

My cousin is three years younger than I am.

EXERCISES

Based on the given information, join these sentences to describe the difference by inserting the adjectives in parentheses and 比 where appropriate. Use exercise 1 as an example.

More exercises

1　我們班有三十個學生，你們班有二十七個
　　學生。（多）

　　→　我們班比你們班多三個學生。

2　小王今年十八歲，小高今年十九歲。（小）

3　藍色的褲子三十號，綠色的褲子三十
　　四號。（大）

Characterize it!

What do the characters mean?
What is the common radical?
What does the radical mean?
How does the radical relate to the overall meaning of the characters?

❶ 　❷ 　❸

More characters

Language Practice

G   Good deal

A furniture store is having a big sale. Compare the original prices and the sale prices. Then,
in pairs, figure out what discount the store is offering on each item, e.g.:

Q: 這張床打幾折？

Zhè zhāng chuáng dǎ jǐ zhé?

A: 這張床打八折。

Zhè zhāng chuáng dǎ bā zhé.

$1000
$800

1 $800 $400

2 $500 $425

3 $80 $40

4 $120 $90

H   Up to you

Ms. Wang has just started dating Mr. Li. She wants to be nice and asks Mr. Li what he would
like to do, where he would like to go, etc. Mr. Li also wants to be nice, so he leaves it up to Ms.
Wang to decide. In pairs, role-play and see if you and your partner can settle on a day, time,
place, and activity, e.g.:

Ms. Wang   你想去哪兒玩兒？

Nǐ xiǎng qù nǎr wánr?

Mr. Li   你想去哪兒玩兒，我們就去哪兒玩兒。

Nǐ xiǎng qù nǎr wánr, wǒmen jiù qù nǎr wánr.

1   Find out what he would like to do.

2   Find out what cuisine he prefers.

3   Find out when he would like to see a movie.

4   Find out which city he would like to travel to.

By the way

In pairs, role-play the following scenarios using 對了 (duì le).

1   You have just said goodbye to your friend, but suddenly it occurs to you that you need to borrow a Chinese book from him. What do you say?

2   You are talking to your mom on the phone to ask for more money, and she says yes. You thank her. It occurs to you that you should mention your plan to travel to China for the summer and ask for her opinion.

3   You are on the phone with your friend discussing booking plane tickets for both of you online. Before you hang up the phone, it occurs to you that you should ask for your friend's seat preferences.

Price-wise

In pairs, compare notes with your partner and find out the difference between what you pay for rent, security deposits, and utilities. Then report to the class.

1 房租

fángzū

2 押金

yājīn

3 水電費

shuǐ diàn fèi

Trip advisor

Divide the class into two groups: travelers and travel agents.

Travelers: As experienced travelers, what questions would you ask when making a flight reservation? Make your list as detailed as possible.

Travel Agents: As experienced travel agents, what questions would you ask customers booking flights? Make your list as detailed as possible.

After each group completes its list, the two groups should compare lists and see if any important questions have been left out. Then the whole class will decide which list is better.

文化

Continue
to explore

A Chinese high-speed train

Rail travel

Rail remains the major means of domestic travel in China. During the Chinese New Year period, railroad stations across the country are overcrowded with travelers waiting for trains or seeking tickets. High-speed trains offer three classes of service: business class (商務座) (shāngwù zuò), which, as the most expensive, offers the most comfort; first class (一等座) (yīděng zuò); and second class (二等座) (èrděng zuò). There are no sleeping berths on high-speed trains. Old-fashioned "regular" trains offer four classes of service: hard seat (硬座) (yìng zuò), soft seat (軟座) (ruǎn zuò), hard sleeper (硬臥) (yìng wò), and soft sleeper (軟臥) (ruǎn wò).

The three oldest and largest travel agencies in China are International Travel Agencies, 國際旅行社 (Guójì Lǚxíngshè) or 國旅 (Guólǚ); China Travel Agencies, 中國旅行社 (Zhōngguó Lǚxíngshè) or 中旅 (Zhōnglǚ); and Youth Travel Agencies, 青年旅行社 (Qīngnián Lǚxíngshè), or 青旅 (Qīnglǚ). While 國旅 (Guólǚ) and 中旅 (Zhōng Lǚ) mainly serve foreign tourists and overseas Chinese, respectively, 青旅 (Qīnglǚ) is primarily oriented toward Chinese citizens. The divisions among types of travel agency, however, have become less distinct in recent years.

Travel agencies

Airlines

Apart from Air China (中國國際航空公司) (*Zhōngguó Guójì Hángkōng Gōngsī*), China's major airlines are China Eastern (中國東方航空) (*Zhōngguó Dōngfāng Hángkōng*), China Southern (中國南方航空) (*Zhōngguó Nánfāng Hángkōng*), and Hainan Airlines (海南航空) (*Hǎinán Hángkōng*). Additionally, there are more than a dozen airline companies specializing in regional routes and half a dozen low-cost carriers.

Attitudes toward travel

In traditional China, the general attitude toward travel was largely ambivalent. As fundamentally an agrarian people, the Chinese were, as expressed in the idiomatic phrase 安土重遷 (*ān tǔ zhòng qiān*), "attached to their native land and reluctant to move." Confucius even admonished that "One should not travel afar while one's parents are still alive, unless there are excellent reasons to do so," 父母在不遠遊，遊必有方 (*fùmǔ zài bù yuǎn yóu, yóu bì yǒu fāng*). On the other hand, however, travel was perceived to be a crucial component of one's intellectual development, a view that is registered in the celebrated saying that a good scholar should "Read ten thousand volumes and travel ten thousand miles," 讀萬卷書，行萬里路 (*dú wàn juàn shū, xíng wàn lǐ lù*). Indeed, many scholars in premodern China were well traveled, as they had to trek, many by boat along the Grand Canal, to take the civil service examinations in the imperial capital.

COMPARE & CONTRAST

1 Compare Beijing with the capital of your country in terms of location, population, political and cultural significance, and famous tourist sites.

2 You may be familiar with Washington, D.C., but how much do you know about Beijing? Both cities are full of monuments. Research the most significant memorial structures on the National Mall in Washington and in Tiananmen Square in Beijing. What historical events and figures do they commemorate? How are the two public spaces used?

Lesson Wrap-Up

Make It Flow

The following sentences are arranged in a logical order. Combine the sentences into a coherent narrative. Replace nouns with pronouns and change periods to commas where appropriate. Avoid unnecessary repetitions of subject pronouns. Add the connective devices 有的…有的…有的… (*yǒu de… yǒu de… yǒu de…*), 也…也… (*yě… yě…*), 不但…而且… (*búdàn… érqiě…*), and …以後 (*…yǐhòu*) where appropriate.

學校馬上就要放暑假了。王朋的一些同學去暑期班學習。王朋的一些同學回家打工。王朋的一些同學去公司實習。王朋告訴李友他要回北京看父母。李友對北京很有興趣。王朋給李友介紹說，北京是中國的首都。王朋給李友介紹說，北京是中國的政治中心。王朋給李友介紹說，北京是中國的文化中心。王朋給李友介紹說，北京有很多名勝古蹟。王朋給李友介紹說，北京好吃的飯館多得不得了。李友聽了王朋的介紹。李友說要是她能去北京就好了。王朋讓李友一起去。王朋說他當導遊。李友很高興。李友說她得趕快辦簽証。王朋說他馬上訂機票。

Presentation

Present a video or slideshow of a destination in China. Include sights you want to see. How is your destination perceived in China? What is it famous for? The class will vote on where to go.

Skit

You're flying to Hong Kong to visit your parents; your partner is a travel agent in Chinatown. Before calling the agent, list key information you'll need: time and city of departure, direct or indirect flight, passport and visa requirement, seat preference, etc. If you're the agent, what information will you need that is not mentioned above? Do travelers need a visa and a passport to enter Hong Kong?

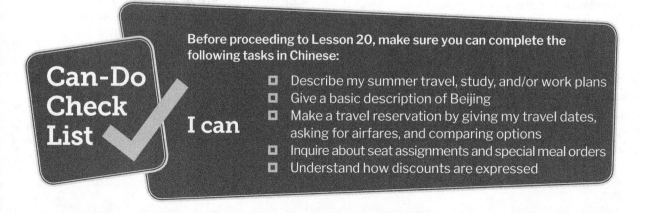

Can-Do Check List

I can

Before proceeding to Lesson 20, make sure you can complete the following tasks in Chinese:

- ☐ Describe my summer travel, study, and/or work plans
- ☐ Give a basic description of Beijing
- ☐ Make a travel reservation by giving my travel dates, asking for airfares, and comparing options
- ☐ Inquire about seat assignments and special meal orders
- ☐ Understand how discounts are expressed

在機場

Zài jīchǎng

AT THE AIRPORT

Learning Objectives

In this lesson, you will learn to:

- Check in at the airport
- Wish departing friends a safe journey and remind them to keep in touch
- Greet guests at the airport
- Compliment someone's language ability
- Ask about someone's health
- Take leave of someone

Relate & Get Ready

In your own culture/community:

- What do people say when seeing someone off on a trip?
- For travel over the summer, is road tripping a popular option?
- What do people say when greeting guests at the airport, train, or bus station?
- What local food should foreign guests try?

Checking in at the Airport

Dialogue 1

（在國航的服務台……）

小姐，這是我們的[1]機票。

請把護照給我看看。你們有幾件行李要托運？

兩件。這個包不托運，我們帶上飛機。

麻煩[a]您把箱子拿上來[2]。

小姐，沒超重吧？

沒有。這是你們的護照、機票，這是登機牌[b]。請到五號登機口[c]上飛機。

謝謝。

……

哥哥，你們去北京了，就我一個人在這兒。

小紅，別哭，我們幾個星期就回來，你好好兒地[1]學英文，別亂跑。

不是幾個星期就回來，是幾個星期以後才回來。

別擔心，我姐姐小音會照顧你。

對，別擔心。

飛機幾點起飛？

中午十二點，還有兩個多小時。

白英愛，你什麼時候去紐約實習？

我不去紐約了。文中幫我在加州找了一份實習工作。

對，我們下個星期開車去加州。

是嗎？一邊兒開車，一邊兒玩兒，太好了。

開車小心。祝你們玩兒得[1]高興。

祝你們一路平安。到了北京以後[3]，別忘了給我們發個電子郵件。

好，那我們秋天見。

下個學期見。

再見！

Pinyin Dialogue

(Zài Guóháng de fúwùtái . . .)

 Xiǎojiě, zhè shì wǒmen de[1] jīpiào.

 Qǐng bǎ hùzhào gěi wǒ kàn kan. Nǐmen yǒu jǐ jiàn

xíngli yào tuōyùn?

 Liǎng jiàn. Zhè ge bāo bù tuōyùn, wǒmen dài

shàng fēijī.

 Máfan[a] nín bǎ xiāngzi ná shàng lai[2].

 Xiǎojiě, méi chāozhòng ba?

 Méiyǒu. Zhè shì nǐmen de hùzhào, jīpiào, zhè shì

dēngjīpái[b]. Qǐng dào wǔ hào dēngjīkǒu[c]

shàng fēijī.

 Xièxie.

. . .

 Gēge, nǐmen qù Běijīng le, jiù wǒ yí ge rén

zài zhèr.

 Xiǎo Hóng, bié kū, wǒmen jǐ ge xīngqī jiù huí lai,

nǐ hǎohāor de[1] xué Yīngwén, bié luàn pǎo.

 Bú shì jǐ ge xīngqī jiù huí lai, shì jǐ ge xīngqī yǐhòu

cái huí lai.

 Bié dān xīn, wǒ jiějie Xiǎoyīn huì zhàogu nǐ.

 Duì, bié dān xīn.

 Fēijī jǐ diǎn qǐfēi?

 Zhōngwǔ shí'èr diǎn, hái yǒu liǎng ge duō xiǎoshí.

 Bái Yīng'ài, nǐ shénme shíhou qù Niǔyuē shíxí?

 Wǒ bú qù Niǔyuē le. Wénzhōng bāng wǒ zài

Jiāzhōu zhǎo le yí fèn shíxí gōngzuò.

 Duì, wǒmen xià ge xīngqī kāi chē qù Jiāzhōu.

 Shì ma? Yìbiānr kāi chē, yìbiānr wánr, tài hǎo le.

 Kāi chē xiǎoxīn. Zhù nǐmen wánr de[1] gāoxìng.

 Zhù nǐmen yí lù píng'ān. Dào le Běijīng yǐhòu[3],

bié wàng le gěi wǒmen fā ge diànzǐ yóujiàn.

 Hǎo, nà wǒmen qiūtiān jiàn.

 Xià ge xuéqī jiàn.

 Zàijiàn!

Language Notes

a 麻煩 (máfan)

When asking others for help, one polite way is to use
麻煩 (máfan) as a verb and begin the request with the
phrase 麻煩你 (máfan nǐ) or 麻煩您 (máfan nín),
e.g.: 麻煩您今天晚上給我打一個電
話 (Máfan nín jīntiān wǎnshang gěi wǒ dǎ yí ge diàn huà)
(Could I trouble you to give me a call this evening?).

b 登機牌 (dēngjīpái)

In Chinese, a boarding pass can be referred to as either
登機牌 (dēngjīpái) (lit. boarding card) or 登機證
(dēngjīzhèng) (lit. boarding certificate).

c 登機口 (dēngjīkǒu)

In Mainland China, boarding gates are called
登機口 (dēngjīkǒu). In Taiwan and Hong Kong,
they are called 登機門 (dēngjīmén) and 閘口
(zhákǒu), respectively.

Vocabulary

No.	Word	Pinyin	Part of Speech	Definition
1	行李	xíngli	n	luggage
2	托運	tuōyùn	v	to check (luggage)
3	包	bāo	n	bag, sack, bundle, package
4	箱子	xiāngzi	n	suitcase, box
5	超重	chāozhòng	v	to be overweight (of luggage, freight, etc.)
	超	chāo	v	to exceed, to surpass
6	登機牌	dēngjīpái	n	boarding pass
	牌	pái	n	plate, tablet, card
7	登機口	dēngjīkǒu	n	boarding gate
	口	kǒu	n	opening, entrance, mouth
8	哭	kū	v	to cry, to weep
9	地	de	p	(particle to link adverbial and verb) [See Grammar 1.]
10	照顧	zhàogu	v	to look after, to care for, to attend to
11	起飛	qǐfēi	v	(of airplanes) to take off
12	小心	xiǎoxīn	v	to be careful
13	一路平安	yí lù píng'ān		have a good trip, bon voyage

Audio

Flashcards

Chinese knots (中國結) (*Zhōngguójié*) like this can be given as gifts for good luck. When would be an appropriate occasion for you to give this knot to someone?

GET
Real
WITH **CHINESE**

坐飛機旅行，什麼東西你不托運？

Zuò fēijī lǚxíng, shénme dōngxi nǐ bù tuōyùn?

What items do you not check in when traveling by plane?

我不會托運 _____ 。
Wǒ bú huì tuōyùn _____ .

See index for corresponding vocabulary or research another term.

Grammar

1   Comparing 的 (de), 得 (de), and 地 (de)

的 (de) usually follows an attributive, which can be formed by an adjective, a noun, or a verb phrase.

A 漂亮的女孩子

piàoliang de nǚ háizi

pretty girl

B 哥哥的公司

gēge de gōngsī

older brother's company

C 我的臥室

wǒ de wòshì

my bedroom

D 剛買的機票

gāng mǎi de jīpiào

a recently purchased plane ticket

E 媽媽給我們做的蛋糕

māma gěi wǒmen zuò de dàngāo

the cake Mom made for us

In most cases, 的 (de) is followed by a noun, as seen in (A) to (E), but it can also precede an adjective or verb if that adjective or verb serves as the subject or object in the sentence.

F 南京的熱[是有名的]。

Nánjīng de rè [shì yǒumíng de].

Nanjing's hot weather [is well known].

G 他的死[讓我們很難受]。

Tā de sǐ [ràng wǒmen hěn nánshòu].

His death [made us very sad].

地 (de) usually links an adverbial to a following verb. An adverbial can be an adjective, an adverb, or a set phrase, and is not always followed by 地 (de).

H	慢慢兒（地）吃		J	一直（地）走

H 慢慢兒（地）吃
mànmānr de chī
eat slowly

J 一直（地）走
yìzhí de zǒu
to walk straight forward

I 很高興地說
hěn gāoxìng de shuō
to say happily

K 好好兒（地）玩兒
hǎohāor de wánr
to have some real fun

得 (de) is used after a verb or an adjective to connect it with a descriptive complement or a complement of degree.

L 跑得很快
pǎo de hěn kuài
to run fast

N 高興得跳起來
gāoxìng de tiào qi lai
to jump up with joy

M 做菜做得很好
zuò cài zuò de hěn hǎo
to cook well

O 危險得不得了
wēixiǎn de bùdéliǎo
unbelievably dangerous

Compare the following two sentences:

P 他高興地唱著歌走回宿舍。
Tā gāoxìng de chàng zhe gē zǒu huí sùshè.
He sang happily on his way back to the dorm.

Q 他高興得唱起歌來了。
Tā gāoxìng de chàng qǐ gē lai le.
He was so happy that he started to sing.

In (P), 高興 (gāoxìng) is used to describe the manner of his singing. In (Q), 高興 (gāoxìng) is the cause of his singing. Patterns for 的 (de), 地 (de), and 得 (de) are provided below.

Attributive + 的 (de) + noun
Adverbial + 地 (de) + verb
Verb/adjective + 得 (de) + adjective/verb

EXERCISES

Fill in the blanks with 的, 得, or 地 where appropriate. Use exercise 1 as an example.

More
exercises

1   公寓 ＿＿＿ 房租貴 ＿＿＿ 不得了。

　　→ 公寓的房租貴得不得了。

2   要是希望游泳游 ＿＿＿ 又快又好，得每天
　　好好兒 ＿＿＿ 練習。

3   他托運 ＿＿＿ 行李被慢慢 ＿＿＿ 送上飛機。

---

2   ┌───┐
　　│   The 把 (bǎ) construction (II)   │
　　└───┘

You can use 把 (bǎ) with a directional complement. The basic constructions are as follows.

把 (bǎ) **with simple directional complements:**

Pattern A
Subject + 把 + object + verb + 來/去
　　　　　(bǎ)　　　　　　　　(lai/qu)

A   請把你的床搬來。

Qǐng bǎ nǐ de chuáng bān lai.

Please move your bed here.

B   小王把冰茶拿去了。

Xiǎo Wáng bǎ bīngchá ná qu le.

Little Wang took the iced tea (with him).

Subject + 把 + object + verb + 上/下/進/出/回/過/起/開/到 + place word
(bǎ) *(shang/xia/jin/chu/hui/guo/qi/kai/dao)*

C 你把孩子送回爺爺家。

Nǐ bǎ háizi sòng hui yéye jiā.

Take the child back to Grandpa's.

D 媽媽把椅子搬上樓了。

Māma bǎ yǐzi bān shang lóu le.

Mom took the chair upstairs.

Note that place words come after the verb and directional complement.

把 (bǎ) with compound directional complements:

Pattern A
Subject + 把 + object + verb + 上/下/進/出/回/過/起/開 + 來/去
(bǎ) *(shang/xia/jin/chu/hui/guo/qi/kai)* *(lai/qu)*

E 你把書拿起來。

Nǐ bǎ shū ná qi lai.

Pick up the book.

F 小李把車開回去了。

Xiǎo Lǐ bǎ chē kāi hui qu le.

Little Li drove the car back.

Pattern B
Subject + 把 + object + verb + 上/下/進/出/回/過/起/到 + place word + 來/去
(bǎ) *(shang/xia/jin/chu/hui/guo/qi/dao)* *(lai/qu)*

G 麻煩把包拿上桌來。

Máfan bǎ bāo ná shang zhuō lai.

Please put the bag on the table.

H 他把剛買的桌子搬進房間來了。

Tā bǎ gang mǎi de zhuōzi bān jin fáng jiān lai le.

He moved the table that he had just bought into the room.

Note that the place word is inserted in the compound directional complement, between 上/下/進/出/回/過/起/到 (shang/xia/jin/chu/hui/guo/qi/dao) and 來/去 (lai/qu).

<u>3</u> | ···的時候 (...de shíhou) **and** ···以後 (...yǐhòu) **compared**

With "Verb 1 + 的時候 (de shíhou), verb 2...," the second action and the first action take place simultaneously.

A 走的時候別忘了帶些錢。

Zǒu de shíhou bié wàng le dài xiē qián.

Don't forget to take some money with you when you leave.

B 我看見他的時候，他正在打球。

Wǒ kàn jiàn tā de shíhou, tā zhèngzài dǎ qiú.

When I saw him, he was playing ball.

C 妹妹看短信的時候，一邊看一邊笑。

Mèimei kàn duǎnxìn de shíhou, yìbiān kàn yìbiān xiào.

When my little sister was reading the text messages, she laughed as she read along.

However, with "Verb 1 以後 (yǐhòu), verb 2...," the second action takes place after the first one.

D 他從家裡走了以後，才想起來忘了帶錢。

Tā cóng jiā li zǒu le yǐhòu, cái xiǎng qi lai wàng le dài qián.

He didn't realize until after he had left home that he'd forgotten to take some money with him.

The "⋯的時候 (. . . de shíhou)" structure describes two simultaneous actions. You may say in English, "When I get to China, I will eat Beijing roast duck," when you really mean, "After I get to China, I'll eat Beijing roast duck." In Chinese, that idea has to be conveyed with 以後 (yǐhòu):

E 我到中國以後要吃北京烤鴨。

Wǒ dào Zhōngguó yǐhòu yào chī Běijīng kǎoyā.

I will eat some Beijing roast duck after I arrive in China.

[烤鴨 [kǎoyā] [roast duck]. See Dialogue 2.]

[✗ 我到中國的時候要吃北京烤鴨。]

(This sentence is incorrect because you won't eat Beijing roast duck until after you arrive in China.)

More
exercises

EXERCISES

Fill in the blanks with ⋯的時候 or ⋯以後 where appropriate. Use exercise 1 as an example.

1 開車 ＿＿＿＿＿＿＿ 發短信太危險了。

→ 開車的時候發短信太危險了。

2 旅行 ＿＿＿＿＿＿＿ 小王不喜歡帶太多行李。

3 大家約好打完球＿＿＿＿＿＿＿去喝咖啡。

Characterize it!

More
characters

| What do the characters mean? |
| What is the common radical? |
| What does the radical mean? |
| How does the radical relate to the overall meaning of the characters? |

Language Practice

Playing by the rules

PRESENTATIONAL

Multitasking can be problematic. In pairs, use the visual prompts to figure out what the rules are in the various contexts provided, e.g.:

做功課的時候，不准／不能
看電視。

Zuò gōngkè de shíhou, bù zhǔn/bù néng kàn diànshì.

1     2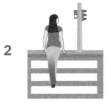

3     4

Could I trouble you?

INTERPERSONAL

In pairs, take turns asking for help from each other using 麻煩你 (*máfan nǐ*). Think of three or four things you would like your partner to help you with, e.g.:

Q: 麻煩你幫我準備考試，好嗎？

Máfan nǐ bāng wǒ zhǔnbèi kǎoshì, hǎo ma?

A: 行，沒問題。

Xíng, méi wèntí.

Big move

You (living on the second floor) and your housemate (living on the third floor) decided to switch rooms with each other. Based on the image below, describe which items need to be moved upstairs and downstairs. For things to be moved upstairs, you should say 把＿＿＿＿搬／拿上（樓）去 *(Bǎ＿＿＿＿ bān/ná shang [lóu] qu)*; for things to be moved downstairs, you should say 把＿＿＿＿搬／拿下（樓）來 *(Bǎ＿＿＿＿ bān/ná xia [lóu] lai)*.

Before

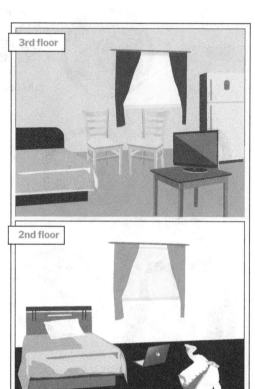

After

1

2

3

4

5

6

7

Positive energy

In pairs, use the prompts to practice giving warm, occasion-appropriate wishes to your partner, e.g.:

On his/her birthday

生日快樂！

Shēngrì kuàilè!

1 Before he/she gets on a plane

2 On New Year's Day

3 Before he/she takes an examination

4 Before he/she goes on a fun date

Don't stress

In pairs, use the prompts to practice giving reassurance to your partner about his/her vexing situation, e.g.:

Your friend is quite anxious before an exam.

別擔心，明天的考試很簡單。

Bié dān xīn, míngtiān de kǎoshì hěn jiǎndān.

1 Your friend hopes his/her dog will be cared for while he/she is away.

2 Your friend isn't sure if his/her date will like him/her.

3 Your friend is worried he/she won't be able to afford clothes at a store.

4 Your friend thinks that his/her baggage might be overweight.

In proper order

INTERPERSONAL

In pairs, form a question-and-answer to find out when Wang Peng takes a shower, takes his medicine, goes online, and cleans his room, e.g.:

Q: 王朋什麼時候做功課？吃飯以前
還是吃飯以後？

Wáng Péng shénme shíhou zuò gōngkè? Chī fàn yǐqián háishi chī fàn yǐhòu?

A: 他吃了晚飯以後做功課。

Tā chī le wǎnfàn yǐhòu zuò gōngkè.

G

Don't do anything I wouldn't do

INTERPERSONAL

Survey each of your classmates about his/her summer plans and how long the activities he/she has planned will last. Remind him/her to keep in touch, and give appropriate good wishes before moving on to the next person.

Counter culture

PRESENTATIONAL

Unlike Li You, you may not have a Chinese friend to accompany you on your trip to China and be your interpreter or tour guide. In pairs, make a list of questions and responses that may come in handy when you check in at a Chinese airline counter.

Chinese Chat

Your friend is going on a trip and is texting you to say goodbye. How would you respond?

Marian

我已經登機，飛機馬上就起飛了。謝謝你開車送我來機場，回去路上開車小心。

7 minutes ago

...

6 minutes ago

對了，也請多照顧我的狗。我到了香港再給你發短信。暑假快樂！

3 minutes ago

...

1 minute ago

📷 Type your message...

Arriving in Beijing

Dialogue 2

Audio

Video

（在北京首都機場……）

小朋！

爸，媽！

累壞了吧？

還好[4]。爸，媽，我給你們介紹一下，這是我的同學李友。

叔叔，阿姨[5a]，你們好。

歡迎你來北京。

李友，你的中文說得真好。

謝謝。是因為王朋教得好。

哪裡，是因為你聰明。

哎，你們倆都聰明。

小朋，你好像瘦了點兒。是不是打工太忙，沒有時間吃飯？

我沒瘦。我常常運動，身體比以前棒多了。

小紅怎麼樣？

她很好，英文水平提高了很多。

走吧，我們上車以後，再慢慢兒地聊吧。爺爺、奶奶在烤鴨店等我們呢！

烤鴨店？

(Zài Běijīng Shǒudū Jīchǎng . . .)

 Xiǎo Péng!

 Bà, mā !

 Lèi huài le ba?

 Hái hǎo [4]. Bà, mā, wǒ gěi nǐmen jièshao yí xià, zhè shì wǒ de tóngxué Lǐ Yǒu.

 Shūshu, āyí [5] [a], nǐmen hǎo.

 Huānyíng nǐ lái Běijīng.

 Lǐ Yǒu, nǐ de Zhōngwén shuō de zhēn hǎo.

 Xièxie. Shì yīnwèi Wáng Péng jiāo de hǎo.

 Nǎli, shì yīnwèi nǐ cōngming.

 Āi, nǐmen liǎ dōu cōngming.

 Xiǎo Péng, nǐ hǎoxiàng shòu le diǎnr. Shì bu shì dǎ gōng tài máng, méiyǒu shíjiān chī fàn?

 Wǒ méi shòu. Wǒ chángcháng yùndòng, shēntǐ bǐ yǐqián bàng duō le.

 Xiǎo Hóng zěnmeyàng?

 Tā hěn hǎo, Yīngwén shuǐpíng tígāo le hěn duō.

 Zǒu ba, wǒmen shàng chē yǐhòu, zài mànmānr de liáo ba. Yéye, nǎinai zài kǎoyā diàn děng wǒmen ne!

 Kǎoyā diàn?

Language Note

a 叔叔 (shūshu) **and** 阿姨 (āyí)

Young people often address a nonrelative as 叔叔 (shūshu) (uncle) or 阿姨 (āyí) (aunt) if the person is approximately the same age as their parents. These respectful forms of address can be applied even to strangers. [See Grammar 5 for additional terms for kin.]

Vocabulary

Audio

Flashcards

No.	Word	Pinyin	Part of Speech	Definition
1	叔叔	shūshu	n	uncle [See Grammar 5.]
2	阿姨	āyí	n	aunt [See Grammar 5.]
3	歡迎	huānyíng	v	to welcome
4	瘦	shòu	adj	thin, skinny, lean
5	爺爺	yéye	n	paternal grandfather [See Grammar 5.]
6	奶奶	nǎinai	n	paternal grandmother [See Grammar 5.]
7	烤鴨	kǎoyā	n	roast duck
8	首都機場	Shǒudū Jīchǎng	pn	the Capital Airport (in Beijing)

等飛機的時候，
你常常做什麼？

Děng fēijī de shíhou, nǐ chángcháng zuò shénme?

What do you often do when waiting for a flight?

How About You?

我 _____ 。

Wǒ _____ .

See index for corresponding vocabulary or research another term.

Grammar

<table>
<tr><td><u>4</u></td><td>還 (hái) + positive adjective</td></tr>
</table>

還 (hái) can be used before a positive adjective to indicate that something is acceptable but not truly outstanding.

A   Q: 你對那家旅館的印象怎麼樣?

Nǐ duì nà jiā lǚguǎn de yìnxiàng zěnmeyàng?

What was your impression of that hotel?

A: 還好。

Hái hǎo.

It's okay.

B   這個廚房還可以，挺乾淨的。

Zhè ge chúfáng hái kěyǐ, tǐng gānjìng de.

This kitchen is all right. It's pretty clean.

C   那套公寓還行，帶傢俱。

Nà tào gōngyù hái xíng, dài jiājù.

That apartment is not too bad. It's furnished.

D   那個飯館的紅燒牛肉和家常豆腐還不錯。

Nà ge fànguǎn de hóngshāo niúròu hé jiācháng dòufu hái búcuò.

That restaurant's beef braised in soy sauce and home-style tofu are pretty good.

EXERCISES

In pairs, form a question-and-answer and indicate something is okay but not great.
Use exercise 1 as an example.

1　這個電影　　好看　可以
　→　Student A　這個電影好看嗎？
　　　Student B　還可以。

2　這碗酸辣湯　好喝　可以

3　這盤餃子　　好吃　不錯

4　這兒的地鐵　方便　行

GET Real WITH CHINESE

This ad for an all-inclusive tour package promises a few tour highlights. What aspects of the trip are covered?

9天晶鑽北京江南

2016年3月1日起，逢週五抵達北京

成人 18歲以上	18歲以下不佔床 （不包早餐）	18歲以下佔床 （包早餐）	單人房附加費	指定自費節目 （大小同價）
$99	**$99**	**$399**	**$300**	**$150**
酒店延住（雙人房/每晚）：**$110**			額外接/送機（2人起）：$30	

不包括北京－－南京高鐵$100，北京/南京機票$140（大小同價）

DAY 4 **北京－南京**（週一）
住宿國際品牌：
南京鉑爾曼酒店或同級
Pullman Nanjing
早餐後搭乘高鐵或飛機前往南京，遊覽【東水關城牆遺址】，接著遊覽莊嚴肅穆的【中山陵】，享用著名的南京特產風味－－南京鹽水鴨，餐後夜遊【夫子廟】十裏秦淮河。當晚品嘗【煙波漁港】正宗淮揚風味（指定自費節目）。　（早，午，晚）

DAY 7 **蘇州－杭州**（週
住宿國際品牌：
杭州皇冠假日酒
Holiday Inn Crowne
早餐後前往蘇州絲綢廠體驗
"天寶之物"絲綢繚染過程
【乘船遊覽西湖】（指定自
魚】、【柳浪聞鶯】等西湖
前往杭州龍井茶園，品嘗著
于杭幫菜博物館品嘗正宗
費節目）。

DAY **南京－無錫**（週二） **DAY** **杭州－上海**

Kinship terms

The system of kinship terms in Chinese is rather complicated, especially because Chinese people distinguish between paternal and maternal relatives, older and younger siblings, etc. The following tables provide Chinese kinship terms. Note that [n] indicates northern usage, [s] indicates southern usage, and [f] indicates a more formal form of address.

Parents

English	Chinese	Pinyin
father, dad	爸爸	bàba
	父親[f]	fùqin
mother, mom	媽媽	māmā
	母親[f]	mǔqin

Grandparents

English	Chinese	Pinyin
[paternal] grandfather	爺爺	yéye
	祖父[f]	zǔfù
[paternal] grandmother	奶奶	nǎinai
	祖母[f]	zǔmǔ
[maternal] grandfather	姥爺[n]	lǎoye
	外公[s]	wàigōng
	外祖父[f]	wàizǔfù
[maternal] grandmother	姥姥[n]	lǎolao
	外婆[s]	wàipó
	外祖母[f]	wàizǔmǔ

Uncles and aunts

English	Chinese	Pinyin
father's older brother	伯伯	*bóbo*
	伯父[f]	*bófù*
father's older brother's wife	大媽	*dàmā*
	大娘[n]	*dàniáng*
	伯母[f]	*bómǔ*
father's younger brother	叔叔	*shūshu*
	叔父[f]	*shūfù*
father's younger brother's wife	嬸嬸	*shěnshen*
	嬸兒[n]	*shěnr*
father's sister	姑姑	*gūgu*
	姑媽	*gūmā*
father's sister's husband	姑父[f]	*gūfù*
	姑丈	*gūzhàng*
mother's brother	舅舅	*jiùjiu*
mother's brother's wife	舅媽	*jiùmā*
mother's sister	姨[n]	*yí*
	阿姨	*āyí*
	姨媽	*yímā*
mother's sister's husband	姨父[f]	*yífu*
	姨丈	*yízhàng*

Brothers, sisters, and their spouses

English	Chinese	Pinyin
older brother	哥哥	gēge
older brother's wife	嫂子	sǎozi
	嫂嫂	sǎosao
older sister	姐姐	jiějie
older sister's husband	姐夫	jiěfu
younger brother	弟弟	dìdi
younger brother's wife	弟妹	dìmèi
younger sister	妹妹	mèimei
younger sister's husband	妹夫	mèifu

Cousins

English	Chinese	Pinyin
father's brother's son (older than you)	堂哥	tánggē
father's brother's son (younger than you)	堂弟	tángdì
father's brother's daughter (older than you)	堂姐	tángjiě
father's brother's daughter (younger than you)	堂妹	tángmèi
other male cousin (older than you)	表哥	biǎogē
other male cousin (younger than you)	表弟	biǎodì
other female cousin (older than you)	表姐	biǎojiě
other female cousin (younger than you)	表妹	biǎomèi

Children and their spouses

English	Chinese	Pinyin
son	兒子	érzi
son's wife	兒媳婦	érxífu
daughter	女兒	nǚ'ér
daughter's husband	女婿	nǚxu

Grandchildren

English	Chinese	Pinyin
son's son	孫子	sūnzi
son's daughter	孫女	sūnnǚ
daughter's son	外孫	wàisūn
daughter's daughter	外孫女	wàisūnnǚ

More
exercises

EXERCISES

Identify kinship terms. Use exercise 1 as an example.

1   媽媽的姐姐我們叫阿姨。

2   媽媽的弟弟我們叫 _____。

3   爸爸的媽媽我們叫 _____。

Language Practice

⫫   **Being diplomatic**   INTERPERSONAL

Your friend has returned from the store with a substantial amount of final-sale merchandise. She wants your opinion on what she's bought. You don't want to hurt her feelings, so you try to be tactful, e.g.:

Friend   你覺得我的大衣怎麼樣？

Nǐ juéde wǒ de dàyī zěnmeyàng?

You   我覺得你的大衣還不錯/還行。

Wǒ juéde nǐ de dàyī hái búcuò/hái xíng.

1

2

3

Characterize it!

| What do the characters mean? |
| What is the common radical? |
| What does the radical mean? |
| How does the radical relate to the overall meaning of the characters? |

1 照   **2** 烤   **3** 煩   **4** 燒   **5** 燈

More characters

Puppy love

PRESENTATIONAL

You've just adopted a puppy that you've decided to name 毛毛 *(Máomao)*. At the vet's office, you want to express your concerns that something is wrong with the puppy, e.g.:

thin

哎，我覺得毛毛好像瘦了。

Āi, wǒ juéde Máomao hǎoxiàng shòu le.

1	tired	**3**	hungry	**5**	has a fever
2	fat	**4**	has a cold		

Bon voyage

PRESENTATIONAL

In pairs, list the things that people say to each other when saying goodbye at the airport or train station, e.g. "Have a safe trip," "Give us a call when you get there," "I'll be back soon," and "Don't worry, I'll be fine." Then sequence the phrases in a logical order. Based on your list, role-play a seeing-off scenario.

Welcome

PRESENTATIONAL

In pairs, list the things that people say to each other when greeting guests at the airport/train station, e.g. "Welcome to . . . ," "Thank you for picking me up," "You must be exhausted after a long trip," "I'm okay, not too tired," and "Let me help you with your luggage." Then sequence the phrases in a logical order. Based on your list, do a role-play between a guest and a person who comes to pick up the guest.

Chinese Chat

Li You just posted about her trip to Beijing on Instagram. What were some of the highlights?

Instagram

 李友   20min

❤ 75 likes

李友 到了北京以後，每天都有人請吃飯。中國菜真好吃，我特別愛吃素餃子！北京城裡、城外都好玩兒極了，我覺得最有意思的名勝古蹟是長城。

20 MINUTES AGO

Comment

文化

Continue
to explore

FLYING
domestic

On domestic flights in China, each passenger is allowed to check only one piece of luggage for free. Snacks or meals are often served on domestic flights.

In addition to 一路平安 *(yí lù píng'ān)* (lit. be peaceful and safe all the way), other expressions in Chinese can be used to wish someone a good journey: 旅途愉快 *(lǚtú yúkuài)* and 旅途快樂 *(lǚtú kuàilè)* mean "happy travels" (lit. be happy on the road), and 一路順風 *(yí lù shùnfēng)* literally means "to travel with a favorable wind all the way." While this expression is frequently heard at railroad stations, some people choose not to use it at airports, for fear of jinxing the flight.

A symbol of Chinese infrastructural development, Beijing Capital Airport has become the second-busiest airport in the world. Its newest terminal, Terminal 3, was completed in early 2008, in time for the Beijing Olympics. At the time of its opening, the terminal covered the largest area of any manmade structure in the world. A second international airport in Beijing, now under construction, is projected to be completed in 2018.

This signboard at Shanghai Hongqiao International Airport shows a selection of popular domestic destinations, including Sanya (三亞) *(Sānyà)*, famous for its sandy beaches, and Chengdu (成都) *(Chéngdū)*, renowned for its spicy food. Which of these places would you like to visit, and why?

COMPARE & CONTRAST

Despite the destructive impact on traditional Chinese culture of twentieth-century social upheavals, especially the Cultural Revolution (1966–1976), the importance of family and family values has not changed for the Chinese people. In Dialogue 2 of the lesson, Wang Peng's mother says to her son after not seeing him for nearly a year, 你好像瘦了點兒 (*Nǐ hǎoxiàng shòu le diǎnr*) (You seem to have lost some weight). That is not true, according to Wang Peng. What is true, however, is the mother's love for the son and concern for his health. Would your mother say something like that in a similar situation? What are the typical expressions of love from your parents when you see them after an extended separation?

The skyline of Pudong, Shanghai

Beijing roast duck

Originally a delicacy on imperial menus, Beijing roast duck boasts a history several centuries long. Now it is arguably the food item most emblematic of the culinary culture of northern China. Indeed, its reputation is well reflected in the Chinese saying that no visit to Beijing is complete without a trip to the Great Wall and a meal at a roast duck restaurant. The most famous roast duck restaurant in Beijing is 全聚德 (*Quánjùdé*), which was established in 1864.

Lesson Wrap-Up

Rearrange the following sentences into a logical sequence. Then combine the sentences into a coherent narrative. Substitute nouns with pronouns and change periods to commas where necessary. Avoid unnecessary repetitions of identical subject pronouns. Add the connective devices 和 (hé), 因為…也…所以… (yīnwèi…yě…suǒyǐ…), 也 (yě), and 祝 (zhù) where appropriate.

   1 王朋和李友要去北京。

_____王朋和李友要到五號登機口上飛機。

_____王朋讓妹妹好好兒學英文。

_____高文中說小音會照顧王紅。

_____白英愛和高文中下個星期要去加州。

_____白英愛祝王朋和李友一路平安。

_____這幾個好朋友要秋天再見。

_____王朋和李友在機場托運了兩件行李。

_____王紅來送王朋和李友。

_____高文中來送王朋和李友。

_____白英愛來送王朋和李友。

_____王紅的爸爸、媽媽在北京。

_____王紅的哥哥也要去北京。

_____王紅哭了。

_____白英愛告訴李友高文中在加州給她找了一個實習的工作。

_____王朋祝他们玩兒得高興。

Off to China

You're going to study in China for a semester and are at the Air China counter at the airport. A ground representative for Air China helps you check in and asks to see your ticket and passport. You search for them and in a moment of panic, think you might have left them at home. Luckily, they are in your bag under a Chinese textbook. He/she asks how many pieces of baggage you are checking. You answer that question. You also want to know if your luggage is overweight. You are reassured that it is not, and receive your passport back and the boarding pass. You want to know the gate number and boarding time. After the Air China representative gives you the information, you thank him/her. He/she wishes you a safe trip.

Welcome to China!

Your host father, Mr. Wang, is holding a placard with your name written on it outside the arrival gate. You greet Mr. Wang and introduce yourself. Mr. Wang welcomes you to Beijing. You have brought your host family a small gift and you give it to Mr. Wang, who thanks you and compliments you on your Chinese. You are too modest to accept Mr. Wang's praise. You ask him if his home is far from the airport. Mr. Wang says it is not close, but it's very convenient by subway. You tell him you have two bags, so Mr. Wang decides to get a taxi. Since it's nearly dinner time, Mr. Wang is taking you to the most famous Peking duck restaurant in the capital!

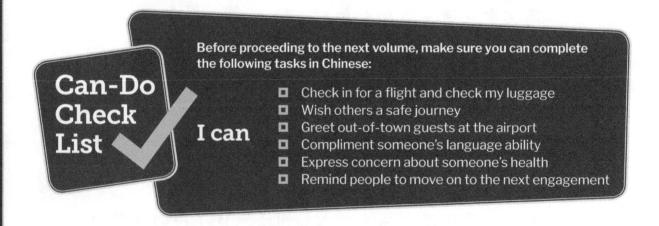

Can-Do Check List

I can

Before proceeding to the next volume, make sure you can complete the following tasks in Chinese:

- ☐ Check in for a flight and check my luggage
- ☐ Wish others a safe journey
- ☐ Greet out-of-town guests at the airport
- ☐ Compliment someone's language ability
- ☐ Express concern about someone's health
- ☐ Remind people to move on to the next engagement

Keeping It Casual (Lessons 16–20)

Before you progress to the next volume, we'll review how some of the functional expressions from Lessons 16–20 are used in casual Chinese. After you complete the review, note any other casual expressions you would like to learn; then share the list with your teacher.

---

1 | 一言為定 *(yì yán wéi dìng)* **(it's a deal, it's decided)**

Say 一言為定 *(yì yán wéi dìng)* when you and your friends or business partners have reached a decision. It indicates that you and the other parties pledge to remember and honor the decision.

A   **Gao Wenzhong**

明年我們去中國，怎麼樣？

Míngnián wǒmen qù Zhōngguó, zěnmeyàng?

We'll go to China next year. How about it?

Bai Ying'ai

好啊！

Hǎo a!

That's great.

Gao Wenzhong

一言為定。

Yì yán wéi dìng.

That settles it.

B   **Wang Peng**

考完試我們出去玩兒，好嗎？

Kǎo wán shì wǒmen chū qu wánr, hǎo ma?

After the exam let's go out and have some fun, all right?

Li You

太好了。你開車？

Tài hǎo le. Nǐ kāi chē?

Wonderful! Will you drive?

Wang Peng

沒問題。

Méi wèntí.

No problem.

Li You

一言為定。

Yì yán wéi dìng.

It's a deal.

Wang Peng

一言為定。

Yì yán wéi dìng.

Deal.

2 | Good, very good, excellent, and extraordinary

Here are some expressions to convey varying degrees of approval, in progressive order of intensity.

A 他的中文不錯。

Tā de Zhōngwén búcuò.

His Chinese is quite good.

B 他的中文很好。

Tā de Zhōngwén hěn hǎo.

His Chinese is very good.

C 他的中文好得很。

Tā de Zhōngwén hǎo de hěn.

His Chinese is very, very good.

D 他的中文非常好。

Tā de Zhōngwén fēicháng hǎo.

His Chinese is unusually good.

E 他的中文好極了。

Tā de Zhōngwén hǎo jí le.

His Chinese is fantastic.

F 他的中文好得不得了。

Tā de Zhōngwén hǎo de bùdéliǎo.

His Chinese is extraordinary.

3 | Greetings

Say these to greet people in different contexts.

A 您好，老師！

Nín hǎo, lǎoshī!

Hello, professor!

B 王先生，早上好！

Wáng xiānsheng, zǎoshang hǎo!

Good morning, Mr. Wang!

C 早！

Zǎo!

Good morning!

In daily life, however, a common way to greet an acquaintance is by asking a casual question about what that person is doing at the moment:

D　老李，上課去呀？

Lǎo Lǐ, shàng kè qu ya?

Old Li, going to class? (It looks like Old Li is going to class.)

E　小王，回家呀？

Xiǎo Wáng, huí jiā ya?

Little Wang, going home? (Upon seeing someone wrapping up his/her things and leaving the office, or someone on his/her way home, for instance.)

F　爸，回來了？

Bà, huí lai le?

Dad, you're home? (Upon seeing one's father walking in the door, for instance.)

4　　　　　　　　　　　　Farewells

Say these to bid someone farewell.

A　再見！

Zàijiàn!

Bye!

C　回頭見！

Huí tóu jiàn!

See you later!

B　明天見！

Míngtiān jiàn!

See you tomorrow!

D　慢走！

Màn zǒu!

Take it easy! (Lit. Walk slowly!)

Mealtime expressions

Say these upon finishing a meal before others or before everyone starts eating.

A　慢吃！

Màn chī!

Take your time (to enjoy the meal)!

B　慢用！

Màn yòng!

Enjoy the meal!

The Chinese-English index is alphabetized according to *pinyin*. Words containing the same Chinese characters are first grouped together. Homonyms appear in the order of their tonal pronunciation (i.e., first tones first, second tones second, third tones third, fourth tones fourth, and neutral tones last).

Traditional	Simplified	Pinyin	Part of Speech	English	Lesson
A					
啊		*a*	p	(a sentence-final particle of exclamation, interrogation, etc.)	6
阿姨		*āyí*	n	aunt	20
哎	哎	*āi*	excl	(exclamatory particle to express surprise or dissatisfaction)	13
愛	爱	*ài*	v	to love, to like, to be fond of	14
安靜	安静	*ānjìng*	adj	quiet	17
B					
把		*bǎ*	m	(measure word for things with handles, for handfuls of things)	14
把		*bǎ*	prep	(indicating disposition, arrangement, or settlement of something)	15
爸爸		*bàba*	n	father, dad	2
吧		*ba*	p	(a sentence-final particle)	5
白英愛	白英爱	*Bái Yīng'ài*	pn	(a personal name)	2
百		*bǎi*	nu	hundred	9
班		*bān*	n	class	14
搬		*bān*	v	to move	16
半		*bàn*	nu	half, half an hour	3
半天		*bàntiān*		half a day, a long time	18
辦	办	*bàn*	v	to handle, to do	11

Traditional	Simplified	Pinyin	Part of Speech	English	Lesson
辦法	办法	bànfǎ	n	method, way (of doing something)	15
辦公室	办公室	bàngōngshì	n	office	6
幫	帮	bāng	v	to help	6
棒		bàng	adj	fantastic, super [colloq.]	18
包		bāo	n	bag, sack, bundle, package	20
保險	保险	bǎoxiǎn	n/adj	insurance; secure	15
抱		bào	v	to hold or carry in the arms	18
報紙	报纸	bàozhǐ	n	newspaper	17
杯		bēi	m	(measure word for things contained in a cup or glass)	5
北		běi	n	north	13
北京		Běijīng	pn	Beijing	1
被		bèi	prep	by	18
本		běn	m	(measure word for books)	14
鼻子		bízi	n	nose	14
筆	笔	bǐ	n	pen	7
比		bǐ	prep/v	compared with (comparison marker); to compare	11
比賽	比赛	bǐsài	n/v	game, match, competition; to compete	18
遍		biàn	m	(measure word for complete courses of an action or instances of an action)	15
表姐		biǎojiě	n	older female cousin	14
別	别	bié	adv	don't	6
別人	别人	biérén	n	other people, another person	4
冰茶	冰茶	bīngchá	n	iced tea	12
冰箱		bīngxiāng	n	refrigerator	15
病人		bìngrén	n	patient	15

Traditional	Simplified	Pinyin	Part of Speech	English	Lesson
不		*bù*	adv	not, no	1
不錯	不错	*búcuò [bùcuò]**	adj	pretty good	4
不但⋯ ， 而且⋯		*búdàn . . . , érqiě . . . [bùdàn . . . , érqiě . . .]*	conj	not only . . . , but also . . .	11
不過	不过	*búguò [bùguò]*	conj	however, but	9
不好意思		*bù hǎoyìsi*		to feel embarrassed	10
不用		*bú yòng [bù yòng]*		need not	9

			C		
才		*cái*	adv	not until, only then	5
菜	菜	*cài*	n	dish, cuisine	3
餐廳	餐厅	*cāntīng*	n	dining room, cafeteria	8
廁所	厕所	*cèsuǒ*	n	restroom, toilet	15
茶	茶	*chá*	n	tea	5
查		*chá*	v	to check, to look into	19
差不多	差不多	*chàbuduō*	adv/adj	almost, nearly; similar	17
常常		*chángcháng*	adv	often	4
常老師	常老师	*Cháng lǎoshī*	pn	Teacher Chang	6
長城	长城	*Chángchéng*	pn	the Great Wall	19
長短	长短	*chángduǎn*	n	length	9
場	场	*chǎng*	n	field	13
唱歌（兒）	唱歌（儿）	*chàng gē(r)*	vo	to sing (a song)	4
超重		*chāozhòng*	v	to be overweight (of luggage, freight, etc.)	20
吵		*chǎo*	v/adj	to quarrel; noisy	17
襯衫	衬衫	*chènshān*	n	shirt	9

* For vocabulary items starting with 不 or 一, we have included the *pinyin* with the stand-alone tone of these two characters in square brackets. However, the *pinyin* listed first indicates how the characters are conventionally pronounced as a lexical unit.

Traditional	Simplified	Pinyin	Part of Speech	English	Lesson
成		*chéng*	v	to become	16
城市		*chéngshì*	n	city	10
吃		*chī*	v	to eat	3
吃壞	吃坏	*chī huài*	vc	to get sick because of bad food	15
寵物	宠物	*chǒngwù*	n	pet	17
初		*chū*	n	beginning	19
出去		*chūqu*	vc	to go out	10
出租		*chūzū*	v	to rent out	17
出租汽車	出租汽车	*chūzū qìchē*	n	taxi	10
廚房	厨房	*chúfáng*	n	kitchen	17
除了⋯以外		*chúle … yǐwài*	conj	in addition to, besides	8
穿		*chuān*	v	to wear, to put on	9
窗戶	窗户	*chuānghu*	n	window	19
春天		*chūntiān*	n	spring	11
次		*cì*	m	(measure word for frequency)	13
聰明	聪明	*cōngming*	adj	smart, bright, clever	14
從	从	*cóng*	prep	from	13
錯	错	*cuò*	adj	wrong	12
D					
打車	打车	*dǎ chē*	vo	to take a taxi	10
打電話	打电话	*dǎ diànhuà*	vo	to make a phone call	6
打工		*dǎ gōng*	vo	to work at a temporary job (often part time)	19
打球		*dǎ qiú*	vo	to play ball	4
打掃	打扫	*dǎsǎo*	v	to clean up (a room, apartment or house)	16

Traditional	Simplified	Pinyin	Part of Speech	English	Lesson
打算		dǎsuàn	v/n	to plan; plan	19
打折		dǎ zhé	vo	to sell at a discount, to give a discount	19
打針	打针	dǎ zhēn	vo	to get an injection	15
大		dà	adj	big, old	3
大哥		dàgē	n	eldest/oldest brother	2
大家		dàjiā	pr	everybody	7
大姐		dàjiě	n	eldest/oldest sister	2
大小		dàxiǎo	n	size	9
大學生	大学生	dàxuéshēng	n	college student	2
帶	带	dài	v	to bring, to take, to carry, to come with	12
單程	单程	dānchéng	n	one-way trip	19
擔心	担心	dān xīn	vo	to worry	18
蛋糕		dàngāo	n	cake	14
但是		dànshì	conj	but	6
當	当	dāng	v	to serve as, to be	17
當然	当然	dāngrán	adv	of course	18
導遊	导游	dǎoyóu	n	tour guide	19
到		dào	v	to go to, to arrive	6
的		de	p	(a possessive or descriptive particle)	2
地		de	p	(particle to link adverbial and verb)	20
得		de	p	(a structural particle)	7
得		děi	av	must, to have to	6
登機口	登机口	dēngjīkǒu	n	boarding gate	20
登機牌	登机牌	dēngjīpái	n	boarding pass	20

Traditional	Simplified	Pinyin	Part of Speech	English	Lesson
等		děng	v	to wait, to wait for	6
第		dì	prefix	(prefix for ordinal numbers)	7
弟弟		dìdi	n	younger brother	2
地方		dìfang	n	place	13
地鐵	地铁	dìtiě	n	subway	10
地圖	地图	dìtú	n	map	13
點	点	diǎn	m	o'clock (lit. dot, point, thus "points on the clock")	3
點菜	点菜	diǎn cài	vo	to order food	12
點（兒）	点（儿）	diǎn(r)	m	a little, a bit, some	5
電	电	diàn	n	electricity	16
電腦	电脑	diànnǎo	n	computer	8
電視	电视	diànshì	n	television	4
電影	电影	diànyǐng	n	movie	4
電子郵件	电子邮件	diànzǐ yóujiàn	n	email/electronic mail	10
訂	订	dìng	v	to reserve, to book (a ticket, a hotel room, etc.)	19
東	东	dōng	n	east	13
東京	东京	Dōngjīng	pn	Tokyo	13
東西	东西	dōngxi	n	things, objects	9
冬天		dōngtiān	n	winter	11
懂	懂	dǒng	v	to understand	7
都		dōu	adv	both, all	2
豆腐		dòufu	n	tofu, bean curd	12
肚子		dùzi	n	belly, abdomen, stomach	15
對	对	duì	adj	right, correct	4

Traditional	Simplified	Pinyin	Part of Speech	English	Lesson
對不起	对不起	*duìbuqǐ*	v	sorry	5
多		*duō*	adv	how many/much, to what extent	3
多		*duō*	adj	many, much	7
多少		*duōshao*	qpr	how much/how many	9

<table>
<tr><td colspan="6" align="center">E</td></tr>
</table>

Traditional	Simplified	Pinyin	Part of Speech	English	Lesson
餓	饿	*è*	adj	hungry	12
兒子	儿子	*érzi*	n	son	2
二姐		*èrjiě*	n	second oldest sister	2

<table>
<tr><td colspan="6" align="center">F</td></tr>
</table>

Traditional	Simplified	Pinyin	Part of Speech	English	Lesson
發短信	发短信	*fā duǎnxìn*	vo	to send a text message (lit. to send a short message)	10
發燒	发烧	*fā shāo*	vo	to have a fever	15
發音	发音	*fāyīn*	n	pronunciation	8
飯	饭	*fàn*	n	meal, (cooked) rice	3
飯館（兒）	饭馆（儿）	*fànguǎn(r)*	n	restaurant	12
飯卡	饭卡	*fànkǎ*	n	meal card	12
飯桌	饭桌	*fànzhuō*	n	dining table	17
方便		*fāngbiàn*	adj	convenient	6
房間	房间	*fángjiān*	n	room	16
房租		*fángzū*	n	rent	17
放		*fàng*	v	to put, to place	12
放假		*fàng jià*	vo	go on vacation, have time off	19
非常		*fēicháng*	adv	very, extremely, exceedingly	11
飛機	飞机	*fēijī*	n	airplane	10
（飛）機場	（飞）机场	*(fēi)jīchǎng*	n	airport	10

Traditional	Simplified	Pinyin	Part of Speech	English	Lesson
費	费	fèi	v	to spend, to take (effort)	16
費	费	fèi	n	fee, expenses	17
分		fēn	m	(measure word for 1/100 of a kuai [equivalent of a cent])	9
分鐘	分钟	fēnzhōng	n	minute	17
份		fèn	m	(measure word for meal orders, jobs)	19
封		fēng	m	(measure word for letters)	8
服務員	服务员	fúwùyuán	n	waiter, attendant	12
附近		fùjìn	n	vicinity, neighborhood, nearby area	17
父母		fùmǔ	n	parents, father and mother	19
付錢	付钱	fù qián	vo	to pay money	9
復習	复习	fùxí	v	to review	7
G					
乾淨	干净	gānjìng	adj	clean	17
趕快	赶快	gǎnkuài	adv	right away, quickly, in a hurry	15
感冒		gǎnmào	v	to have a cold	15
剛	刚	gāng	adv	just	12
剛才	刚才	gāngcái	t	just now, a moment ago	11
高速公路		gāosù gōnglù	n	highway	10
高文中		Gāo Wénzhōng	pn	(a personal name)	2
高小音		Gāo Xiǎoyīn	pn	(a personal name)	5
高興	高兴	gāoxìng	adj	happy, pleased	5
告訴	告诉	gàosu	v	to tell	8
哥哥		gēge	n	older brother	2

Traditional	Simplified	Pinyin	Part of Speech	English	Lesson
個	个	*gè/ge*	m	(measure word for many common everyday objects)	2
給	给	*gěi*	v	to give	5
給	给	*gěi*	prep	to, for	6
跟		*gēn*	prep	with	6
更		*gèng*	adv	even more	11
公共汽車	公共汽车	*gōnggòng qìchē*	n	bus	10
公司		*gōngsī*	n	company	19
公寓		*gōngyù*	n	apartment	17
公園	公园	*gōngyuán*	n	park	11
功課	功课	*gōngkè*	n	homework, schoolwork	7
工作		*gōngzuò*	n/v	job; to work	2
狗		*gǒu*	n	dog	14
夠	够	*gòu*	adj	enough	12
谷歌		*Gǔgē*	pn	Google	13
拐	拐	*guǎi*	v	to turn	13
廣告	广告	*guǎnggào*	n	advertisement	17
貴	贵	*guì*	adj	honorable, expensive	1
國際	国际	*guójì*	adj	international	18
過	过	*guò*	v	to live (a life), to observe (a holiday), to celebrate (a festival), to pass	14
過敏	过敏	*guòmǐn*	v	to be allergic to	15
過	过	*guo*	p	(particle used after a verb to indicate a past experience)	13

H

| 還 | 还 | *hái* | adv | also, too, as well | 3 |

Traditional	Simplified	Pinyin	Part of Speech	English	Lesson
還是	还是	háishi	conj	or	3
孩子		háizi	n	child	2
海倫	海伦	Hǎilún	pn	Helen	14
寒假		hánjià	n	winter vacation	10
漢字	汉字	Hànzì	n	Chinese characters	7
航班		hángbān	n	scheduled flight	19
航空		hángkōng	n	aviation	19
好		hǎo	adj	fine, good, nice, OK, it's settled	1
好吃		hǎochī	adj	delicious	12
好幾	好几	hǎo jǐ		quite a few	15
好久		hǎo jiǔ		a long time	4
好玩兒	好玩儿	hǎowánr	adj	fun, amusing, interesting	11
好像	好像	hǎoxiàng	v	to seem, to be like	12
號	号	hào	m	(measure word for a position in a numerical series, day of the month)	3
號	号	hào	n	size	9
號碼	号码	hàomǎ	n	number	16
喝		hē	v	to drink	5
和		hé	conj	and	2
合適	合适	héshì	adj	suitable	9
黑		hēi	adj	black	9
很		hěn	adv	very	3
紅	红	hóng	adj	red	9
紅綠燈	红绿灯	hónglǜdēng	n	traffic light	13

Traditional	Simplified	Pinyin	Part of Speech	English	Lesson
紅燒	红烧	*hóngshāo*	v	to braise in soy sauce (to red-cook)	12
後來	后来	*hòulái*	t	later	8
後天	后天	*hòutiān*	t	the day after tomorrow	16
護照	护照	*hùzhào*	n	passport	19
花	花	*huā*	v	to spend	10
花	花	*huā*	n	flower	14
滑冰	滑冰	*huá bīng*	vo	to ice skate	11
歡迎	欢迎	*huānyíng*	v	to welcome	20
還	还	*huán*	v	to return (something)	17
換	换	*huàn*	v	to exchange, to change	9
黃	黄	*huáng*	adj	yellow	9
黃瓜	黄瓜	*huánggua*	n	cucumber	12
回家		*huí jiā*	vo	to go home	5
回來	回来	*huí lai*	vc	to come back	6
回去		*huí qu*	vc	to go back, to return	11
會	会	*huì*	mv	can, know how to	8
會	会	*huì*	mv	will	11
活動	活动	*huódòng*	n	activity	13
或者		*huòzhě*	conj	or	10

			J		
極	极	*jí*	adv	extremely	12
幾	几	*jǐ*	nu	how many, some, a few	2
記得	记得	*jìde*	v	to remember	16
計劃	计划	*jìhuà*	v/n	to plan; plan	19

Traditional	Simplified	Pinyin	Part of Speech	English	Lesson
家		*jiā*	n	family, home	2
家常		*jiācháng*	n	home-style	12
傢俱	家具	*jiājù*	n	furniture	17
加州		*Jiāzhōu*	pn	California	11
檢查	检查	*jiǎnchá*	v	to examine	15
簡單	简单	*jiǎndān*	adj	simple	18
件		*jiàn*	m	(measure word for shirts, dresses, jackets, coats, etc.)	9
見	见	*jiàn*	v	to see	3
見面	见面	*jiàn miàn*	vo	to meet up, to meet with	6
健康		*jiànkāng*	adj/n	healthy; health	15
教		*jiāo*	v	to teach	7
腳	脚	*jiǎo*	n	foot	18
餃子	饺子	*jiǎozi*	n	dumplings (with vegetable and/or meat filling)	12
叫		*jiào*	v	to be called, to call	1
教室		*jiàoshì*	n	classroom	8
接		*jiē*	v	to catch, to meet, to welcome	14
節	节	*jié*	m	(measure word for class periods)	6
姐姐		*jiějie*	n	older sister	2
介紹	介绍	*jièshào*	v	to introduce	5
今年		*jīnnián*	t	this year	3
今天		*jīntiān*	t	today	3
緊張	紧张	*jǐnzhāng*	adj	nervous, anxious	10
近		*jìn*	adj	near	13
進	进	*jìn*	v	to enter	5

Traditional	Simplified	Pinyin	Part of Speech	English	Lesson
進來	进来	jìn lai	vc	to come in	5
九月		jiǔyuè	n	September	3
就		jiù	adv	precisely, exactly	6
就		jiù	adv	just, only (indicating a small number)	16
覺得	觉得	juéde	v	to feel, to think	4

			K		
咖啡		kāfēi	n	coffee	5
咖啡色		kāfēisè	n	brown, coffee color	9
開車	开车	kāi chē	vo	to drive a car	10
開會	开会	kāi huì	vo	to have a meeting	6
開始	开始	kāishǐ	v/n	to begin, to start; beginning	7
看		kàn	v	to watch, to look, to read	4
看病		kàn bìng	vo	to see a doctor	15
考試	考试	kǎo shì	vo/n	to give or take a test; test	6
烤鴨	烤鸭	kǎoyā	n	roast duck	20
靠		kào	v	to lean on, to lean against, to be next to	19
渴		kě	adj	thirsty	12
可愛	可爱	kě'ài	adj	cute, lovable	14
可樂	可乐	kělè	n	cola	5
可能		kěnéng	mv/adj	may; possible	17
可是		kěshì	conj	but	3
可以		kěyǐ	mv	can, may	5
刻		kè	m	quarter (of an hour)	3
課	课	kè	n	class, course, lesson	6

Traditional	Simplified	Pinyin	Part of Speech	English	Lesson
課文	课文	kèwén	n	text of a lesson	7
客氣	客气	kèqi	adj	polite	6
客廳	客厅	kètīng	n	living room	17
空（兒）	空（儿）	kòng(r)	n	free time	6
口		kǒu	m	(measure word for number of family members)	2
哭		kū	v	to cry, to weep	20
酷		kù	adj	cool (appearance, behavior)	7
褲子	裤子	kùzi	n	pants	9
塊	块	kuài	m	(measure word for the basic Chinese monetary unit [equivalent of a dollar])	9
快		kuài	adj/adv	fast, quick; quickly	5
快樂	快乐	kuàilè	adj	happy	10
		L			
來	来	lái	v	to come	5
藍	蓝	lán	adj	blue	10
籃球	篮球	lánqiú	n	basketball	18
懶	懒	lǎn	adj	lazy	15
老師	老师	lǎoshī	n	teacher	1
了		le	p	(a dynamic particle)	5
累		lèi	adj	tired	8
冷		lěng	adj	cold	11
離	离	lí	prep	away from	13
梨		lí	n	pear	14
裡邊	里边	lǐbian	n	inside	13
禮物	礼物	lǐwù	n	gift, present	14

Traditional	Simplified	Pinyin	Part of Speech	English	Lesson
李友		Lǐ Yǒu	pn	(a personal name)	1
力氣	力气	lìqi	n	strength, effort	16
倆	俩	liǎ	nu+m	two [colloq.]	16
連	连	lián	prep	even	17
臉	脸	liǎn	n	face	14
練習	练习	liànxí	v	to practice	6
涼拌	凉拌	liángbàn	v	(of food) cold "blended", cold tossed	12
兩	两	liǎng	nu	two, a couple of	2
聊天（兒）	聊天（儿）	liáo tiān(r)	vo	to chat	5
另外		lìngwài	conj	furthermore, in addition	17
樓	楼	lóu	n	multi-storied building, floor (of a multi-level building)	14
路		lù	n	route, road	10
路口		lùkǒu	n	intersection	13
錄音	录音	lùyīn	n/vo	sound recording; to record	7
旅館	旅馆	lǚguǎn	n	hotel	19
旅行		lǚxíng	v	to travel	16
旅行社		lǚxíngshè	n	travel agency	19
綠	绿	lǜ	adj	green	10
律師	律师	lǜshī	n	lawyer	2
亂	乱	luàn	adv	randomly, arbitrarily, messily	15

M

Traditional	Simplified	Pinyin	Part of Speech	English	Lesson
媽媽	妈妈	māma	n	mother, mom	2
麻煩	麻烦	máfan	adj	troublesome	10
馬上	马上	mǎshàng	adv	immediately, right away	19

Traditional	Simplified	Pinyin	Part of Speech	English	Lesson
嗎	吗	ma	qp	(question particle)	1
買	买	mǎi	v	to buy	9
賣完	卖完	mài wán	vc	to be sold out	12
慢		màn	adj	slow	7
忙		máng	adj	busy	3
毛		máo	m	(measure word for 1/10 of a kuai [equivalent of a dime])	9
沒	没	méi	adv	not	2
沒關係	没关系	méi guānxi		it doesn't matter	12
每		měi	pr	every, each	10
美國	美国	Měiguó	pn	America	1
美式		Měishì	adj	American-style	18
美元		Měiyuán	n	American dollar (USD)	17
妹妹		mèimei	n	younger sister	2
米飯	米饭	mǐfàn	n	cooked rice	12
面試	面试	miànshì	v/n	to interview; interview (for a job or school admission)	11
名勝古蹟	名胜古迹	míngshèng gǔjì		famous scenic spots and historic sites	19
明天		míngtiān	t	tomorrow	3
名字		míngzi	n	name	1
		N			
拿		ná	v	to take, to get	13
哪		nǎ/něi	qpr	which	6
哪裡	哪里	nǎli	pr	where	7
哪兒	哪儿	nǎr	qpr	where	5
那		nà	pr	that	2

Traditional	Simplified	Pinyin	Part of Speech	English	Lesson
那		*nà*	conj	in that case, then	4
那裡	那里	*nàli*	pr	there	17
那麼	那么	*nàme*	pr	(indicating degree) so, such	11
那兒	那儿	*nàr*	pr	there	8
奶奶		*nǎinai*	n	paternal grandmother	20
男		*nán*	adj	male	2
南		*nán*	n	south	13
難	难	*nán*	adj	difficult	7
難受	难受	*nánshòu*	adj	hard to bear, uncomfortable	18
呢		*ne*	qp	(question particle)	1
能		*néng*	mv	can, to be able to	8
你		*nǐ*	pr	you	1
年級	年级	*niánjí*	n	grade in school	6
念		*niàn*	v	to read aloud	7
您		*nín*	pr	you (honorific for 你)	6
牛肉		*niúròu*	n	beef	12
紐約	纽约	*Niǔyuē*	pn	New York	1
暖和		*nuǎnhuo*	adj	warm	11
女		*nǚ*	adj	female	2
女兒	女儿	*nǚ'ér*	n	daughter	2
P					
怕		*pà*	v	to fear, to be afraid of	18
拍		*pāi*	n	racket	18
盤	盘	*pán*	n	plate, dish	12

Traditional	Simplified	Pinyin	Part of Speech	English	Lesson
旁邊	旁边	pángbiān	n	side	13
胖		pàng	adj	fat	18
跑步		pǎo bù	vo	to jog	18
朋友		péngyou	n	friend	3
篇		piān	m	(measure word for essays, articles, etc.)	8
便宜		piányi	adj	cheap, inexpensive	9
片		piàn	m	(measure word for tablets, slices, etc.)	15
票		piào	n	ticket	10
漂亮	漂亮	piàoliang	adj	pretty	5
瓶		píng	m/n	(measure word for bottled liquid, etc.)	5
平常		píngcháng	adv	usually	7
蘋果	苹果	píngguǒ	n	apple	14
Q					
起床	起床	qǐ chuáng	vo	to get up	8
起飛	起飞	qǐfēi	v	(of airplanes) to take off	20
千		qiān	nu	thousand	19
簽證	签证	qiānzhèng	n	visa	19
錢	钱	qián	n	money	9
前		qián	n	forward, ahead	13
前面		qiánmiàn	n	ahead, in front of	13
青菜	青菜	qīngcài	n	green, leafy vegetable	12
清楚		qīngchu	adj	clear	12
請	请	qǐng	v	please (polite form of request), to treat or to invite (somebody)	1

Traditional	Simplified	Pinyin	Part of Speech	English	Lesson
請客	请客	qǐng kè	vo	to invite someone (to dinner, coffee, etc.), to play the host	4
秋天		qiūtiān	n	autumn, fall	11
去		qù	v	to go	4
去年		qùnián	t	last year	14

Traditional	Simplified	Pinyin	Part of Speech	English	Lesson
然後	然后	ránhòu	adv	then	10
讓	让	ràng	v	to allow or cause (somebody to do something)	10
熱	热	rè	adj	hot	11
人		rén	n	people, person	1
人民幣	人民币	rénmínbì	n	renminbi (RMB, Chinese currency)	17
認識	认识	rènshi	v	to be acquainted with, to recognize	3
日本		Rìběn	pn	Japan	13
日記	日记	rìjì	n	diary	8
日文		Rìwén	pn	Japanese (language)	13
容易		róngyì	adj	easy	7
肉		ròu	n	meat	12
如果…的話	如果…的话	rúguǒ…de huà	conj	if	9

Traditional	Simplified	Pinyin	Part of Speech	English	Lesson
沙發	沙发	shāfā	n	sofa	17
商店		shāngdiàn	n	store, shop	9
上		shàng	v	to go [colloq.]	13
上菜	上菜	shàng cài	vo	to serve food	12
上次		shàng cì		last time	15

Traditional	Simplified	Pinyin	Part of Speech	English	Lesson
上大學	上大学	shàng dàxué	vo	to attend college/university	18
上個	上个	shàng ge		previous, last	7
上海		Shànghǎi	pn	Shanghai	12
上課	上课	shàng kè	vo	to go to a class, to start a class, to be in class	7
上網	上网	shàng wǎng	vo	to go online, to surf the internet	8
上午		shàngwǔ	t	morning	6
誰	谁	shéi	qpr	who, whom	2
身體	身体	shēntǐ	n	body, health	15
什麼	什么	shénme	qpr	what	1
生病		shēng bìng	vo	to get sick	15
生詞	生词	shēngcí	n	new words, vocabulary	7
生日		shēngrì	n	birthday	3
師傅	师傅	shīfu	n	master worker	12
十八		shíbā	nu	eighteen	3
十二		shí'èr	nu	twelve	3
時候	时候	shíhou	n	(a point in) time, moment, (a duration of) time	4
時間	时间	shíjiān	n	time	6
實習	实习	shíxí	v	to intern	19
是		shì	v	to be	1
試	试	shì	v	to try	9
事（兒）	事（儿）	shì(r)	n	matter, affair, event	3
收		shōu	v	to receive, to accept	9
手		shǒu	n	hand	18
手機	手机	shǒujī	n	cell phone	10

Traditional	Simplified	Pinyin	Part of Speech	English	Lesson
首都		shǒudū	n	capital city	19
首都機場	首都机场	Shǒudū Jīchǎng	pn	the Capital Airport (in Beijing)	20
瘦		shòu	adj	thin, skinny, lean	20
售貨員	售货员	shòuhuòyuán	n	shop assistant, salesclerk	9
書	书	shū	n	book	4
書店	书店	shūdiàn	n	bookstore	13
書架	书架	shūjià	n	bookcase, bookshelf	17
書桌	书桌	shūzhuō	n	desk	17
舒服		shūfu	adj	comfortable	11
叔叔		shūshu	n	uncle	20
屬	属	shǔ	v	to belong to	14
暑假		shǔjià	n	summer vacation	19
暑期		shǔqī	n	summer term	14
刷卡		shuā kǎ	vo	to pay with a credit card	9
帥	帅	shuài	adj	handsome	7
雙	双	shuāng	m	(measure word for a pair)	9
水		shuǐ	n	water	5
水果		shuǐguǒ	n	fruit	14
水平		shuǐpíng	n	level, standard	18
睡覺	睡觉	shuì jiào	vo	to sleep	4
說	说	shuō	v	to say, to speak	6
說話	说话	shuō huà	vo	to talk	7
送		sòng	v	to see off or out, to take (someone somewhere)	10
送		sòng	v	to give as a gift	14

Traditional	Simplified	Pinyin	Part of Speech	English	Lesson
素		*sù*	adj	vegetarian (lit. plain)	12
素餐		*sùcān*	n	vegetarian meal	19
宿舍		*sùshè*	n	dormitory	8
酸		*suān*	adj	sour	12
酸辣湯	酸辣汤	*suānlàtāng*	n	hot-and-sour soup	12
算了		*suàn le*		forget it, never mind	4
雖然	虽然	*suīrán*	conj	although	9
歲	岁	*suì*	n	year (of age)	3
所以		*suǒyǐ*	conj	so	4
T					
他		*tā*	pr	he, him	2
她		*tā*	pr	she, her	2
它		*tā*	pr	it	9
台北		*Táiběi*	pn	Taipei	19
太⋯了		*tài . . . le*		too, extremely	3
湯姆	汤姆	*Tāngmǔ*	pn	Tom	14
糖醋魚	糖醋鱼	*tángcùyú*	n	sweet-and-sour fish	12
躺下		*tǎng xià*	vc	to lie down	15
套		*tào*	m	(measure word for things that come in a set/sets)	17
特別	特别	*tèbié*	adv	especially	10
疼死		*téng sǐ*	adj + c	really painful	15
踢		*tī*	v	to kick	18
提高		*tígāo*	v	to improve, to raise, to heighten	18
天		*tiān*	n	day	3

Traditional	Simplified	Pinyin	Part of Speech	English	Lesson
天氣	天气	*tiānqì*	n	weather	11
甜		*tián*	adj	sweet	12
條	条	*tiáo*	m	(measure word for pants and long, thin objects)	9
跳舞		*tiào wǔ*	vo	to dance	4
聽	听	*tīng*	v	to listen	4
聽說	听说	*tīngshuō*	v	to be told, to hear of	13
挺		*tǐng*	adv	very, rather	9
同		*tóng*	adj	same	16
同學	同学	*tóngxué*	n	classmate	3
圖書館	图书馆	*túshūguǎn*	n	library	5
托運	托运	*tuōyùn*	v	to check (luggage)	20
W					
外國	外国	*wàiguó*	n	foreign country	4
玩（兒）	玩（儿）	*wán(r)*	v	to have fun, to play	5
碗		*wǎn*	n	bowl	12
晚		*wǎn*	adj	late	7
晚飯	晚饭	*wǎnfàn*	n	dinner, supper	3
晚上		*wǎnshang*	t	evening, night	3
王紅	王红	*Wáng Hóng*	pn	a personal name	14
王朋		*Wáng Péng*	pn	(a personal name)	1
往		*wǎng*	prep	towards	13
往返		*wǎngfǎn*	v	make a round trip, go there and back	19
網球	网球	*wǎngqiú*	n	tennis	18
網上	网上	*wǎng shang*		on the Internet	11

Traditional	Simplified	Pinyin	Part of Speech	English	Lesson
忘		wàng	v	to forget	12
危險	危险	wēixiǎn	adj	dangerous	18
喂		wéi/wèi	interj	(on the phone) Hello!, Hey!	6
位		wèi	m	(polite measure word for people)	6
位子		wèizi	n	seat	12
味精		wèijīng	n	monosodium glutamate (MSG)	12
為了	为了	wèile	prep	for the sake of	18
為什麼	为什么	wèishénme	qpr	why	3
衛生間	卫生间	wèishēngjiān	n	bathroom	17
文化		wénhuà	n	culture	19
問	问	wèn	v	to ask (a question)	1
問題	问题	wèntí	n	question, problem	6
我		wǒ	pr	I, me	1
我們	我们	wǒmen	pr	we, us	3
臥室	卧室	wòshì	n	bedroom	17
午飯	午饭	wǔfàn	n	lunch, midday meal	8
舞會	舞会	wǔhuì	n	dance party, ball	14

X

Traditional	Simplified	Pinyin	Part of Speech	English	Lesson
西		xī	n	west	13
西北航空公司		Xīběi Hángkōng Gōngsī	pn	Northwest Airlines	19
西瓜		xīguā	n	watermelon	14
希望	希望	xīwàng	v/n	to hope; hope	8
喜歡	喜欢	xǐhuan	v	to like	3
洗澡		xǐ zǎo	vo	to take a bath/shower	8

Traditional	Simplified	Pinyin	Part of Speech	English	Lesson
下車	下车	xià chē	vo	to get off (a bus, train, etc.)	10
下個	下个	xià ge		next	6
下午		xiàwǔ	t	afternoon	6
下雪		xià xuě	vo	to snow	11
下雨		xià yǔ	vo	to rain	11
夏天		xiàtiān	n	summer	11
先		xiān	adv	first	10
先生		xiānsheng	n	Mr., husband, teacher	1
線	线	xiàn	n	line	10
現在	现在	xiànzài	t	now	3
香港		Xiānggǎng	pn	Hong Kong	19
箱子		xiāngzi	n	suitcase, box	20
想		xiǎng	av	to want to, would like to	4
想		xiǎng	v	to think	16
想起來	想起来	xiǎng qi lai	vc	to remember, to recall	16
像	像	xiàng	v	to be like, to look like, to take after	14
小		xiǎo	adj	small, little	4
小白菜	小白菜	xiǎo báicài	n	baby bok choy	12
小姐		xiǎojiě	n	Miss, young lady	1
小時	小时	xiǎoshí	n	hour	15
小心		xiǎoxīn	v	to be careful	20
笑		xiào	v	to laugh at, to laugh, to smile	8
些		xiē	m	(measure word for an indefinite amount), some	12
鞋		xié	n	shoes	9

Traditional	Simplified	Pinyin	Part of Speech	English	Lesson
寫	写	xiě	v	to write	7
謝謝	谢谢	xièxie	v	to thank	3
新		xīn	adj	new	8
新年		xīnnián	n	new year	10
信		xìn	n	letter (correspondence)	8
信用卡		xìnyòngkǎ	n	credit card	9
星期		xīngqī	n	week	3
星期四		xīngqīsì	n	Thursday	3
行		xíng	v	all right, OK	6
行李		xíngli	n	luggage	20
姓		xìng	v/n	(one's) family name is . . .; family name	1
興趣	兴趣	xìngqù	n	interest	17
休息		xiūxi	v	to take a break, to rest	15
學	学	xué	v	to study, to learn	7
學期	学期	xuéqī	n	school term, semester, quarter	8
學生	学生	xuésheng	n	student	1
學習	学习	xuéxí	v	to study, to learn	7
學校	学校	xuéxiào	n	school	5

Y

Traditional	Simplified	Pinyin	Part of Speech	English	Lesson
壓	压	yā	v	to press, to hold down, to weigh down	18
押金		yājīn	n	security deposit	17
呀		ya	p	(interjectory particle used to soften a question)	5
淹死		yān sǐ	vc	to drown	18

Traditional	Simplified	Pinyin	Part of Speech	English	Lesson
鹽	盐	*yán*	n	salt	12
顏色	颜色	*yánsè*	n	color	9
演		*yǎn*	v	to show (a film), to perform	16
眼睛		*yǎnjing*	n	eye	14
癢	痒	*yǎng*	adj	itchy	15
養	养	*yǎng*	v	to raise	17
樣子	样子	*yàngzi*	n	style	9
藥	药	*yào*	n	medicine	15
藥店	药店	*yàodiàn*	n	pharmacy	15
要		*yào*	v	to want	5
要		*yào*	mv	will, to be going to; to want to, to have a desire to	6
要不然		*yàobùrán*	conj	otherwise	15
要是		*yàoshi*	conj	if	6
爺爺	爷爷	*yéye*	n	paternal grandfather	20
也		*yě*	adv	too, also	1
夜裡	夜里	*yè lǐ*	n	at night	15
衣服		*yīfu*	n	clothes	9
醫生	医生	*yīshēng*	n	doctor, physician	2
醫院	医院	*yīyuàn*	n	hospital	15
一定		*yídìng [yīdìng]*	adj/adv	certain, definite; certainly, definitely	14
一共		*yígòng [yīgòng]*	adv	altogether	9
一路平安		*yí lù píng'ān [yī lù píng'ān]*		have a good trip, bon voyage	20
一下		*yí xià [yī xià]*	n+m	once, a bit	5

Traditional	Simplified	Pinyin	Part of Speech	English	Lesson
一樣	一样	yíyàng [yīyàng]	adj	same, alike	9
一邊	一边	yìbiān [yībiān]	adv	simultaneously, at the same time	8
一房一廳	一房一厅	yì fáng yì tīng [yī fáng yī tīng]		one bedroom and one living room	17
一起	一起	yìqǐ [yīqǐ]	adv	together	5
一言為定	一言为定	yì yán wéi dìng [yī yán wéi dìng]		that settles it, that's settled, it's decided	16
一直		yìzhí [yīzhí]	adv	straight, continuously	13
以後	以后	yǐhòu	t	after, from now on, later on	6
以前		yǐqián	t	before	8
以為	以为	yǐwéi	v	to assume erroneously	14
已經	已经	yǐjīng	adv	already	8
椅子		yǐzi	n	chair	17
因為	因为	yīnwèi	conj	because	3
音樂	音乐	yīnyuè	n	music	4
音樂會	音乐会	yīnyuèhuì	n	concert	8
飲料	饮料	yǐnliào	n	beverage	14
印象	印象	yìnxiàng	n	impression	16
應該	应该	yīnggāi	mv	should, ought to	18
英國	英国	Yīngguó	pn	Britain	3
英文	英文	Yīngwén	n	the English language	2
用		yòng	v	to use	8
用功		yònggōng	adj	hard-working, diligent, studious	14
游泳		yóu yǒng	vo	to swim	18
有		yǒu	v	to have, to exist	2
有的		yǒude	pr	some	4

Traditional	Simplified	Pinyin	Part of Speech	English	Lesson
有名		yǒumíng	adj	famous, well-known	19
有意思		yǒu yìsi	adj	interesting	4
又		yòu	adv	again	11
右		yòu	n	right	13
魚	鱼	yú	n	fish	12
語法	语法	yǔfǎ	n	grammar	7
預報	预报	yùbào	v/n	to forecast; forecast	11
預習	预习	yùxí	v	to preview	7
圓	圆	yuán	adj	round	14
元		yuán	m	(measure word for the basic Chinese monetary unit), *yuan*	17
遠	远	yuǎn	adj	far	13
願意	愿意	yuànyì	mv	to be willing	18
約	约	yuē	v	to make an appointment	11
月		yuè	n	month	3
越來越	越来越	yuè lái yuè	adv	more and more	15
運動	运动	yùndòng	n	sports	13
運動服	运动服	yùndòngfú	n	sportswear, athletic clothing	18
Z					
在		zài	prep	at, in, on	5
在		zài	v	to be present, to be at (a place)	6
再		zài	adv	again	9
再見	再见	zàijiàn	v	goodbye, see you again	3
再說	再说	zàishuō	conj	moreover	15

Traditional	Simplified	Pinyin	Part of Speech	English	Lesson
糟糕		zāogāo	adj	in a terrible mess, how terrible	11
早		zǎo	adj	early	7
早飯	早饭	zǎofàn	n	breakfast	8
早上		zǎoshang	t	morning	7
怎麼	怎么	zěnme	qpr	how, how come	7
怎麼樣	怎么样	zěnmeyàng	qpr	Is it OK? How is that? How does that sound?	3
站		zhàn	m	(measure word for bus stops, train stops, etc.)	10
張	张	zhāng	m	(measure word for flat objects such as paper, pictures, etc.)	7
長	长	zhǎng	v	to grow, to appear	14
長大	长大	zhǎng dà	vc	to grow up	14
找		zhǎo	v	to look for	4
找（錢）	找（钱）	zhǎo (qián)	v(o)	to give change	9
照顧	照顾	zhàogu	v	to look after, to care for, to attend to	20
照片		zhàopiàn	n	picture, photo	2
這	这	zhè	pr	this	2
這麼	这么	zhème	pr	so, this (late, etc.)	7
這兒	这儿	zhèr	pr	here	9
真		zhēn	adv	really	7
整理		zhěnglǐ	v	to put in order	16
正在		zhèngzài	adv	in the middle of (doing something)	8
政治		zhèngzhì	n	politics	19
枝		zhī	m	(measure word for long, thin, inflexible objects such as pens, pencils, etc.)	7

Traditional	Simplified	Pinyin	Part of Speech	English	Lesson
知道		*zhīdao*	v	to know	8
直飛	直飞	*zhí fēi*		fly directly	19
只		*zhǐ*	adv	only	4
紙	纸	*zhǐ*	n	paper	7
中		*zhōng*	adj	medium, middle	9
中國	中国	*Zhōngguó*	pn	China	1
中國城	中国城	*Zhōngguóchéng*	n	Chinatown	13
中國國際航空公司	中国国际航空公司	*Zhōngguó Guójì Hángkōng Gōngsī*	pn	Air China	19
中間	中间	*zhōngjiān*	n	middle	13
中文		*Zhōngwén*	n	the Chinese language	6
中午		*zhōngwǔ*	t	noon	8
中心		*zhōngxīn*	n	center	13
中學	中学	*zhōngxué*	n	middle school, secondary school	14
鐘頭	钟头	*zhōngtóu*	n	hour	14
種	种	*zhǒng*	m	(measure word for kinds, sorts, types)	9
重		*zhòng*	adj	heavy, serious	14
週末	周末	*zhōumò*	n	weekend	4
祝		*zhù*	v	to wish (well)	8
住		*zhù*	v	to live (in a certain place)	14
專業	专业	*zhuānyè*	n	major (in college), specialty	8
轉機	转机	*zhuǎn jī*	vo	change planes	19
准		*zhǔn*	v	to allow, to be allowed	17
準備	准备	*zhǔnbèi*	v	to prepare	6

Traditional	Simplified	Pinyin	Part of Speech	English	Lesson
桌子		zhuōzi	n	table	12
字		zì	n	character	7
自己		zìjǐ	pr	oneself	10
走		zǒu	v	to go by way of, to walk	10
走道		zǒudào	n	aisle	19
走路		zǒu lù	vo	to walk	17
租		zū	v	to rent	19
足球		zúqiú	n	soccer, football	18
嘴		zuǐ	n	mouth	14
最		zuì	adv	most, (of superlative degree) -est	14
最好		zuìhǎo	adv	had better	15
最後	最后	zuìhòu		final, last	10
最近		zuìjìn	t	recently	8
昨天		zuótiān	t	yesterday	4
左		zuǒ	n	left	13
做		zuò	v	to do	2
做飯	做饭	zuò fàn	vo	to cook, to prepare a meal	17
坐		zuò	v	to sit	5
坐		zuò	v	to travel by	10

The English-Chinese index is organized based on the alphabetical order of the English definitions. For ease of reference, indefinite articles and definite articles are omitted when they are the beginning of a phrase.

English	Traditional	Simplified	Pinyin	Part of Speech	Lesson
A					
activity	活動	活动	huódòng	n	13
advertisement	廣告	广告	guǎnggào	n	17
after, from now on, later on	以後	以后	yǐhòu	t	6
afternoon	下午		xiàwǔ	t	6
again	再		zài	adv	9
again	又		yòu	adv	11
ahead, in front of	前面		qiánmiàn	n	13
Air China	中國國際航空公司	中国国际航空公司	Zhōngguó Guójì Hángkōng Gōngsī	pn	19
airplane	飛機	飞机	fēijī	n	10
airport	（飛）機場	（飞）机场	(fēi)jīchǎng	n	10
aisle	走道		zǒudào	n	19
all right, OK	行		xíng	v	6
allow, be allowed	准		zhǔn	v	17
allow or cause (somebody to do something)	讓	让	ràng	v	10
almost, nearly; similar	差不多	差不多	chàbuduō	adv/adj	17
already	已經	已经	yǐjīng	adv	8
also, too, as well	還	还	hái	adv	3
although	雖然	虽然	suīrán	conj	9

English	Traditional	Simplified	Pinyin	Part of Speech	Lesson
altogether	一共		yígòng	adv	9
America	美國	美国	Měiguó	pn	1
American-style	美式		Měishì	adj	18
American dollar (USD)	美元		Měiyuán	n	17
and	和		hé	conj	2
apartment	公寓		gōngyù	n	17
apple	蘋果	苹果	píngguǒ	n	14
ask (a question)	問	问	wèn	v	1
assume erroneously	以為	以为	yǐwéi	v	14
at, in, on	在		zài	prep	5
at night	夜裡	夜里	yè lǐ	n	15
aunt	阿姨		āyí	n	20
autumn, fall	秋天		qiūtiān	n	11
aviation	航空		hángkōng	n	19
away from	離	离	lí	prep	13
B					
baby bok choy	小白菜	小白菜	xiǎo báicài	n	12
bag, sack, bundle, package	包		bāo	n	20
Bai Ying'ai	白英愛	白英爱	Bái Yīng'ài	pn	2
basketball	籃球	篮球	lánqiú	n	18
bathroom	衛生間	卫生间	wèishēngjiān	n	17
be	是		shì	v	1
be acquainted with, recognize	認識	认识	rènshi	v	3
be allergic to	過敏	过敏	guòmǐn	v	15

English	Traditional	Simplified	Pinyin	Part of Speech	Lesson
be called, call	叫		jiào	v	1
be careful	小心		xiǎoxīn	v	20
be like, look like, take after	像	像	xiàng	v	14
be overweight (of luggage, freight, etc.)	超重		chāozhòng	v	20
be present, be at (a place)	在		zài	v	6
be sold out	賣完	卖完	mài wán	vc	12
be told, hear of	聽說	听说	tīngshuō	v	13
be willing	願意	愿意	yuànyì	mv	18
because	因為	因为	yīnwèi	conj	3
become	成		chéng	v	16
bedroom	臥室	卧室	wòshì	n	17
beef	牛肉		niúròu	n	12
before	以前		yǐqián	t	8
begin, start; beginning	開始	开始	kāishǐ	v/n	7
beginning	初		chū	n	19
Beijing	北京		Běijīng	pn	1
belly, abdomen, stomach	肚子		dùzi	n	15
belong to	屬	属	shǔ	v	14
beverage	飲料	饮料	yǐnliào	n	14
big, old	大		dà	adj	3
birthday	生日		shēngrì	n	3
black	黑		hēi	adj	9
blue	藍	蓝	lán	adj	10
boarding gate	登機口	登机口	dēngjīkǒu	n	20

English	Traditional	Simplified	Pinyin	Part of Speech	Lesson
boarding pass	登機牌	登机牌	dēngjīpái	n	20
body, health	身體	身体	shēntǐ	n	15
book	書	书	shū	n	4
bookcase, bookshelf	書架	书架	shūjià	n	17
bookstore	書店	书店	shūdiàn	n	13
both, all	都		dōu	adv	2
bowl	碗		wǎn	n	12
braise in soy sauce (to red-cook)	紅燒	红烧	hóngshāo	v	12
breakfast	早飯	早饭	zǎofàn	n	8
bring, take, carry, come with	帶	带	dài	v	12
Britain	英國	英国	Yīngguó	pn	3
brown, coffee color	咖啡色		kāfēisè	n	9
bus	公共汽車	公共汽车	gōnggòng qìchē	n	10
busy	忙		máng	adj	3
but	可是		kěshì	conj	3
but	但是		dànshì	conj	6
buy	買	买	mǎi	v	9
by	被		bèi	prep	18
C					
cake	蛋糕		dàngāo	n	14
California	加州		Jiāzhōu	pn	11
can, able to	能		néng	mv	8
can, know how to	會	会	huì	mv	8
can, may	可以		kěyǐ	mv	5

English	Traditional	Simplified	Pinyin	Part of Speech	Lesson
Capital Airport (in Beijing)	首都機場	首都机场	Shǒudū Jīchǎng	pn	20
capital city	首都		shǒudū	n	19
catch, meet, welcome	接		jiē	v	14
cell phone	手機	手机	shǒujī	n	10
center	中心		zhōngxīn	n	13
certain, definite; certainly, definitely	一定		yídìng	adj/adv	14
chair	椅子		yǐzi	n	17
change planes	轉機	转机	zhuǎn jī	vo	19
character	字		zì	n	7
chat	聊天（兒）	聊天（儿）	liáo tiān(r)	vo	5
cheap, inexpensive	便宜		piányi	adj	9
check, look into	查		chá	v	19
check (luggage)	托運	托运	tuōyùn	v	20
child	孩子		háizi	n	2
China	中國	中国	Zhōngguó	pn	1
Chinatown	中國城	中国城	Zhōngguóchéng	n	13
Chinese characters	漢字	汉字	Hànzì	n	7
Chinese language	中文		Zhōngwén	n	6
city	城市		chéngshì	n	10
class	班		bān	n	14
class, course, lesson	課	课	kè	n	6
classmate	同學	同学	tóngxué	n	3
classroom	教室		jiàoshì	n	8
clean	乾淨	干净	gānjìng	adj	17

English	Traditional	Simplified	Pinyin	Part of Speech	Lesson
clean up (a room, apartment or house)	打掃	打扫	*dǎsǎo*	v	16
clear	清楚		*qīngchu*	adj	12
clothes	衣服		*yīfu*	n	9
coffee	咖啡		*kāfēi*	n	5
cola	可樂	可乐	*kělè*	n	5
cold	冷		*lěng*	adj	11
college student	大學生	大学生	*dàxuéshēng*	n	2
color	顏色	颜色	*yánsè*	n	9
come	來	来	*lái*	v	5
come back	回來	回来	*huí lai*	vc	6
come in	進來	进来	*jìn lai*	vc	5
comfortable	舒服		*shūfu*	adj	11
company	公司		*gōngsī*	n	19
compared with (comparison marker), to compare	比		*bǐ*	prep/v	11
computer	電腦	电脑	*diànnǎo*	n	8
concert	音樂會	音乐会	*yīnyuèhuì*	n	8
convenient	方便		*fāngbiàn*	adj	6
cook, prepare a meal	做飯	做饭	*zuò fàn*	vo	17
cooked rice	米飯	米饭	*mǐfàn*	n	12
cool (appearance, behavior)	酷		*kù*	adj	7
credit card	信用卡		*xìnyòngkǎ*	n	9
cry, weep	哭		*kū*	v	20
cucumber	黃瓜	黄瓜	*huánggua*	n	12

English	Traditional	Simplified	Pinyin	Part of Speech	Lesson
culture	文化		wénhuà	n	19
cute, lovable	可愛	可爱	kě'ài	adj	14

			D		
dance	跳舞		tiào wǔ	vo	4
dance party, ball	舞會	舞会	wǔhuì	n	14
dangerous	危險	危险	wēixiǎn	adj	18
daughter	女兒	女儿	nǚ'ér	n	2
day	天		tiān	n	3
day after tomorrow	後天	后天	hòutiān	t	16
delicious	好吃		hǎochī	adj	12
desk	書桌	书桌	shūzhuō	n	17
diary	日記	日记	rìjì	n	8
difficult	難	难	nán	adj	7
dining room, cafeteria	餐廳	餐厅	cāntīng	n	8
dining table	飯桌	饭桌	fànzhuō	n	17
dinner, supper	晚飯	晚饭	wǎnfàn	n	3
dish, cuisine	菜	菜	cài	n	3
do	做		zuò	v	2
doctor, physician	醫生	医生	yīshēng	n	2
dog	狗		gǒu	n	14
don't	別	别	bié	adv	6
dormitory	宿舍		sùshè	n	8
drink	喝		hē	v	5
drive a car	開車	开车	kāi chē	vo	10

English	Traditional	Simplified	Pinyin	Part of Speech	Lesson
drown	淹死		*yān sǐ*	vc	18
dumplings (with vegetable and/or meat filling)	餃子	饺子	*jiǎozi*	n	12
(dynamic particle)	了		*le*	p	5
E					
early	早		*zǎo*	adj	7
east	東	东	*dōng*	n	13
easy	容易		*róngyì*	adj	7
eat	吃		*chī*	v	3
eighteen	十八		*shíbā*	nu	3
eldest/oldest brother	大哥		*dàgē*	n	2
eldest/oldest sister	大姐		*dàjiě*	n	2
electricity	電	电	*diàn*	n	16
email/electronic mail	電子郵件	电子邮件	*diànzǐ yóujiàn*	n	10
English language	英文	英文	*Yīngwén*	n	2
enough	夠	够	*gòu*	adj	12
enter	進	进	*jìn*	v	5
especially	特別	特别	*tèbié*	adv	10
even	連	连	*lián*	prep	17
even more	更		*gèng*	adv	11
evening, night	晚上		*wǎnshang*	t	3
every, each	每		*měi*	pr	10
everybody	大家		*dàjiā*	pr	7
examine	檢查	检查	*jiǎnchá*	v	15

English	Traditional	Simplified	Pinyin	Part of Speech	Lesson
exchange, change	換	换	*huàn*	v	9
(exclamatory particle to express surprise or dissatisfaction)	哎	哎	*āi*	excl	13
extremely	極	极	*jí*	adv	12
eye	眼睛		*yǎnjing*	n	14
F					
face	臉	脸	*liǎn*	n	14
family, home	家		*jiā*	n	2
famous, well-known	有名		*yǒumíng*	adj	19
famous scenic spots and historic sites	名勝古蹟	名胜古迹	*míngshèng gǔjì*	n	19
fantastic, super [colloq.]	棒		*bàng*	adj	18
far	遠	远	*yuǎn*	adj	13
fast, quick; quickly	快		*kuài*	adj/adv	5
fat	胖		*pàng*	adj	18
father, dad	爸爸		*bàba*	n	2
fear, be afraid of	怕		*pà*	v	18
fee, expenses	費	费	*fèi*	n	17
feel, think	覺得	觉得	*juéde*	v	4
feel embarrassed	不好意思		*bù hǎoyìsi*		10
female	女		*nǚ*	adj	2
field	場	场	*chǎng*	n	13
final, last	最後	最后	*zuìhòu*		10
fine, good, nice, OK, it's settled	好		*hǎo*	adj	1
first	先		*xiān*	adv	10

English	Traditional	Simplified	Pinyin	Part of Speech	Lesson
fish	魚	鱼	yú	n	12
flower	花	花	huā	n	14
fly directly	直飛	直飞	zhí fēi		19
foot	腳	脚	jiǎo	n	18
for the sake of	為了	为了	wèile	prep	18
forecast; forcast	預報	预报	yùbào	v/n	11
foreign country	外國	外国	wàiguó	n	4
forget	忘		wàng	v	12
forget it, never mind	算了		suàn le		4
forward, ahead	前		qián	n	13
free time	空（兒）	空（儿）	kòng(r)	n	6
friend	朋友		péngyou	n	3
from	從	从	cóng	prep	13
fruit	水果		shuǐguǒ	n	14
fun, amusing, interesting	好玩兒	好玩儿	hǎowánr	adj	11
furniture	傢俱	家具	jiājù	n	17
furthermore, in addition	另外		lìngwài	conj	17
G					
game, match, competition; to compete	比賽	比赛	bǐsài	n/v	18
Gao Wenzhong	高文中		Gāo Wénzhōng	pn	2
Gao Xiaoyin	高小音		Gāo Xiǎoyīn	pn	5
get an injection	打針	打针	dǎ zhēn	vo	15
get off (a bus, train, etc.)	下車	下车	xià chē	vo	10

English	Traditional	Simplified	Pinyin	Part of Speech	Lesson
get sick	生病		shēng bìng	vo	15
get sick because of bad food	吃壞	吃坏	chī huài	vc	15
get up	起床	起床	qǐ chuáng	vo	8
gift, present	禮物	礼物	lǐwù	n	14
give	給	给	gěi	v	5
give as a gift	送		sòng	v	14
give change	找（錢）	找（钱）	zhǎo (qián)	v(o)	9
give or take a test; test	考試	考试	kǎo shì	vo/n	6
go	去		qù	v	4
go [colloq.]	上		shàng	v	13
go back, return	回去		huí qu	vc	11
go by way of, walk	走		zǒu	v	10
go home	回家		huí jiā	vo	5
go on vacation, have time off	放假		fàng jià	vo	19
go online, surf the internet	上網	上网	shàng wǎng	vo	8
go out	出去		chūqu	vc	10
go to, arrive	到		dào	v	6
go to a class, start a class, be in class	上課	上课	shàng kè	vo	7
goodbye, see you again	再見	再见	zàijiàn	v	3
Google	谷歌		Gǔgē	pn	13
grade in school	年級	年级	niánjí	n	6
grammar	語法	语法	yǔfǎ	n	7
Great Wall	長城	长城	Chángchéng	pn	19
green	綠	绿	lǜ	adj	10

English	Traditional	Simplified	Pinyin	Part of Speech	Lesson
green, leafy vegetable	青菜	青菜	*qīngcài*	n	12
grow, appear	長	长	*zhǎng*	v	14
grow up	長大	长大	*zhǎng dà*	vc	14
H					
had better	最好		*zuìhǎo*	adv	15
half, half an hour	半		*bàn*	nu	3
half a day, a long time	半天		*bàntiān*		18
hand	手		*shǒu*	n	18
handle, do	辦	办	*bàn*	v	11
handsome	帥	帅	*shuài*	adj	7
happy	快樂	快乐	*kuàilè*	adj	10
happy, pleased	高興	高兴	*gāoxìng*	adj	5
hard to bear, uncomfortable	難受	难受	*nánshòu*	adj	18
hard-working, diligent, studious	用功		*yònggōng*	adj	14
have, exist	有		*yǒu*	v	2
have a cold	感冒		*gǎnmào*	v	15
have a fever	發燒	发烧	*fā shāo*	vo	15
have a good trip, bon voyage	一路平安		*yí lù píng'ān*		20
have a meeting	開會	开会	*kāi huì*	vo	6
have fun, play	玩（兒）	玩（儿）	*wán(r)*	v	5
he, him	他		*tā*	pr	2
healthy; health	健康		*jiànkāng*	adj/n	15
heavy, serious	重		*zhòng*	adj	14

English	Traditional	Simplified	Pinyin	Part of Speech	Lesson
Helen	海倫	海伦	*Hǎilún*	pn	14
Hello!, Hey! (on the phone)	喂		*wéi/wèi*	interj	6
help	幫	帮	*bāng*	v	6
here	這兒	这儿	*zhèr*	pr	9
highway	高速公路		*gāosù gōnglù*	n	10
hold or carry in the arms	抱		*bào*	v	18
home-style	家常		*jiācháng*	n	12
homework, schoolwork	功課	功课	*gōngkè*	n	7
Hong Kong	香港		*Xiānggǎng*	pn	19
honorable, expensive	貴	贵	*guì*	adj	1
hope; hope	希望	希望	*xīwàng*	v/n	8
hospital	醫院	医院	*yīyuàn*	n	15
hot	熱	热	*rè*	adj	11
hot-and-sour soup	酸辣湯	酸辣汤	*suānlàtāng*	n	12
hotel	旅館	旅馆	*lǚguǎn*	n	19
hour	鐘頭	钟头	*zhōngtóu*	n	14
hour	小時	小时	*xiǎoshí*	n	15
how, how come	怎麼	怎么	*zěnme*	qpr	7
how many, some, a few	幾	几	*jǐ*	nu	2
how many/much, to what extent	多		*duō*	adv	3
how much/many	多少		*duōshao*	qpr	9
however, but	不過	不过	*búguò*	conj	9
hundred	百		*bǎi*	nu	9
hungry	餓	饿	*è*	adj	12

English	Traditional	Simplified	Pinyin	Part of Speech	Lesson
		I			
I, me	我		wǒ	pr	1
ice skate	滑冰	滑冰	huá bīng	vo	11
iced tea	冰茶	冰茶	bīngchá	n	12
if	要是		yàoshi	conj	6
if	如果…的話	如果…的话	rúguǒ…de huà	conj	9
immediately, right away	馬上	马上	mǎshàng	adv	19
impression	印象	印象	yìnxiàng	n	16
improve, raise, heighten,	提高		tígāo	v	18
in a terrible mess, how terrible	糟糕		zāogāo	adj	11
in addition to, besides	除了…以外		chúle…yǐwài	conj	8
in that case, then	那		nà	conj	4
in the middle of (doing something)	正在		zhèngzài	adv	8
(indicating degree) so, such	那麼	那么	nàme	pr	11
(indicating disposition, arrangement, or settlement of something)	把		bǎ	prep	15
inside	裡邊	里边	lǐbian	n	13
insurance; secure	保險	保险	bǎoxiǎn	n/adj	15
interest	興趣	兴趣	xìngqù	n	17
interesting	有意思		yǒu yìsi	adj	4
(interjectory particle used to soften a question)	呀		ya	p	5
intern	實習	实习	shíxí	v	19

English	Traditional	Simplified	Pinyin	Part of Speech	Lesson
international	國際	国际	*guójì*	adj	18
intersection	路口		*lùkǒu*	n	13
interview, interview (for a job or school admission)	面試	面试	*miànshì*	v/n	11
introduce	介紹	介绍	*jièshào*	v	5
invite someone (to dinner, coffee, etc.), play the host	請客	请客	*qǐng kè*	vo	4
Is it OK? How is that? How does that sound?	怎麼樣	怎么样	*zěnmeyàng*	qpr	3
it	它		*tā*	pr	9
it doesn't matter	沒關係	没关系	*méi guānxi*		12
itchy	癢	痒	*yǎng*	adj	15

			J		
Japan	日本		*Rìběn*	pn	13
Japanese (language)	日文		*Rìwén*	pn	13
job; to work	工作		*gōngzuò*	n/v	2
jog	跑步		*pǎo bù*	vo	18
just	剛	刚	*gāng*	adv	12
just, only (indicating a small number)	就		*jiù*	adv	16
just now, a moment ago	剛才	刚才	*gāngcái*	t	11

			K		
kick	踢		*tī*	v	18
kitchen	廚房	厨房	*chúfáng*	n	17
know	知道		*zhīdao*	v	8

English	Traditional	Simplified	Pinyin	Part of Speech	Lesson
L					
last time	上次		*shàng cì*		15
last year	去年		*qùnián*	t	14
late	晚		*wǎn*	adj	7
later	後來	后来	*hòulái*	t	8
laugh at, laugh, smile	笑		*xiào*	v	8
lawyer	律師	律师	*lǜshī*	n	2
lazy	懶	懒	*lǎn*	adj	15
lean on, lean against, be next to	靠		*kào*	v	19
left	左		*zuǒ*	n	13
length	長短	长短	*chángduǎn*	n	9
letter (correspondence)	信		*xìn*	n	8
level, standard	水平		*shuǐpíng*	n	18
Li You	李友		*Lǐ Yǒu*	pn	1
library	圖書館	图书馆	*túshūguǎn*	n	5
lie down	躺下		*tǎng xià*	vc	15
like	喜歡	喜欢	*xǐhuan*	v	3
line	線	线	*xiàn*	n	10
listen	聽	听	*tīng*	v	4
little, a bit, some	點（兒）	点（儿）	*diǎn(r)*	m	5
live (a life), observe (a holiday), celebrate (a festival), pass	過	过	*guò*	v	14
live (in a certain place)	住		*zhù*	v	14
living room	客廳	客厅	*kètīng*	n	17
long time	好久		*hǎo jiǔ*		4

English	Traditional	Simplified	Pinyin	Part of Speech	Lesson
look after, care for, attend to	照顧	照顾	zhàogu	v	20
look for	找		zhǎo	v	4
love, like, be fond of	愛	爱	ài	v	14
luggage	行李		xíngli	n	20
lunch, midday meal	午飯	午饭	wǔfàn	n	8
M					
major (in college), specialty	專業	专业	zhuānyè	n	8
make a phone call	打電話	打电话	dǎ diànhuà	vo	6
make a round trip, go there and back	往返		wǎngfǎn	v	19
make an appointment	約	约	yuē	v	11
male	男		nán	adj	2
many, much	多		duō	adj	7
map	地圖	地图	dìtú	n	13
master worker	師傅	师傅	shīfu	n	12
matter, affair, event	事（兒）	事（儿）	shì(r)	n	3
may; possible	可能		kěnéng	mv/adj	17
meal, (cooked) rice	飯	饭	fàn	n	3
meal card	飯卡	饭卡	fànkǎ	n	12
(measure word for a pair)	雙	双	shuāng	m	9
(measure word for a position in a numerical series, day of the month)	號	号	hào	m	3
(measure word for an indefinite amount), some	些		xiē	m	12
(measure word for books)	本		běn	m	14

English	Traditional	Simplified	Pinyin	Part of Speech	Lesson
(measure word for bottled liquid, etc.)	瓶		*píng*	m/n	5
(measure word for bus stops, train stops, etc.)	站		*zhàn*	m	10
(measure word for class periods)	節	节	*jié*	m	6
(measure word for complete courses of an action or instances of an action)	遍		*biàn*	m	15
(measure word for essays, articles, etc.)	篇		*piān*	m	8
(measure word for flat objects such as paper, pictures, etc.)	張	张	*zhāng*	m	7
(measure word for frequency)	次		*cì*	m	13
(measure word for kinds, sorts, types)	種	种	*zhǒng*	m	9
(measure word for letters)	封		*fēng*	m	8
(measure word for long, thin, inflexible objects such as pens, pencils, etc.)	枝		*zhī*	m	7
(measure word for many common everyday objects)	個	个	*gè/ge*	m	2
(measure word for meal orders, jobs)	份		*fèn*	m	19
(measure word for number of family members)	口		*kǒu*	m	2
(measure word for pants and long, thin objects)	條	条	*tiáo*	m	9
(measure word for people [polite])	位		*wèi*	m	6
(measure word for shirts, dresses, jackets, coats, etc.)	件		*jiàn*	m	9
(measure word for tablets, slices, etc.)	片		*piàn*	m	15

English	Traditional	Simplified	Pinyin	Part of Speech	Lesson
(measure word for the basic Chinese monetary unit [equivalent of a dollar])	塊	块	*kuài*	m	9
(measure word for the basic Chinese monetary unit), *yuan*	元		*yuán*	m	17
(measure word for things contained in a cup or glass)	杯		*bēi*	m	5
(measure word for things that come in a set/sets)	套		*tào*	m	17
(measure word for things with handles, for handfuls of things)	把		*bǎ*	m	14
(measure word for 1/100 of a kuai [equivalent of a cent])	分		*fēn*	m	9
(measure word for 1/10 of a kuai [equivalent of a dime])	毛		*máo*	m	9
meat	肉		*ròu*	n	12
medicine	藥	药	*yào*	n	15
medium, middle	中		*zhōng*	adj	9
meet up/with	見面	见面	*jiàn miàn*	vo	6
method, way (of doing something)	辦法	办法	*bànfǎ*	n	15
middle	中間	中间	*zhōngjiān*	n	13
middle school, secondary school	中學	中学	*zhōngxué*	n	14
minute	分鐘	分钟	*fēnzhōng*	n	17
Miss, young lady	小姐		*xiǎojiě*	n	1
money	錢	钱	*qián*	n	9
monosodium glutamate (MSG)	味精		*wèijīng*	n	12
month	月		*yuè*	n	3

English	Traditional	Simplified	Pinyin	Part of Speech	Lesson
more and more	越來越	越来越	yuè lái yuè	adv	15
moreover	再說	再说	zàishuō	conj	15
morning	上午		shàngwǔ	t	6
morning	早上		zǎoshang	t	7
most, (of superlative degree) -est	最		zuì	adv	14
mother, mom	媽媽	妈妈	māma	n	2
mouth	嘴		zuǐ	n	14
move	搬		bān	v	16
movie	電影	电影	diànyǐng	n	4
Mr., husband, teacher	先生		xiānsheng	n	1
multi-story building, floor (of a multi-level building)	樓	楼	lóu	n	14
music	音樂	音乐	yīnyuè	n	4
must, have to	得		děi	av	6

			N		
name	名字		míngzi	n	1
near	近		jìn	adj	13
need not	不用		bú yòng		9
nervous, anxious	緊張	紧张	jǐnzhāng	adj	10
new	新		xīn	adj	8
new words, vocabulary	生詞	生词	shēngcí	n	7
new year	新年		xīnnián	n	10
New York	紐約	纽约	Niǔyuē	pn	1
newspaper	報紙	报纸	bàozhǐ	n	17

English	Traditional	Simplified	Pinyin	Part of Speech	Lesson
next one	下個	下个	xià ge		6
noon	中午		zhōngwǔ	t	8
north	北		běi	n	13
Northwest Airlines	西北航空公司		Xīběi Hángkōng Gōngsī	pn	19
nose	鼻子		bízi	n	14
not	沒	没	méi	adv	2
not, no	不		bù	adv	1
not only ..., but also ...	不但… ，而且…		búdàn ..., érqiě ...	conj	11
not until, only then	才		cái	adv	5
now	現在	现在	xiànzài	t	3
number	號碼	号码	hàomǎ	n	16

			O		
o'clock (lit. dot, point, thus "points on the clock")	點	点	diǎn	m	3
(of airplanes) take off	起飛	起飞	qǐfēi	v	20
of course	當然	当然	dāngrán	adv	18
(of food) cold "blended", cold tossed	涼拌	凉拌	liángbàn	v	12
office	辦公室	办公室	bàngōngshì	n	6
often	常常		chángcháng	adv	4
older brother	哥哥		gēge	n	2
older female cousin	表姐		biǎojiě	n	14
older sister	姐姐		jiějie	n	2
on the Internet	網上	网上	wǎng shang		11
once, a bit	一下		yí xià	n+m	5

English	Traditional	Simplified	Pinyin	Part of Speech	Lesson
one bedroom and one living room	一房一廳	一房一厅	yì fáng yì tīng		17
(one's) family name is . . . ; family name	姓		xìng	v/n	1
oneself	自己		zìjǐ	pr	10
one-way trip	單程	单程	dānchéng	n	19
only	只		zhǐ	adv	4
or	還是	还是	háishi	conj	3
or	或者		huòzhě	conj	10
order food	點菜	点菜	diǎn cài	vo	12
other people, another person	別人	别人	biérén	n	4
otherwise	要不然		yàobùrán	conj	15

P

English	Traditional	Simplified	Pinyin	Part of Speech	Lesson
pants	褲子	裤子	kùzi	n	9
paper	紙	纸	zhǐ	n	7
parents, father and mother	父母		fùmǔ	n	19
park	公園	公园	gōngyuán	n	11
(particle to link adverbial and verb)	地		de	p	20
(particle used after a verb to indicate a past experience)	過	过	guo	p	13
passport	護照	护照	hùzhào	n	19
paternal grandfather	爺爺	爷爷	yéye	n	20
paternal grandmother	奶奶		nǎinai	n	20
patient	病人		bìngrén	n	15
pay money	付錢	付钱	fù qián	vo	9
pay with a credit card	刷卡		shuā kǎ	vo	9

English	Traditional	Simplified	Pinyin	Part of Speech	Lesson
pear	梨		*lí*	n	14
pen	筆	笔	*bǐ*	n	7
people, person	人		*rén*	n	1
pet	寵物	宠物	*chǒngwù*	n	17
pharmacy	藥店	药店	*yàodiàn*	n	15
picture, photo	照片		*zhàopiàn*	n	2
place	地方		*dìfang*	n	13
plan; plan	打算		*dǎsuàn*	v/n	19
plan; plan	計劃	计划	*jìhuà*	v/n	19
plate, dish	盤	盘	*pán*	n	12
play ball	打球		*dǎ qiú*	vo	4
please (polite form of request), to treat or to invite (somebody)	請	请	*qǐng*	v	1
polite	客氣	客气	*kèqi*	adj	6
politics	政治		*zhèngzhì*	n	19
(possessive or descriptive particle)	的		*de*	p	2
practice	練習	练习	*liànxí*	v	6
precisely, exactly	就		*jiù*	adv	6
(prefix for ordinal numbers)	第		*dì*	prefix	7
prepare	準備	准备	*zhǔnbèi*	v	6
press, hold down, weigh down	壓	压	*yā*	v	18
pretty	漂亮	漂亮	*piàoliang*	adj	5
pretty good	不錯	不错	*búcuò*	adj	4
preview	預習	预习	*yùxí*	v	7

English	Traditional	Simplified	Pinyin	Part of Speech	Lesson
previous one	上個	上个	shàng ge		7
pronunciation	發音	发音	fāyīn	n	8
put, place	放		fàng	v	12
put in order	整理		zhěnglǐ	v	16
Q					
quarrel; noisy	吵		chǎo	v/adj	17
quarter (of an hour)	刻		kè	m	3
(question particle)	嗎	吗	ma	qp	1
(question particle)	呢		ne	qp	1
question, problem	問題	问题	wèntí	n	6
quiet	安靜	安静	ānjìng	adj	17
quite a few	好幾	好几	hǎo jǐ		15
R					
racket	拍		pāi	n	18
rain	下雨		xià yǔ	vo	11
raise	養	养	yǎng	v	17
randomly, arbitrarily, messily	亂	乱	luàn	adv	15
read aloud	念		niàn	v	7
really	真		zhēn	adv	7
really painful	疼死		téng sǐ	adj+c	15
receive, accept	收		shōu	v	9
recently	最近		zuìjìn	t	8
red	紅	红	hóng	adj	9
refrigerator	冰箱		bīngxiāng	n	15

English	Traditional	Simplified	Pinyin	Part of Speech	Lesson
remember	記得	记得	*jìde*	v	16
remember, recall	想起來	想起来	*xiǎng qi lai*	vc	16
renminbi (RMB, Chinese currency)	人民幣	人民币	*rénmínbì*	n	17
rent	房租		*fángzū*	n	17
rent	租		*zū*	v	19
rent out	出租		*chūzū*	v	17
reserve, book (a ticket, a hotel room, etc.)	訂	订	*dìng*	v	19
restaurant	飯館（兒）	饭馆（儿）	*fànguǎn(r)*	n	12
restroom, toilet	廁所	厕所	*cèsuǒ*	n	15
return	還	还	*huán*	v	17
review	復習	复习	*fùxí*	v	7
right	右		*yòu*	n	13
right, correct	對	对	*duì*	adj	4
right away, quickly, in a hurry	趕快	赶快	*gǎnkuài*	adv	15
roast duck	烤鴨	烤鸭	*kǎoyā*	n	20
room	房間	房间	*fángjiān*	n	16
round	圓	圆	*yuán*	adj	14
route, road	路		*lù*	n	10

S

English	Traditional	Simplified	Pinyin	Part of Speech	Lesson
salt	鹽	盐	*yán*	n	12
same, alike	一樣	一样	*yíyàng*	adj	9
same, alike	同		*tóng*	adj	16
say, speak	說	说	*shuō*	v	6
scheduled flight	航班		*hángbān*	n	19

English	Traditional	Simplified	Pinyin	Part of Speech	Lesson
school	學校	学校	xuéxiào	n	5
school term, semester, quarter	學期	学期	xuéqī	n	8
seat	位子		wèizi	n	12
second oldest sister	二姐		èrjiě	n	2
security deposit	押金		yājīn	n	17
see	見	见	jiàn	v	3
see a doctor	看病		kàn bìng	vo	15
see off or out, take (someone somewhere)	送		sòng	v	10
seem, be like	好像	好像	hǎoxiàng	adv	12
sell at a discount, give a discount	打折		dǎ zhé	vo	19
send a text message (lit. send a short message)	發短信	发短信	fā duǎnxìn	vo	10
(sentence-final particle of exclamation, interrogation, etc.)	啊		a	p	6
(sentence-final particle)	吧		ba	p	5
September	九月		jiǔyuè	p	3
serve as, to be	當	当	dāng	v	17
serve food	上菜	上菜	shàng cài	vo	12
Shanghai	上海		Shànghǎi	pn	12
she, her	她		tā	pr	2
shirt	襯衫	衬衫	chènshān	n	9
shoes	鞋		xié	n	9
shop assistant, salesclerk	售貨員	售货员	shòuhuòyuán	n	9
should, ought to	應該	应该	yīnggāi	mv	18
show (a film), perform	演		yǎn	v	16

English	Traditional	Simplified	Pinyin	Part of Speech	Lesson
side	旁邊	旁边	*pángbiān*	n	13
simple	簡單	简单	*jiǎndān*	adj	18
simultaneously, at the same time	一邊	一边	*yìbiān*	adv	8
sing (a song)	唱歌（兒）	唱歌（儿）	*chàng gē(r)*	vo	4
sit	坐		*zuò*	v	5
size	大小		*dàxiǎo*	n	9
size	號	号	*hào*	n	9
sleep	睡覺	睡觉	*shuì jiào*	vo	4
slow	慢		*màn*	adj	7
small, little	小		*xiǎo*	adj	4
smart, bright, clever	聰明	聪明	*cōngming*	adj	14
snow	下雪		*xià xuě*	vo	11
so	所以		*suǒyǐ*	conj	4
so, this (late, etc.)	這麼	这么	*zhème*	pr	7
soccer, football	足球		*zúqiú*	n	18
sofa	沙發	沙发	*shāfā*	n	17
some	有的		*yǒude*	pr	4
son	兒子	儿子	*érzi*	n	2
sorry	對不起	对不起	*duìbuqǐ*	v	5
sound recording; record	錄音	录音	*lùyīn*	n/vo	7
sour	酸		*suān*	adj	12
south	南		*nán*	n	13
spend	花	花	*huā*	v	10
spend, take (effort)	費	费	*fèi*	v	16

English	Traditional	Simplified	Pinyin	Part of Speech	Lesson
sports	運動	运动	*yùndòng*	n	13
sportswear, athletic clothing	運動服	运动服	*yùndòngfú*	n	18
spring	春天		*chūntiān*	n	11
store, shop	商店		*shāngdiàn*	n	9
straight, continuously	一直		*yìzhí*	adv	13
strength, effort	力氣	力气	*lìqi*	n	16
(structural particle)	得		*de*	p	7
student	學生	学生	*xuésheng*	n	1
study, learn	學	学	*xué*	v	7
study, learn	學習	学习	*xuéxí*	v	7
style	樣子	样子	*yàngzi*	n	9
subway	地鐵	地铁	*dìtiě*	n	10
suitable	合適	合适	*héshì*	adj	9
suitcase, box	箱子		*xiāngzi*	n	20
summer	夏天		*xiàtiān*	n	11
summer term	暑期		*shǔqī*	n	14
summer vacation	暑假		*shǔjià*	n	19
sweet	甜		*tián*	adj	12
sweet-and-sour fish	糖醋魚	糖醋鱼	*tángcùyú*	n	12
swim	游泳		*yóu yǒng*	vo	18

T

English	Traditional	Simplified	Pinyin	Part of Speech	Lesson
table	桌子		*zhuōzi*	n	12
Taipei	台北		*Táiběi*	pn	19
take, get	拿		*ná*	v	13

English	Traditional	Simplified	Pinyin	Part of Speech	Lesson
take a bath/shower	洗澡		xǐ zǎo	vo	8
take a break, to rest	休息		xiūxi	v	15
take a taxi	打車	打车	dǎ chē	vo	10
talk	說話	说话	shuō huà	vo	7
taxi	出租汽車	出租汽车	chūzū qìchē	n	10
tea	茶	茶	chá	n	5
teach	教		jiāo	v	7
teacher	老師	老师	lǎoshī	n	1
Teacher Chang	常老師	常老师	Cháng lǎoshī	pn	6
television	電視	电视	diànshì	n	4
tell	告訴	告诉	gàosu	v	8
tennis	網球	网球	wǎngqiú	n	18
text of a lesson	課文	课文	kèwén	n	7
thank	謝謝	谢谢	xièxie	v	3
that	那		nà	pr	2
that settles it, that's settled, it's decided	一言為定	一言为定	yì yán wéi dìng		16
then	然後	然后	ránhòu	adv	10
there	那兒	那儿	nàr	pr	8
there	那裡	那里	nàli	pr	17
thin, skinny, lean	瘦		shòu	adj	20
things, objects	東西	东西	dōngxi	n	9
think	想		xiǎng	v	16
thirsty	渴		kě	adj	12
this	這	这	zhè	pr	2

English	Traditional	Simplified	Pinyin	Part of Speech	Lesson
this year	今年		jīnnián	t	3
thousand	千		qiān	nu	19
Thursday	星期四		xīngqīsì	n	3
ticket	票		piào	n	10
time	時間	时间	shíjiān	n	6
time (a point in), moment, time (a duration of)	時候	时候	shíhou	n	4
tired	累		lèi	adj	8
to, for	給	给	gěi	prep	6
today	今天		jīntiān	t	3
tofu, bean curd	豆腐		dòufu	n	12
together	一起	一起	yìqǐ	adv	5
Tokyo	東京	东京	Dōngjīng	pn	13
Tom	湯姆	汤姆	Tāngmǔ	pn	14
tomorrow	明天		míngtiān	t	3
too, also	也		yě	adv	1
too, extremely	太…了		tài … le		3
tour guide	導遊	导游	dǎoyóu	n	19
towards	往		wǎng	prep	13
traffic light	紅綠燈	红绿灯	hónglǜdēng	n	13
travel	旅行		lǚxíng	v	16
travel agency	旅行社		lǚxíngshè	n	19
travel by	坐		zuò	v	10
troublesome	麻煩	麻烦	máfan	adj	10
try	試	试	shì	v	9

English	Traditional	Simplified	Pinyin	Part of Speech	Lesson
turn	拐	拐	*guǎi*	v	13
twelve	十二		*shí'èr*	nu	3
two [colloq.]	倆	俩	*liǎ*	nu+m	16
two, a couple of	兩	两	*liǎng*	nu	2
U					
uncle	叔叔		*shūshu*	n	20
understand	懂	懂	*dǒng*	v	7
use	用		*yòng*	v	8
usually	平常		*píngcháng*	adv	7
V					
vegetarian (lit. plain)	素		*sù*	adj	12
vegetarian meal	素餐		*sùcān*	n	19
very	很		*hěn*	adv	3
very, extremely, exceedingly	非常		*fēicháng*	adv	11
very, rather	挺		*tǐng*	adv	9
vicinity, neighborhood, nearby area	附近		*fùjìn*	n	17
visa	簽證	签证	*qiānzhèng*	n	19
W					
wait, wait for	等		*děng*	v	6
waiter, attendant	服務員	服务员	*fúwùyuán*	n	12
walk	走路		*zǒu lù*	vo	17
Wang Hong	王紅	王红	*Wáng Hóng*	pn	14
Wang Peng	王朋		*Wáng Péng*	pn	1
want	要		*yào*	v	5

English	Traditional	Simplified	Pinyin	Part of Speech	Lesson
want to, would like to	想		*xiǎng*	av	4
warm	暖和		*nuǎnhuo*	adj	11
watch, look, read	看		*kàn*	v	4
water	水		*shuǐ*	n	5
watermelon	西瓜		*xīgua*	n	14
we, us	我們	我们	*wǒmen*	pr	3
wear, put on	穿		*chuān*	v	9
weather	天氣	天气	*tiānqì*	n	11
week	星期		*xīngqī*	n	3
weekend	週末	周末	*zhōumò*	n	4
welcome	歡迎	欢迎	*huānyíng*	v	20
west	西		*xī*	n	13
what	什麼	什么	*shénme*	qpr	1
where	哪兒	哪儿	*nǎr*	qpr	5
where	哪裡	哪里	*nǎli*	pr	7
which	哪		*nǎ/něi*	qpr	6
who, whom	誰	谁	*shéi*	qpr	2
why	為什麼	为什么	*wèishénme*	qpr	3
will	會	会	*huì*	mv	11
will, be going to; want to, have a desire to	要		*yào*	mv	6
window	窗戶	窗户	*chuānghu*	n	19
winter	冬天		*dōngtiān*	n	11
winter vacation	寒假		*hánjià*	n	10

English	Traditional	Simplified	Pinyin	Part of Speech	Lesson
wish (well)	祝		*zhù*	v	8
with	跟		*gēn*	prep	6
work at a temporary job (often part time)	打工		*dǎ gōng*	vo	19
worry	擔心	担心	*dān xīn*	vo	18
write	寫	写	*xiě*	v	7
wrong	錯	错	*cuò*	adj	12
		Y			
year (of age)	歲	岁	*suì*	n	3
yellow	黃	黄	*huáng*	adj	9
yesterday	昨天		*zuótiān*	t	4
you	你		*nǐ*	pr	1
you (honorific for 你)	您		*nín*	pr	6
younger brother	弟弟		*dìdi*	n	2
younger sister	妹妹		*mèimei*	n	2

Lesson 11

L11-1

Noun:	天氣，公園
Verb:	下雪，約，滑冰，預報，辦會
Modal Verb:	會
Adjective:	冷，暖和
Adverb:	更
Preposition:	比
Conjunction:	不但…，而且…
Time Word:	剛才
Others:	網上

L11-2

Noun:	冬天，夏天，春天，秋天
Pronoun:	那麼
Verb:	下雨，面試，回去
Adjective:	好玩兒，糟糕，熱，舒服
Adverb:	非常，又
Proper Noun:	加州

Lesson 12

L12-1

Noun:	飯館（兒），位子，服務員，桌子，盤，餃子，家常，豆腐，肉，碗，酸辣湯，味精，鹽，小白菜，青菜，冰茶
Measure Word:	些
Verb:	點菜，放，賣完，上菜
Adjective:	素，渴，夠，餓
Adverb:	好像，剛

L12-2

Noun:	師傅，糖醋魚，牛肉，魚，黃瓜，米飯，飯卡
Verb:	紅燒，涼拌，忘，帶
Adjective:	好吃，甜，酸，錯，清楚
Adverb:	極
Others:	沒關係
Proper Noun:	上海

Lesson 13	L13-1	Noun:	中心，運動場，旁邊，活動，中間，書店，地方，裡邊
		Verb:	上，聽說
		Adjective:	遠，近
		Preposition:	離

	L13-2	Noun:	中國城，地圖，南，路口，西，東，北，前，紅綠燈，右，左，前面
		Measure Word:	次
		Verb:	拿，拐
		Adverb:	一直
		Preposition:	從，往
		Particle:	過
		Others:	哎
		Proper Noun:	谷歌，日文，東京，日本

Lesson 14	L14-1	Noun:	舞會，表姐，中學，禮物，飲料，水果，花，蘋果，梨，西瓜，樓
		Measure Word:	本，把
		Verb:	過，送，愛，住，接
		Adjective:	重
		Proper Noun:	王紅

	L14-2	Noun:	鐘頭，暑期班，狗，臉，眼睛，鼻子，嘴，蛋糕
		Verb:	以為，長，屬，像，長大
		Adjective:	聰明，用功，可愛，圓
		Adverb:	一定，最
		Time Word:	去年
		Proper Noun:	海倫，湯姆

Lesson 15 　(L15-1)

Noun:	病人，醫院，肚子，夜裡，廁所，冰箱，藥，小時，辦法
Measure Word:	片，遍
Verb:	看病，發燒，躺下，檢查，吃壞，打針
Adverb:	最好
Preposition:	把
Others:	疼死，好幾

(L15-2)

Noun:	身體，藥店，保險
Verb:	生病，感冒，過敏，休息
Adjective:	癢，健康，懶
Adverb:	趕快，越來越，亂
Conjunction:	要不然，再說
Others:	上次

Lesson 16 　(L16-1)

Noun:	印象，力氣
Verb:	成，演，費
Adjective:	同
Adverb:	就
Time Word:	後天
Others:	倆，一言為定

(L16-2)

Noun:	號碼，房間，電
Verb:	記得，想，想起來，搬，打掃，整理，旅行

Lesson 17　L17-1

Noun:	報紙，廣告，附近，公寓，分鐘，臥室，廚房，衛生間，客廳，傢俱
Measure Word:	套
Verb:	吵，做飯，出租，走路
Adverb:	可能
Preposition:	連

L17-2

Noun:	沙發，飯桌，椅子，書桌，書架，房租，美元，人民幣，費，押金，寵物，興趣
Measure Word:	元
Pronoun:	那裡
Verb:	當，還，准，養
Adjective:	乾淨，安靜
Adverb:	差不多
Conjunction:	另外
Others:	一房一廳

Lesson 18　L18-1

Noun:	網球，拍，籃球
Verb:	怕，跑步，游泳，淹死
Modal Verb:	願意
Adjective:	胖，簡單，難受，危險
Adverb:	當然

L18-2

Noun:	水平，足球，比賽，腳，手，運動服
Verb:	上大學，提高，踢，抱，壓，擔心
Modal Verb:	應該
Adjective:	國際，美式，棒
Preposition:	為了，被
Others:	半天

Lesson 19 L19-1

Noun:	公司，計劃，暑假，父母，首都，政治，文化，導遊，護照，簽證，旅行社
Verb:	放假，實習，打工，打算，訂
Adjective:	有名
Adverb:	馬上
Others:	名勝古蹟
Proper Noun:	長城，香港，台北

L19-2

Noun:	初，單程，航空，航班，窗戶，走道，素餐，旅館
Measure Word:	份
Numeral:	千
Verb:	往返，查，打折，轉機，靠，租
Others:	直飛
Proper Noun:	中國國際航空公司，西北航空公司

Lesson 20 L20-1

Noun:	行李，包，箱子，登機牌，登機口
Verb:	托運，超重，哭，照顧，起飛，小心
Particle:	地
Others:	一路平安

L20-2

Noun:	叔叔，阿姨，爺爺，奶奶，烤鴨
Verb:	歡迎
Adjective:	瘦
Proper Noun:	首都機場

Vocabulary Index (How About You?), Volume 2

The How About You? vocabulary index is sequenced according to the order of the corresponding images, horizontally from left to right.

English	Traditional	Simplified	Pinyin	Part of Speech
Lesson 11: Dialogue 1				
windy	刮大風	刮大风	*guā dà fēng*	vo
cloudy	多雲	多云	*duō yún*	
sunny	出太陽（了）	出太阳（了）	*chū tàiyang (le)*	vo
Lesson 11: Dialogue 2				
play games on the Internet	上網玩兒遊戲	上网玩儿游戏	*shàng wàng wánr yóuxì*	
wash clothes	洗衣服		*xǐ yīfu*	vo
clean the room	打掃房間	打扫房间	*dǎsǎo fángjiān*	vo
Lesson 12: Dialogue 1				
small steamed bun	小籠包	小笼包	*xiǎolóngbāo*	n
fried noodles	炒麵	炒面	*chǎomiàn*	n
mapo tofu	麻婆豆腐		*mápó dòufu*	n
Lesson 12: Dialogue 2				
curry	咖喱		*gāli*	n
ramen	拉麵	拉面	*lāmiàn*	n
fried rice	炒飯	炒饭	*chǎofàn*	n
Lesson 13: Dialogue 1				
to an art gallery	去美術館看展覽	去美术馆看展览	*qù měishùguǎn kàn zhǎnlǎn*	
to exercise at the gym	去健身房運動	去健身房运动	*qù jiànshēnfáng yùndòng*	
to the music hall	去音樂廳看演出	去音乐厅看演出	*qù yīnyuètīng kàn yǎnchū*	

English	Traditional	Simplified	Pinyin	Part of Speech
Lesson 13: Dialogue 2				
southeast	東南	东南	*dōngnán*	n
southwest	西南		*xīnán*	n
northeast	東北	东北	*dōngběi*	n
northwest	西北		*xīběi*	n
Lesson 14: Dialogue 1				
banana	香蕉	香蕉	*xiāngjiāo*	n
strawberry	草莓	草莓	*cǎoméi*	n
grapes	葡萄	葡萄	*pútao*	n
Lesson 14: Dialogue 2				
cookies	餅乾	饼干	*bǐnggān*	n
balloon	氣球	气球	*qìqiú*	n
popcorn	爆米花	爆米花	*bàomǐhuā*	n
Lesson 15: Dialogue 1				
lower back pain	腰疼		*yāo téng*	
cough	咳嗽		*késòu*	v
have a runny nose	流鼻涕		*liú bítì*	vo
Lesson 15: Dialogue 2				
peanuts	花生	花生	*huāshēng*	n
cats	貓	猫	*māo*	n
pollen	花粉	花粉	*huāfěn*	n
Lesson 16: Dialogue 1				
go fishing	釣魚	钓鱼	*diào yú*	vo
go for a drive	開車兜風	开车兜风	*kāi chē dōu fēng*	
have a picnic	野餐		*yěcān*	v

English	Traditional	Simplified	Pinyin	Part of Speech
Lesson 16: Dialogue 2				
fix the car	修車	修车	*xiū chē*	vo
do volunteer work	做義工	做义工	*zuò yìgōng*	vo
mow the lawn	割草	割草	*gē cǎo*	vo
Lesson 17: Narrative				
coffee table	咖啡桌		*kāfēizhuō*	n
barstools	吧檯凳	吧台凳	*bātáidèng*	n
recliner	躺椅		*tǎngyǐ*	n
Lesson 17: Dialogue				
bird	鳥	鸟	*niǎo*	n
guinea pig	天竺鼠		*tiānzhúshǔ*	n
turtle	烏龜	乌龟	*wūguī*	n
Lesson 18: Dialogue 1				
play baseball	打棒球		*dǎ bàngqiú*	vo
play ice hockey	打冰球		*dǎ bīngqiú*	vo
go skateboarding	玩兒滑板	玩儿滑板	*wánr huábǎn*	vo
Lesson 18: Dialogue 2				
table tennis competition	乒乓球比賽	兵乓球比赛	*pīngpāngqiú bǐsài*	n
gymnastics competition	體操比賽	体操比赛	*tǐcāo bǐsài*	n
car-racing competition	賽車比賽	赛车比赛	*sàichē bǐsài*	n
Lesson 19: Dialogue 1				
Africa	非洲		*Fēizhōu*	pn
Asia	亞洲	亚洲	*Yàzhōu*	pn
Europe	歐洲	欧洲	*Ōuzhōu*	pn

English	Traditional	Simplified	Pinyin	Part of Speech
Lesson 19: Dialogue 2				
driver's license	駕（駛執）照	驾（驶执）照	*jià(shǐ zhí)zhào*	n
camera	照相機	照相机	*zhàoxiàngjī*	n
cash	現金	现金	*xiànjīn*	n
Lesson 20: Dialogue 1				
keys	鑰匙	钥匙	*yàoshi*	n
jewelry	珠寶首飾	珠宝首饰	*zhūbǎo shǒushì*	n
tablet computer	平板電腦	平板电脑	*píngbǎn diànnǎo*	n
Lesson 20: Dialogue 2				
charge one's cell phone	給手機充電	给手机充电	*gěi shǒujī chōng diàn*	
go shopping at duty-free shops	逛免稅商店	逛免税商店	*guàng miǎnshuì shāngdiàn*	vo
take and post a selfie	自拍打卡		*zì pāi dǎ kǎ*	

Appendix 1: Lesson Texts in Simplified Characters

Lesson 11

(Dialogue 1)

Tomorrow's Weather
Will Be Even Better!

（高小音跟弟弟高文中聊到天气……）

高小音： 今天天气比[1]昨天好，不下雪了[2]。

高文中： 我约了朋友明天去公园滑冰，不知道天气会[3]怎么样，冷不冷？

高小音： 我刚才看了网上的天气预报，明天天气比今天更好。不但不会下雪，而且[a]会暖和一点儿[4]。

高文中： 是吗？太好了！

高小音： 你约了谁去滑冰？

高文中： 白英爱。

高小音： 你约了白英爱？可是她今天早上坐飞机去纽约了。

高文中： 真的啊？那我明天怎么办？

高小音： 你还是在家看电视吧！

(Dialogue 2)

The Weather
Here Is Awful!

（高文中在网上找白英爱聊天儿。）

高文中： 英爱，纽约那么好玩儿，你怎么在网上，没出去？

白英爱： 这儿的天气非常糟糕。

高文中： 怎么了[a]?

白英爱： 昨天下大雨，今天又[5]下雨了。

高文中： 这个周末这儿天气很好，你快一点儿回来吧。

白英爱： 这个周末纽约也会暖和一点儿。我下个星期有一个面试，还不能回去。

高文中： 我在加州找了一个工作，你也去吧。加州冬天不冷，夏天不热，春天和秋天更舒服。

白英爱： 加州好是好[6]，可是我更喜欢纽约。

（在饭馆儿……）

服务员： 请进，请进。

李友： 人怎么这么[a]多？好像一个位子[b]都
没[1]有了。

王朋： 服务员，请问，还有没有位子？

服务员： 有，有，有。那张桌子没有人。

……

服务员： 两位想吃点儿什么？

李友： 王朋，你点菜吧。

王朋： 好。先给我们两盘饺子，要素的。

服务员： 除了饺子以外，还要什么？

王朋： 李友，你说呢？

李友： 还要一盘家常豆腐，不要放肉，
我吃素。

服务员： 我们的家常豆腐没有肉。

李友： 还要两碗[c]酸辣汤，请别放味精，
少[2]放点儿盐。有小白菜吗？

服务员： 对不起，小白菜刚[3]卖完[4]。

王朋： 那就不要青菜了。

服务员： 那喝点儿什么呢？

王朋： 我要一杯冰茶。李友，你喝什么？

李友： 我很渴，请给我一杯可乐，多放
点儿冰。

服务员： 好，两盘饺子，一盘家常豆腐，
两碗酸辣汤，一杯冰茶，一杯可
乐，多放冰。还要别的吗？

李友： 不要别的了，这些够[d]了。服务
员，我们都饿了，请上菜快一
点儿[e]。

服务员： 没问题，菜很快就能做好[5]。

Dialogue 2

At the Dining Hall

（今天是星期四，学生餐厅有中国菜，师傅是
上海人。）

王朋：师傅ᵃ，请问今天晚饭有什么好吃的?

师傅：我们今天有糖醋鱼，甜甜的ᵇ、酸酸的，
好吃极了ᵇ，你买一个吧。

王朋：好。今天有没有红烧牛肉?

师傅：没有。你已经要鱼了，别吃肉了。
来ᶻ个凉拌黄瓜吧?

王朋：好。再来一碗米饭。一共多少钱?

师傅：糖醋鱼，四块五，凉拌黄瓜，一块七;
一碗米饭，五毛钱。一共六块七。

王朋：师傅，糟糕，我忘了带饭卡了。这是
十块钱。

师傅：找你三块三。

王朋：师傅，钱你找错了，多找了我一块钱。

师傅：对不起，我没有看清楚。

王朋：没关系ᶜ。

师傅：下个星期四再来。

王朋：好，再见。

Lesson 13

Dialogue 1

Where Are You
Off To?

（白英爱刚下课……）

常老师：小白，下课了? 上哪儿去ᵃ?

白英爱：您好，常老师。我想去学校的电脑
中心，不知道怎么走，听说就在运
动场旁边¹。

常老师：电脑中心没有²运动场那么³远。
你知道学校图书馆在哪里ᵇ吗?

白英爱：知道，离王朋的宿舍不远。

常老师：电脑中心离图书馆很近，就在图书
馆和学生活动中心中间。

白英爱：常老师，您去哪儿呢?

常老师：我想到学校书店去买书⁴。

白英爱：书店在什么地方ᶜ?

常老师：就在学生活动中心里边。我们一起
走吧。

白英爱：好。

Dialogue 2

Going to
Chinatown

（高文中找王朋去中国城吃饭……）

高文中：　我们去中国城吃中国饭吧！

王朋：　　我没去过[5]中国城，不知道中国城
　　　　　在哪儿。

高文中：　没问题[a]，你开车，我告诉你怎
　　　　　么走。

王朋：　　你有谷歌地图吗？拿给我看看[6]。

高文中：　手机在宿舍里，我忘了带了。

王朋：　　没有地图，走错了怎么办？

高文中：　没有地图没关系，中国城我去过
　　　　　很多次，不用地图也能找到[7]。你
　　　　　从这儿一直往南开，到第三个路
　　　　　口，往西一拐[b]就[8]到了。

王朋：　　哎，我不知道东南西北[c]。

高文中：　那你一直往前开，到第三个红绿
　　　　　灯，往右一拐就到了。

（到了第三个路口……）

王朋：　　不对，不对。你看，这个路口只
　　　　　能往左拐，不能往右拐。

高文中：　那就是下一个路口。往右拐，
　　　　　再往前开。到了，到了，你看见
　　　　　了吗？前面有很多中国字。

王朋：　　那不是中文，那是日文，我们到
　　　　　了小东京了。

高文中：　是吗？那我们不吃中国饭了，吃
　　　　　日本饭吧！

Lesson 14 (Dialogue 1)

Let's Go to
a Party!

（李友给王朋打电话。）

李友： 王朋，你做什么呢[1]?

王朋： 我看书呢。

李友： 今天高小音过生日[a]，晚上我们在她
家开舞会，你能去吗?

王朋： 能去。几点?

李友： 七点。我们先吃饭，吃完饭再唱歌
跳舞。

王朋： 有哪些人?

李友： 小音和她的男朋友，小音的表姐[b]，
白英爱，你妹妹王红，听说还有
小音的中学同学。

王朋： 你要送给小音什么生日礼物?

李友： 我买了一本书送给她。

王朋： 那我带什么东西?

李友： 饮料或者水果都可以。

王朋： 那我带一些饮料，再买一把花儿。

李友： 小音爱吃水果，我再买一些苹果、
梨和西瓜吧。

王朋： 你住的地方[2]离小音家很远，水果
很重，我开车去接你，我们一起
去吧。

李友： 好，我六点半在楼下等你。

Dialogue 2 Birthday Bash	（在高小音家……） 高小音： 王朋，李友，快进来。 李友： 小音，祝你生日快乐！这是送给你的生日礼物。 高小音： 谢谢！……太好了！我一直想买这本书。带这么多东西，你们太客气了。 王红： 哥哥，李友，你们来了[a]。 李友： 啊[b]。小红，你怎么样？ 王红： 我很好。每天都在学英文。 王朋： 小红，你每天练习英文练习多长时间[3]？ 王红： 三个半钟头[c]。还看两个钟头的英文电视。 高文中： 哎，你们两个是什么时候到的[4]？ 李友： 刚到。 高文中： 白英爱没跟你们一起来吗？ 李友： 她还[5]没来？我以为[d]她已经来了。 高小音： 王朋，李友，来，我给你们介绍一下，这是我表姐海伦，这是她的儿子汤姆。 王朋： 你好，海伦。 海伦： 你好，王朋。文中和小音都说你又聪明[e]又用功[6]。 王朋： 哪里，哪里。你的中文说得真好，是在哪儿学的？ 海伦： 在暑期班[f]学的。 王朋： 哎，汤姆长[g]得真可爱！你们看，他笑了。他几岁了？ 海伦： 刚一岁，是去年生的，属狗。 李友： 你们看，他的脸圆圆的，眼睛大大的，鼻子高高的，嘴不大也不小，长得很像海伦。 王红： 妈妈这么漂亮，儿子长大一定也很帅。 高小音： 来，来，来，我们吃蛋糕吧。 高文中： 等等白英爱吧。她最爱吃蛋糕。

Lesson 15

Dialogue 1

My Stomach Is Killing Me!

（病人去医院看病……）

高文中： 医生，我肚子疼死[1]了。

医生： 你昨天吃什么东西了？

高文中： 我姐姐上个星期过生日，蛋糕没吃完。昨天晚上我吃了几口[2]，夜里肚子就疼起来[2]了，今天早上上了好几次[3]厕所。

医生： 你把[4]蛋糕放在哪儿了？

高文中： 放在冰箱里了。

医生： 放了几天了？

高文中： 五、六天[a]了。

医生： 发烧吗？

高文中： 不发烧。

医生： 你躺下。先检查一下。

……

医生： 你吃蛋糕把肚子吃坏了。

高文中： 得打针吗？

医生： 不用打针，吃这种药[b]就可以。一天三次，一次两片。

高文中： 医生，一天吃几次？请您再说一遍。

医生： 一天三次，一次两片。

高文中： 好！饭前[c]吃还是饭后吃？

医生： 饭前饭后都可以。不过，你最好二十四小时不要吃饭。

高文中： 那我要饿死了。不行，这个办法不好！

Dialogue 2

Allergies

李友：王朋，你怎么了？眼睛怎么红红的，感冒了吗？

王朋：没感冒。我也不知道怎么了，最近这几天身体很不舒服。眼睛又红又痒。

李友：你一定是对⁵什么过敏了。

王朋：我想也是，所以去药店买了一些药。已经吃了四、五种了，花了不少钱，都没有用。

李友：把你买的药拿出来给我看看。

王朋：这些就是。

李友：这些药没有用。为什么不去看病？你没有健康保险吗？

王朋：我有保险。可是我这个学期功课很多，看病太花时间。

李友：那你也得赶快去看病ª。要不然病会越来越⁶重。

王朋：我想再吃点儿别的药试试ᵇ。我上次生病，没去看医生ª，休息了两天，最后也好了。

李友：不行，不行，你太懒了。再说⁷，你不能自己乱吃药。走，我跟你看病去。

Lesson 16

Dialogue 1

Seeing a Movie

王朋跟李友在同ª一个学校学习，他们认识已经快半年了。王朋常常帮李友练习说中文。他们也常常一起出去玩儿，每次都玩儿得¹很高兴。李友对王朋的印象ᵇ很好，王朋也很喜欢李友，他们成了好朋友。

王朋：这个周末学校演一个中国电影ᶜ，我们一起去看，好吗？

李友：好啊！不过，听说看电影的人很多，买得到²票吗？

王朋：票已经买好了，我费了很大的力气才买到。

李友：好极了！我早ᵈ就想看中国电影了。还有别人跟我们一起去吗？

王朋：没有，就³我们俩ᵉ。

李友：好。什么时候？

王朋：后天晚上八点。

李友：看电影以前，我请你吃晚饭。

王朋：太好了！一言为定ᶠ。

Dialogue 2

Turning Down
an Invitation

（费先生给李友打电话⋯⋯）

费先生： 喂，请问李友小姐在吗？

李友： 我就是。请问你是哪一位？

费先生： 我姓费，你还记得ᵃ我吗？

李友： 姓费？

费先生： 你还记得上个月高小音的生日舞会吗？我就是最后请你跳舞的那个人。你再想想。想起来了吗？

李友： 对不起，我想不起来。

费先生： 我是高小音的中学同学。

李友： 是吗？你是怎么知道我的电话号码的？

费先生： 是小音告诉我的。

李友： 费先生，你有事吗？

费先生： 这个周末你有空儿吗？我想请你去跳舞。

李友： 这个周末不行，下个星期我有三个考试。

费先生： 没关系，下个周末怎么样？你考完试，我们好好儿ᵇ玩儿玩儿。

李友： 下个周末也不行，我要从宿舍搬出去ᴬ，得打扫、整理房间。

费先生： 你看下下个周末，好不好？

李友： 对不起，下下个周末更不行了，我要跟我的男朋友去纽约旅行。

费先生： ⋯⋯那⋯⋯

李友： 费先生，对不起，我的手机没电了。再见！

费先生： 喂⋯⋯喂⋯⋯

Narrative

Finding a Better Place

Dialogue

Calling about an Apartment for Rent

王朋在学校的宿舍住了两个学期了[1]。他觉得宿舍太吵，睡不好觉，房间太小，连电脑都[2]放不下[3]，再说也没有地方可以做饭，很不方便，所以准备下个学期搬出去住。他找房子找了一个多[4]月了，可是还没有找到合适的。刚才他在报纸上看到了一个广告，说学校附近有一套公寓出租，离学校很近，走路只要五分钟，很方便。公寓有一个[a]卧室，一个厨房，一个卫生间[b]，一个客厅，还带家具。王朋觉得这套公寓可能对他很合适。

（王朋打电话问租房子的事儿……）

王朋：喂，请问你们是不是[a]有公寓出租？

房东：有啊，一房一厅[b]，非常干净，还带家具。

王朋：有什么家具？

房东：客厅里有一套沙发、一张饭桌跟四把椅子。卧室里有一张床、一张书桌和一个书架。

王朋：你们那里安静不安静？

房东：非常安静。

王朋：每个月房租多少钱？

房东：八百五十元。

王朋：八百五十美元？人民币差不多是……有一点儿贵，能不能便宜点儿？

房东：那你不用付水电费。

王朋：要不要付押金？

房东：要多付一个月的房租当押金，搬出去的时候还给你。另外，我们公寓不准养宠物。

王朋：没关系，我对养宠物没有兴趣[c]，什么宠物都[b]不养。

房东：那太好了。你今天下午来看看吧。

王朋：好。

Lesson 18 (Dialogue 1)

Getting in Shape

（高文中跟王朋聊天儿……）

高文中： 你看，我的肚子越来越大了。

王朋： 你平常吃得那么多，又[a]不运动，
当然越来越胖了。

高文中： 那怎么办呢？

王朋： 如果怕胖，你一个星期运动两、三
次，每次半个小时，肚子就会小了。

高文中： 我两年没运动了[1]，做什么运动呢？

王朋： 最简单的运动是跑步。

高文中： 冬天那么冷，夏天那么热，跑步太
难受[2]了。

王朋： 你打网球吧。

高文中： 打网球得买网球拍、网球鞋，你知
道，网球拍、网球鞋贵极了！

王朋： 找几个人打篮球吧。买个篮球很便
宜。

高文中： 那每次都得打电话约人，麻烦死了。

王朋： 你去游泳吧。不用找人，也不用花
很多钱，什么时候去都可以。

高文中： 游泳？我怕水，太危险了，淹死了
怎么办？

王朋： 我也没办法了。你不愿意运动，那
就胖下去[3]吧。

王朋的妹妹王红刚从北京来，要在美国上ª大学，现在住在高小音家里学英文。为了ᵇ提高英文水平，她每天都看两个小时的电视⁴。

高小音： 快把电视打开，足球比赛开始了。

王红： 是吗？我也喜欢看足球赛ᶜ。……这是什么足球ᵈ啊？怎么不是圆的？

高小音： 这不是国际ᵉ足球，这是美式足球。

王红： 足球应该用脚踢，为什么那个人用手抱着⁵跑呢？

高小音： 美式足球可以用手。

王红： 你看，你看，那么多人都压在一起，下面的人不是要被⁶压坏ᶠ了吗？

高小音： 别担心，他们的身体都很棒，而且还穿特别的运动服，没问题。

王红： 我看了半天ᵍ也看不懂。还是看别的吧。

高小音： 你在美国住半年就会喜欢了。我男朋友看美式足球的时候，常常连饭都忘了吃。

（暑假快要到了……）

王朋： 李友，时间过得真快，马上就要放假了，我们的同学，有的去暑期班学习，有的去公司实习，有的回家打工，你有什么计划？

李友： 我还没有想好。你呢，王朋？

王朋： 我暑假打算ª回北京去看父母。

李友： 是吗？我听说北京这个城市很有意思。

王朋： 当然。北京是中国的首都，也是中国的政治、文化中心，有很多名胜古迹。

李友： 对啊，长城很有名。

王朋： 还有，北京的好饭馆多得不得了¹。

李友： 真的？我去过香港、台北，还没去过北京，要是能去北京就好了。

王朋： 那你跟我一起回去吧，我当你的导游。

李友： 真的吗？那太好了！护照我已经有了，我得赶快办ᵇ签证。

王朋： 那我马上给旅行社打电话订飞机票。

（王朋给旅行社打电话订机票……）

旅行社： 天一旅行社，你好。

王朋： 你好。请问六月初[a]到北京的机票多少钱？

旅行社： 您要买单程票还是往返票？

王朋： 我要买两张往返票。

旅行社： 你想买哪家航空公司的？

王朋： 哪家的便宜，就买哪[2]家的。

旅行社： 请等等，我查一下……好几家航空公司都有航班[b]。中国国际航空公司，一千五[3]，直飞。西北航空公司正在打折[c]，差不多一千四百六十，可是要转机。

王朋： 西北只比国航[d]便宜四十几块钱[4]，我还是买国航吧。

旅行社： 哪一天走[e]？哪一天回来？

王朋： 六月十号走，七月十五号回来。现在可以订位子吗？

旅行社： 可以。你们喜欢靠窗户的还是靠走道的？

王朋： 靠走道的。对了[f]，我朋友吃素，麻烦帮她订一份素餐。

旅行社： 没问题……您在北京要订旅馆、租车吗？

王朋： 不用，谢谢！

Lesson 20 (Dialogue 1)

Checking in at the Airport

（在国航的服务台……）

王朋：	小姐，这是我们的[1]机票。
航空公司：	请把护照给我看看。你们有几件行李要托运？
王朋：	两件。这个包不托运，我们带上飞机。
航空公司：	麻烦[a]您把箱子拿上来[2]。
王朋：	小姐，没超重吧？
航空公司：	没有。这是你们的护照、机票，这是登机牌[b]。请到五号登机口[c]上飞机。
李友和王朋：	谢谢。

……

王红：	哥哥，你们去北京了，就我一个人在这儿。
王朋：	小红，别哭，我们几个星期就回来，你好好儿地[1]学英文，别乱跑。
王红：	不是几个星期就回来，是几个星期以后才回来。
高文中：	别担心，我姐姐小音会照顾你。
李友：	对，别担心。
白英爱：	飞机几点起飞？
王朋：	中午十二点，还有两个多小时。
李友：	白英爱，你什么时候去纽约实习？
白英爱：	我不去纽约了。文中帮我在加州找了一份实习工作。
高文中：	对，我们下个星期开车去加州。
李友：	是吗？一边儿开车，一边儿玩儿，太好了。
王朋：	开车小心。祝你们玩儿得[1]高兴。
白英爱：	祝你们一路平安。到了北京以后[3]，别忘了给我们发个电子邮件。
王朋：	好，那我们秋天见。
高文中：	下个学期见。
白英爱和王红：	再见！

（在北京首都机场……）

王父：小朋！

王朋：爸，妈！

王母：累坏了吧？

王朋：还好[4]。爸，妈，我给你们介绍一下，这是我的同学李友。

李友：叔叔，阿姨[5a]，你们好。

王父：欢迎你来北京。

王母：李友，你的中文说得真好。

李友：谢谢。是因为王朋教得好。

王朋：哪里，是因为你聪明。

王父：哎，你们俩都聪明。

王母：小朋，你好像瘦了点儿。是不是打工太忙，没有时间吃饭？

王朋：我没瘦。我常常运动，身体比以前棒多了。

王母：小红怎么样？

王朋：她很好，英文水平提高了很多。

王父：走吧，我们上车以后，再慢慢儿地聊吧。爷爷、奶奶在烤鸭店等我们呢！

李友：烤鸭店？

Lesson 11

Dialogue 1

Tomorrow's Weather
Will Be Even Better!

(Gao Xiaoyin and her younger brother Gao Wenzhong are discussing the weather . . .)

Gao Xiaoyin: Today's weather is better than yesterday's. It's not snowing anymore.

Gao Wenzhong: I asked a friend to go ice skating with me in the park tomorrow. I wonder what the weather is going to be like. Will it be cold?

Gao Xiaoyin: I just looked up the forecast on the Internet. Tomorrow's weather will be even better than today's. Not only will it not snow, it'll be a bit warmer, too.

Gao Wenzhong: Really? Great!

Gao Xiaoyin: Who did you ask to go ice skating with?

Gao Wenzhong: Bai Ying'ai.

Gao Xiaoyin: You asked Bai Ying'ai? But she flew to New York this morning.

Gao Wenzhong: Really? Then what do I do tomorrow?

Gao Xiaoyin: Why don't you stay home and watch TV?

Dialogue 2

The Weather
Here Is Awful!

(Gao Wenzhong is chatting with Bai Ying'ai online.)

Gao Wenzhong: Ying'ai, New York is so much fun. How come you're online and not out and about?

Bai Ying'ai: The weather here is awful.

Gao Wenzhong: How come?

Bai Ying'ai: Yesterday it poured. It rained again today.

Gao Wenzhong: The weather here is great this weekend. You'd better come back as soon as you can.

Bai Ying'ai: It's going to be warmer in New York this weekend. I have an interview next week, I can't come back just yet.

Gao Wenzhong: I found a job in California. Go with me. It's not cold in the winter in California, or hot in the summer. Spring and fall are even more comfortable.

Bai Ying'ai: California is great, but I like New York more.

Lesson 12 — Dialogue 1

Dining Out

(In a restaurant . . .)

Waiter: Come in! Please come in!

Li You: How come there are so many people? It looks like there isn't a single seat left.

Wang Peng: Waiter, are there any tables left?

Waiter: Yes, yes. That table is not taken.

. . .

Waiter: What would you like to order?

Li You: Wang Peng, why don't you order?

Wang Peng: All right. To start, give us two plates of dumplings—vegetarian ones.

Waiter: What else would you like besides dumplings?

Wang Peng: Li You, what do you say?

Li You: Home-style tofu with no meat in it. I'm vegetarian.

Waiter: Our home-style tofu has no meat in it.

Li You: Also, two bowls of hot and sour soup with no MSG. Not too salty. Do you have baby bok choy?

Waiter: I'm sorry. We've just sold out of the baby bok choy.

Wang Peng: Then we'll do without green vegetables.

Waiter: What would you like to drink?

Wang Peng: I'd like a glass of iced tea. Li You, what would you like to drink?

Li You: I'm really thirsty. Please give me a cola, with lots of ice.

Waiter: OK. Two plates of dumplings, home-style tofu, two hot-and-sour soups, a glass of iced tea, and a cola with lots of ice. Anything else?

Li You: That's good, that's enough. Waiter, we're both really hungry. Could you please bring out the food as soon as possible?

Waiter: No problem. The dishes will be done in no time.

Dialogue 2

At the Dining Hall

(It's Thursday. The student cafeteria is serving Chinese food. The chef is from Shanghai.)

Wang Peng: Chef, what do you have for dinner today that's tasty?

Chef: We've got sweet-and-sour fish. It's a little sweet and a little sour. It's delicious. Why don't you get that?

Wang Peng: Great. Do you have beef braised in soy sauce today?

Chef: No, we don't. You've already got fish, so there's no need to have meat. How about a cucumber salad?

Wang Peng: All right. I'd also like a bowl of rice. How much is everything together?

Chef: Sweet-and-sour fish is $4.50, cucumber salad is $1.70, and one bowl of rice is fifty cents. All together, it's $6.70.

Wang Peng: Shoot, Chef. I forgot my meal card. Here's $10.

Chef: $3.30 is your change.

Wang Peng: Chef, you've given the wrong change. You gave me one dollar extra.

Chef: I'm sorry. I didn't see it clearly.

Wang Peng: That's all right.

Chef: Come again next Thursday.

Wang Peng: OK. Bye.

Lesson 13

Dialogue 1

Where Are You Off To?

(Bai Ying'ai has just gotten out of class . . .)

Teacher Chang: Are classes over, Little Bai? Where are you off to?

Bai Ying'ai: Hello, Teacher Chang. I want to go to the school computer center, but I don't know how to get there. I heard it's next to the sports field.

Teacher Chang: The computer center is not as far as the sports field. Do you know where the school library is?

Bai Ying'ai: I do. It's not far from Wang Peng's dorm.

Teacher Chang: The computer center is near the library. It's between the library and the student activity center.

Bai Ying'ai: Teacher Chang, where are you headed?

Teacher Chang: I'd like to get some books at the school bookstore.

Bai Ying'ai: Where's the bookstore?

Teacher Chang: It's in the student activity center. We can walk together.

Bai Ying'ai: OK.

Dialogue 2

Going to Chinatown

(Gao Wenzhong takes Wang Peng to Chinatown to eat . . .)

Gao Wenzhong: Let's go to Chinatown to have some Chinese food!

Wang Peng: I've never been to Chinatown. I don't know where it is.

Gao Wenzhong: No problem. You drive, and I'll tell you how to get there.

Wang Peng: You have Google Maps, right? Let me take a look.

Gao Wenzhong: Shoot, my phone's in the dorm. I forgot to bring it.

Wang Peng: Without a map, what do we do if we go the wrong way?

Gao Wenzhong: We're fine without a map. I've been to Chinatown a bunch of times, I don't need a map to get there. Go south from here. At the third intersection, turn west, and we'll be there.

Wang Peng: Oh, I don't have a sense of direction.

Gao Wenzhong: Then drive straight ahead. At the third traffic light, turn right, and you'll be there.

(At the third intersection . . .)

Wang Peng: This isn't right. See, you can only turn left here. You can't turn right.

Gao Wenzhong: Then it'll be the next block. Turn right. Keep going further. We're here! See, there are lots of Chinese characters out in front.

Wang Peng: That's not Chinese, that's Japanese. We're in Little Tokyo.

Gao Wenzhong: Really? Then let's not eat Chinese food, let's eat Japanese food instead!

Lesson 14 — Dialogue 1

Let's Go to a Party!

(Li You calls Wang Peng.)

Li You: Wang Peng, what are you doing?

Wang Peng: I'm reading.

Li You: Today is Gao Xiaoyin's birthday. Tonight we're having a dance party at her place. Can you go?

Wang Peng: Yes. What time?

Li You: Seven o'clock. We'll eat first. After dinner we'll sing and dance.

Wang Peng: Who will be there?

Li You: Xiaoyin and her boyfriend, Xiaoyin's cousin, Bai Ying'ai, your sister Wang Hong, and Xiaoyin's middle school classmates, I hear.

Wang Peng: What birthday gift are you giving Xiaoyin?

Li You: I bought a book to give her.

Wang Peng: What should I bring?

Li You: Either beverages or fruit would do.

Wang Peng: Then I'll bring some beverages. I'll also get some flowers.

Li You: Xiaoyin loves fruit. I'll get some apples, pears, and a watermelon.

Wang Peng: Your place is very far from Xiaoyin's house, and the fruit will be heavy. I'll come pick you up. Let's go together.

Li You: OK, I'll wait for you downstairs at six-thirty.

(At Gao Xiaoyin's house . . .)

Gao Xiaoyin:	Wang Peng, Li You, come in.
Li You:	Happy birthday, Xiaoyin. This is a birthday gift for you.
Gao Xiaoyin:	Thank you! . . I always wanted to buy this book. You've brought so many things with you. You're really too kind.
Wang Hong:	Brother! Li You! You're here.
Li You:	Xiao Hong, how are you?
Wang Hong:	I'm good. I've been studying English every day.
Wang Peng:	Xiao Hong, how much time do you spend practicing English every day?
Wang Hong:	Three and a half hours, plus I watch two hours of English-language TV.
Gao Wenzhong:	When did you two get here?
Li You:	Just now.
Gao Wenzhong:	Didn't Bai Ying'ai come with you?
Li You:	She's still not here? I thought she'd already gotten here.
Gao Xiaoyin:	Wang Peng, Li You, let me introduce you. This is my cousin Helen. This is her son, Tom.
Wang Peng:	Hello, Helen.
Helen:	Hello, Wang Peng. Wenzhong and Xiaoyin say that you're very smart and very hardworking.
Wang Peng:	You flatter me. Your Chinese is great. Where did you learn it?
Helen:	At summer school.
Wang Peng:	Hey, Tom is really cute. Look, he's smiling now. How old is he?
Helen:	He just turned one. He was born last year, the year of the dog.
Li You:	Look, he's got a round face, big eyes, and a straight nose. His mouth is not too big, and not too small. He looks just like Helen.
Wang Hong:	With such a gorgeous mom, the son will definitely be very handsome.
Gao Xiaoyin:	Come, let's eat the cake.
Gao Wenzhong:	Why don't we wait for Bai Ying'ai? She loves cake.

Lesson 15

Dialogue 1

My Stomach Is Killing Me!

(A patient is at a hospital for treatment ...)

Gao Wenzhong:	Doctor, my stomach is killing me!
Doctor:	What did you have to eat yesterday?
Gao Wenzhong:	It was my sister's birthday last week. We didn't finish the cake. Last night I had a few bites. My stomach began to hurt at night, and this morning I went to the bathroom several times.
Doctor:	Where did you put the cake?
Gao Wenzhong:	In the refrigerator.
Doctor:	How long had it been there?
Gao Wenzhong:	About five or six days.
Doctor:	Do you have a fever?
Gao Wenzhong:	No, I don't.
Doctor:	Please lie down. Let me check.

. . .

Doctor:	You upset your stomach by eating that cake.
Gao Wenzhong:	Do I need an injection?
Doctor:	No, you don't need an injection. Just take this medicine, three times a day, two pills at a time.
Gao Wenzhong:	Doctor, how many times a day? Could you please repeat that?
Doctor:	Three times a day, two pills at a time.
Gao Wenzhong:	All right. Before or after meals?
Doctor:	Either before or after meals is fine, but you'd better not eat anything for twenty-four hours.
Gao Wenzhong:	Then I'll be starving. That's not a good idea. That's not a good remedy!

Dialogue 2

Allergies

(The past few days, Wang Peng has seemed to be sick ...)

Li You:	Wang Peng, what's the matter? How come your eyes are red? Did you catch a cold?
Wang Peng:	No, I didn't catch a cold. I don't know what's wrong with me. I haven't been feeling well the last few days. My eyes are red and itchy.
Li You:	You must be allergic to something.
Wang Peng:	I think so, too. That's why I went to the pharmacy and got some medicine. I've taken four or five kinds and spent quite a bit of money, but none of them has been effective.
Li You:	Take out the medicines you bought. Let me take a look.
Wang Peng:	Here you are.
Li You:	These medicines are useless. Why didn't you go to the doctor? Don't you have health insurance?
Wang Peng:	I do have health insurance. I have too much homework this semester. Going to the doctor takes too much time.
Li You:	Even so, you still need to go see a doctor as soon as possible. Otherwise, you'll get sicker and sicker.
Wang Peng:	I'd like to try some other medicines first. Last time I was sick I didn't go to the doctor. After a couple of days' rest, I was fine.
Li You:	No way, no way, you're too lazy. Besides, you can't just randomly take medicine by yourself. Let's go. I'll go to the doctor with you.

Lesson 16

Dialogue 1

Seeing a Movie

Wang Peng and Li You go to the same school. They have known each other for almost six months now. Wang Peng often helps Li You practice speaking Chinese. They also often go out for fun, and they always have a good time. Li You has a very good impression of Wang Peng, and Wang Peng likes Li You very much, too. So they've become good friends.

Wang Peng: This weekend they're showing a Chinese film at school. How about we go together?

Li You: Okay! But I hear that many people are going to see that film. Will we be able to get tickets?

Wang Peng: I already got the tickets. It took a lot of effort.

Li You: Fantastic. I've wanted to see a Chinese film for a long time. Anyone else going with us?

Wang Peng: No one else. Just the two of us.

Li You: OK. When?

Wang Peng: The day after tomorrow, eight o'clock.

Li You: Before the movie, I'll take you to dinner.

Wang Peng: Great! It's a deal.

Dialogue 2

Turning Down an Invitation

(Mr. Fei calls Li You . . .)

Mr. Fei: Hello, is Miss Li You there?

Li You: This is she. Who is this, please?

Mr. Fei: My name is Fei. Do you remember me?

Li You: Mr. Fei?

Mr. Fei: Do you still remember Gao Xiaoyin's birthday party last month? I was the last person to ask you to dance. Think again. Do you remember now?

Li You: I'm sorry. I can't recall.

Mr. Fei: I was Gao Xiaoyin's high school classmate.

Li You: Is that so? How did you get my number?

Mr. Fei: Xiaoyin gave it to me.

Li You: Mr. Fei, can I help you?

Mr. Fei: Are you free this weekend? I'd like to ask you out to dance.

Li You: This weekend won't do. Next week I have three tests.

Mr. Fei: No problem. What about the following weekend? After your tests are over, we'll go have a good time.

Li You: Next weekend won't work, either. I'm moving out of the dorm. I have to clean my room.

Mr. Fei: How about two weeks from now?

Li You: I'm sorry, two weeks from now would be even more impossible. I'm going on a trip to New York with my boyfriend.

Mr. Fei: In that case . . .

Li You: Mr. Fei, I'm sorry, my cell phone is out of power. Bye.

Mr. Fei: Hello . . . hello . . .

Lesson 17

Narrative

Finding a Better Place

Wang Peng has been living in the school dorm for two semesters. He thinks that the dorm is too noisy, and he can't sleep well. His room is too small, and he can't even fit a computer there. Besides, he has nowhere to cook. It's really inconvenient, so he plans to move out next semester. He has been looking for a place for a month now, but he hasn't found anything suitable yet. He just saw an ad in the newspaper saying there's an apartment for rent. It's very close to school, only a five-minute walk—very convenient. The apartment includes a bedroom, a kitchen, a bathroom, and a living room, and it's furnished. Wang Peng thinks this apartment may be just right for him.

Dialogue

Calling about an Apartment for Rent

(Wang Peng makes a call to ask about renting an apartment . . .)

Wang Peng: Hi, do you have an apartment for rent?

Landlord: Yes, we do. One bedroom with a living room. It's very clean, and also furnished.

Wang Peng: What kind of furniture does it have?

Landlord: In the living room there are a sofa set, a dining table, and four chairs. The bedroom has a bed, a desk, and a bookcase.

Wang Peng: Is it quiet over there?

Landlord: Extremely quiet.

Wang Peng: How much is the monthly rent?

Landlord: Eight hundred and fifty dollars.

Wang Peng: Eight hundred and fifty U.S. dollars? In renminbi that's almost . . .

That's a little bit expensive. Could you come down a little bit?

Landlord: All right. You won't have to pay for the utilities.

Wang Peng: Do I have to pay a deposit?

Landlord: An extra month's rent as a security deposit, which will be returned to you when you move out. And another thing, no pets are allowed in our apartments.

Wang Peng: That doesn't matter. I'm not interested in keeping pets. I don't have pets of any kind.

Landlord: Great. Why don't you come over this afternoon and take a look?

Wang Peng: OK.

Lesson 18

Dialogue 1
Getting in Shape

(Gao Wenzhong and Wang Peng are chatting . . .)

Gao Wenzhong: Look, my gut is getting bigger and bigger.

Wang Peng: You usually overeat, and on top of that you don't exercise; of course you're putting on more and more weight.

Gao Wenzhong: What should I do?

Wang Peng: If you're afraid of being overweight, you should exercise two or three times a week, for half an hour each time. Then your belly will get smaller.

Gao Wenzhong: I haven't exercised for two years. What kind of exercise should I do?

Wang Peng: The simplest exercise is jogging.

Gao Wenzhong: It's so cold in winter, and so hot in summer. Jogging is too uncomfortable.

Wang Peng: How about playing tennis?

Gao Wenzhong: Then I'd have to get a tennis racket and tennis shoes. You know tennis rackets and tennis shoes are very expensive!

Wang Peng: How about getting a few people together to play basketball? Buying a basketball is very inexpensive.

Gao Wenzhong: Then every time I'd have to call people and arrange to meet. That's way too much hassle.

Wang Peng: Then why don't you swim? There's no need to look for people, it wouldn't cost much money, and you could go any time.

Gao Wenzhong: Swimming? I'm afraid of water. That's too dangerous. What if I drown?

Wang Peng: There's nothing I can do [to help]. If you're not willing to exercise, then keep packing on the pounds.

Dialogue 2
Watching American Football

Wang Peng's younger sister, Wang Hong, just came from Beijing. She will be going to college in the United States. Right now she is staying at Gao Xiaoyin's place, studying English. To improve her English, she watches two hours of TV every day.

Gao Xiaoyin: Hurry, turn the TV on. The football game is starting.

Wang Hong: Really? I like watching football games too...What kind of football is this? How come it's not round?

Gao Xiaoyin: This is not international football, this is American football.

Wang Hong: To play football you should kick (the ball) with your feet. Why is that guy running with the ball in his hands?

Gao Xiaoyin: In American football you can use your hands.

Wang Hong: Look! All those people are piling on top of each other. Wouldn't the people underneath be crushed to pieces?

Gao Xiaoyin: Don't worry, they're really strong. Besides, they wear special sports clothing, so everything's fine.

Wang Hong: I've been watching for a while and I still don't get it. Let's watch something else.

Gao Xiaoyin: You only have to live in America for half a year before you will begin to like American football. When my boyfriend is watching a football game, often he will even forget to eat.

Lesson 19

Dialogue 1
Traveling to Beijing

(It's almost summer break . . .)

Wang Peng: Li You, time flies. It'll be break soon. Some of our class-mates are going to summer school; some of them are going to intern at different companies. Some will go home and work. What are your plans?

Li You: I haven't decided. What about you, Wang Peng?

Wang Peng: I plan to go back to Beijing to see my parents.

Li You: Really? I hear that Beijing is a really interesting city.

Wang Peng: Of course. Beijing is China's capital, and it's also China's political and cultural center with lots of famous historic sites.

Li You: That's right. The Great Wall is very famous.

Wang Peng: And there are tons of great restaurants in Beijing.

Li You: Really? I've been to Hong Kong and Taipei, but I've never been to Beijing. I wish I could go to Beijing.

Wang Peng: Why don't you go with me? I could be your guide.

Li You: Really? That would be great! I already have a passport. I'll have to apply for a visa at once.

Wang Peng: I'll get the plane tickets online right away.

Li You: It's not secure to make payments online. Let's rather call a travel agency instead.

Dialogue 2
Planning an Itinerary

(Wang Peng calls a travel agency to make flight reservations . . .)

Travel Agent: Tianyi Travel Agency, good morning.

Wang Peng: Good morning. How much is a ticket to Beijing for the beginning of June?

Travel Agent: One-way or roundtrip?

Wang Peng: Two roundtrip tickets.

Travel Agent: Which airline?

Wang Peng: I'll take whichever airline is the least expensive.

Travel Agent: Please wait a moment. Let me check. Quite a few airlines fly there. Air China, $1,500, direct flight. Northwest Airlines is having a sale. About $1,460, but you have to change planes.

Wang Peng: Northwest Airlines is only $40 cheaper than Air China. I'll go with Air China.

Travel Agent: What are the dates for departure and return?

Wang Peng: Departing on June 10, returning on July 15. Can I reserve seats now?

Travel Agent: Yes, you can. Do you prefer window or aisle seats?

Wang Peng: Aisle seats. Oh, that's right, my friend is a vegetarian. Could you please order vegetarian meals for her?

Travel Agent: No problem. While in Beijing, do you need to make reservations for a hotel or car rental?

Wang Peng: No, thank you.

Lesson 20   (Dialogue 1)

Checking in at the Airport

(At the Air China Counter . . .)

Wang Peng:	Miss, these are our tickets.
Airline staff:	Please show me your passports. How many pieces of checked luggage do you have?
Wang Peng:	Two. We won't check this bag. We'll take it on board.
Airline staff:	Please put the suitcases up here.
Li You:	Miss, they are not over the weight limit, I hope.
Airline staff:	No, they're not. Here are your passports and tickets. These are your boarding passes. Please go to Gate 5 to board the plane.
Li You and Wang Peng:	Thank you.

. . .

Wang Hong:	You're both leaving for Beijing. I'll be all alone here.
Wang Peng:	Xiao Hong, don't cry. We'll be back in just a few weeks. Work hard on your English. Don't go running around.
Wang Hong:	Be back in a few weeks? Won't be back till a few weeks later!
Gao Wenzhong:	Don't worry. My sister Xiaoyin will take good care of you.
Li You:	That's right. Don't worry.
Bai Ying'ai:	When does the plane leave?
Wang Peng:	12:00 noon. There are two hours left.
Li You:	Bai Ying'ai, when are you going to New York for your internship?
Bai Ying'ai:	I'm not going to New York anymore. Wenzhong helped me get an internship in California.
Gao Wenzhong:	That's right. We're driving to California next week.
Li You:	Really? Driving and sightseeing at the same time, that's really wonderful.
Wang Peng:	Drive carefully. Have fun!
Bai Ying'ai:	Have a safe trip. Don't forget to email us after you arrive in Beijing.
Wang Peng:	OK. See you in the fall then.
Gao Wenzhong:	See you next semester.
Bai Ying'ai and Wang Hong:	Goodbye!

Dialogue 2

Arriving in Beijing

(At Beijing Capital International Airport ...)

Dad:	Xiao Peng!
Wang Peng:	Dad, Mom!
Mom:	You must be really tired.
Wang Peng:	Not really. Dad, Mom, let me introduce you ... This is my classmate Li You.
Li You:	Uncle, Aunt, how do you do?
Dad:	Welcome to Beijing.
Mom:	Li You, you speak Chinese wonderfully.
Li You:	Thank you. It's because Wang Peng is a good teacher.
Wang Peng:	You flatter me. It's because you're smart.
Dad:	Hey, you're both smart.
Mom:	Xiao Peng, you seem to have lost some weight. Is it because you were too busy working and had no time to eat?
Wang Peng:	Mom, I haven't lost any weight. I exercise a lot. I'm much stronger than before.
Mom:	How is Xiao Hong?
Wang Peng:	She's great. Her English has really improved.
Dad:	Let's go. We'll talk at leisure after we get in the car. Grandpa and Grandma are waiting for us at the roast duck restaurant.
Li You:	Roast duck restaurant?